Buddhism in Contemporary Tibet

Religious Revival and Cultural Identity

EDITED BY

Melvyn C. Goldstein

AND

Matthew T. Kapstein

WITH A FOREWORD BY

Orville Schell

UNIVERSITY OF CALIFORNIA PRESS

Berkeley   Los Angeles   London

University of California Press
Berkeley and Los Angeles, California

University of California Press, Ltd.
London, England

© 1998 by
The Regents of the University of California

Library of Congress Cataloging-in-Publication Data
Buddhism in contemporary Tibet : religious revival and cultural
   identity / Melvyn C. Goldstein, Matthew T. Kapstein, editors.
       p. cm.
   Includes bibliographical references and index.
   ISBN 0-520-21130-8 (alk. paper).—ISBN 0-520-21131-6 (alk.
paper)
       1. Buddhism—China—Tibet—History—20th century.   2. Tibet
(China)—Religion—20th century.   I. Goldstein, Melvyn C.
II. Kapstein, Matthew.
BQ7590.B84   1998
294.3′923′0951509048—dc21   97-26851
                                                       CIP

Printed in the United States of America
9 8 7 6 5 4 3 2 1

The paper used in this publication meets the minimum requirements of American National
Standards for Information Sciences—Permanence of Paper for Printed Library Materials,
ANSI Z39.48 – 1984.

CONTENTS

ILLUSTRATIONS

All photographs were taken by the authors of the chapters in which they occur.

FOREWORD

Mao Zedong was fond of analyzing political situations in terms of their "contradictions," but he was also enamored of the notion of "the unity of opposites." As
he wrote in "On Contradiction" in 1937, "All contrary things are interconnected;
not only do they coexist in a single entity in given conditions, but in other given
conditions they also transform themselves into each other. This is the full meaning
of the unity of opposites."

When trying to make sense out of the highly politicized and polemicized debate that has raged over recent events in Tibet, Mao's notion of the unity of opposites is not a bad analytical mode to call into service. For if contemporary Tibet
is anything, it is contradictory. While the atrocities committed by Mao in carrying
out his grand plan to reunite China by occupying Tibet with the People's Liberation Army and the savagery visited on Tibetans subsequently during the Cultural
Revolution are undeniable and unpardonable, the Chinese Communist party's
policies toward Tibet became more nuanced with the death of Mao and Deng
Xiaoping's enunciation of his reform platform late in 1978. While political and religious repression continued, a pulse of reform-minded sentiment from Beijing in
the early 1980s did presage a period of hopeful liberality that harkened back to the
early 1950s. The party's revised policies allowed for a recrudescence of Tibetan
Buddhism and traditional culture, albeit under the ever-watchful eye of party
overlords. To understand the past two decades is to understand a paradox of al-
ternating currents—interludes of what the Chinese refer to as *fang*, loosening up,
and *shou*, tightening down.

Buddhism in Contemporary Tibet is organized around this paradox that even as
things have gotten better in Tibet, they have also gotten worse; even as Beijing has
"loosened up" and allowed a religious revival to arise, it has also relentlessly "tightened down," especially whenever this same religious revival has manifested politically dissident or separatist tendencies. Just as Deng and other architects of

China's reform post-Mao movement imagined that they could keep politics detached from economics, so they hope that religion and politics in Tibet can be kept separated into two discrete universes. As Matthew T. Kapstein writes in his "Concluding Reflections," "The religious revival in Tibet following the Cultural Revolution has . . . been a matter of great delicacy: to the extent that it appears to foster Tibetan national identity, within the context of Tibetan inclusion in the multinational Chinese state, it remains (in principle at least) ideologically unobjectionable, and on this basis local governments have been able to protect and in some cases even support revival movements. At the same time, when religious revival has provided the background for the emergence of genuinely nationalistic expression, the Chinese state has brought its instruments of control, and, if it deems necessary, repression, to bear."

With this book Melvyn C. Goldstein and Matthew T. Kapstein, two Tibetologists who know the culture, language, people, and geography of this unusual land, have added another important volume to the small but growing collection of work that offers readers informative scholarly research rather than nostalgia or polemics. By doing so, they have helped to refoliate the landscape of Tibetan studies—a landscape that had been denuded by China's earlier reluctance to grant access to outside researchers and that had consequently become overrun with bitter polemics rather than concrete information about what has actually been happening within Tibet's religious institutions.

Buddhism in Contemporary Tibet is cultural anthropology at its best. It provides a rare doorway through which ordinary people and specialists alike can enter Tibet and learn something of what has been happening behind the shroud that separates most visitors from Tibetan reality. Be forewarned, however, that because it is presented in an even-handed unapologetic way, what lies through this doorway may sometimes seem contradictory and confusing. In this sense, it is a perfect embodiment of the notion of the unity of opposites that Mao sought to describe in his 1937 essay. It is also a realistic representation of the contradictory nature of China's relationship to Tibet.

One thing is clear. This book will make interesting reading not only for Westerners who are trying to discern what has been happening in Tibet over the past two decades but for Tibetans and Chinese as well.

Orville Schell

ONE

Introduction

Melvyn C. Goldstein

One of the most dramatic transformations in twentieth-century Chinese history was the shift in policy launched by the Third Plenum of the Eleventh Chinese Communist Party (CCP) Congress in Beijing in December 1978. This historic meeting ushered in a series of wide-ranging reforms dealing with key issues such as decollectivization and the marketization of China's economy as well as cultural issues such as the freedom to practice religion. After more than a decade of vehement attacks on traditional culture and the total suppression of religious practices, the CCP reversed course.

That decision, however, was not without precedent. In the early years of the People's Republic of China (PRC) the party concluded that, in the stage of development the Chinese people had reached, it was not reasonable to expect them readily to accept communist ideology as a replacement for religion. Consequently, a pragmatic strategy was adopted which allowed religion to continue until such a time that conditions for change were more fully present. An editorial in the *People's Daily* in 1950 conveys some of the thinking behind this:

> The religious policy of the Chinese Communist Party and the People's Government . . . . provides that the people have freedom of religious belief, that is, freedom to believe in a religion and freedom to refuse to believe in a religion. Both aspects of this freedom receive the protection of the law. . . . Some people ask, since Communists are thorough-going atheists, then why do they advocate permitting freedom of religious belief? This is because religion came into being and has continued to exist during the time when mankind has been faced with natural and social forces that it felt it could not contend with and so looked to the mystical for help. Therefore only when man has adequate means to put nature at his disposal and thoroughly destroy the exploitative class system and its remnants—only then will religion go to its destruction. Until that time, so long as a part of mankind is technologically backward and hence continues to be dependent on natural forces and so long as a part of

mankind has been unable to win its release from capitalist and feudal slavery, it will be impossible to bring about the universal elimination of religious phenomena from human society. Therefore with regard to the problem of religious belief as such, any idea about taking coercive action is useless and positively harmful. This is the reason why we advocate protecting freedom of religious belief just as we advocate protecting freedom to reject religious belief.[1]

Mao Zedong himself explicitly wrote on this issue, stating, "It is the peasants who put up idols and, when the time comes, they will throw the idols out with their own hands. . . . It is wrong for anybody else to do it for them."[2] And in his famous "On the Correct Handling of Contradictions" (1957), Mao further elaborated:

All attempts to use administrative orders or coercive measures to settle ideological questions or questions of right and wrong are not only ineffective but harmful. We cannot abolish religion by administrative decree or force people not to believe in it. We cannot compel people to give up idealism, any more than we can force them to believe in Marxism. The only way to settle questions of an ideological nature or controversial issues among the people is by the democratic method, the method of discussion, of criticism, of persuasion and education, and not by the method of coercion or repression.[3]

Thus, despite the CCP's adherence to a Marxist, atheist ideology, it initially adopted a flexible policy regarding the place of religion in its new state. This policy was institutionalized on 29 September 1949 in article 5 of the "Common Program"[4] and then officially codified in 1954 in China's first constitution, which declared that "every citizen of the PRC shall have freedom of religious belief."[5]

"Freedom of religious belief," however, was never operationalized in a systematic fashion. In fact, its practical meaning was complicated by the government's articulation of a distinction between religion, which was allowed, and superstition, which was to be discouraged if not prohibited. The latter included a range of activities such as fortune telling, shamanistic trances, casting horoscopes, exorcising evil spirits, geomancy, and physiognomy, although no formal listing was ever produced. These diverse activities were lumped together into the residual category "superstition," mainly because they were not part of a formal religion with an organization, activities, and a doctrine, but also because they were considered exploitive—that is, they were felt to be manipulated by a class of "superstition trade" practitioners (such as fortune tellers and shamans) to exploit the masses financially.[6]

Over and above such ambiguities, religious freedom was also circumscribed with respect to politics. The new government specified that religious practitioners could not interfere with or challenge the political power and authority of the CCP. The following comment made in 1951 by the editor-in-chief of the (government) journal *Modern Buddhism* illustrates this view.

Freedom of religious belief is stated as clear as day in the Common Program and it will not be compromised. However, one must realize that the Common Program is a charter for the era of the New Democracy; and the New Democracy takes as its premises the struggle against imperialism, feudalism and bureaucratic capitalism, the overthrow of the reactionary power of the Kuomintang, and the purge of open and hidden counterrevolutionary forces. Buddhists who do not accept these premises are either reactionaries or backward elements. Reactionaries have no political rights; backward elements do not understand the times and, since in their thinking there is not much trust of the government, the government cannot treat them with the respect and concern that would otherwise be appropriate. Only if they become progressive and join the people of the era of the New Democracy can they fully enjoy all the freedoms of the Common Program. . . . Some Buddhists think that, because the Common Program provides for freedom of belief, they can do anything they like and that anyone who corrects their thinking or actions is infringing on their freedom of religion. This is a very big mistake and really is the thinking of backward elements. . . . [I]t must be corrected as forcefully as possible. Anyone who does not listen must be denounced to the government.[7]

Even more explicit is the report made by Liu Shaoqi in 1954 on China's draft constitution: "Safeguarding freedom of religious belief is quite a different matter from safeguarding freedom of counter-revolutionary activities; these two cannot be mixed up. Nor, similarly, will our constitution and laws ever provide the slightest facility for those elements who engage in counter-revolutionary activities under the cloak of religion."[8]

Notwithstanding such restrictions, the practice of religion was allowed to continue to some degree in the new communist state until the onset of the Great Proletarian Cultural Revolution in 1966. At that time all religious practices were banned, priests and monks were defrocked, and most religious buildings and paraphernalia were demolished. Religion, in essence, ceased to exist in the People's Republic of China.

The death of Mao and the rise of Deng Xiaoping in 1978, therefore, shifted the CCP's religious policy back to the more pragmatic viewpoint that had been dominant in the 1950s. The beliefs and practices that had been ridiculed and denigrated and the institutions that had been reviled and destroyed during the violent years of the Cultural Revolution were suddenly again possible and acceptable, and in the two decades since 1978 religion has reappeared throughout China. However, as in the 1950s, there were clear constraints on the practice of religion. A section in the 1982 revision of the Chinese constitution articulates these:

In our country, citizens may believe in religion or disbelieve, but politically they have one thing in common, that is, they are all patriotic and support socialism. . . . The State protects legitimate religious activities, but no one may use religion to carry out counter-revolutionary activities or activities that disrupt public order, harm the health of citizens, or obstruct the educational system of the State . . . [and] no religious affairs may be controlled by any foreign power.[9]

Tibetans have taken advantage of the decisions of 1978 to enact a vibrant Buddhist revival that is one of the most extensive and dramatic examples of religious revitalization in contemporary China. The nature of that revival is the focus of this book.

WHAT IS "TIBET"?

To understand the Tibetan Buddhist revival, what we mean when we speak of Tibet needs clarification. Ethnic Tibetan populations are distributed over an area the size of Western Europe. They are found not only in China but also in neighboring countries such as India (in Ladakh, Sikkim, northern Uttar Pradesh, and Arunachal Pradesh), Nepal, and Bhutan.[10]

This volume deals with the 4.6 million ethnic Tibetans who are now part of China, that is, those living in the heartland of Tibetan Buddhism. The regions these Tibetans inhabit are differentiated into two broad geopolitical categories known as "political" and "ethnographic" Tibet as a result of their differing historical experiences. Political Tibet refers to the polity that was ruled by the Dalai Lamas and is equivalent to today's Tibet Autonomous Region (TAR). Ethnographic Tibet refers to the ethnic Tibetan areas of Amdo and Kham that are today part of Qinghai, Sichuan, Gansu, and Yunnan provinces. Hugh Richardson articulated the historical rationale for this distinction as follows:

> In "political" Tibet the Tibetan government has ruled continuously from the earliest times down to 1951. The region beyond that to the north and east [Amdo and Kham] . . . is its "ethnographic" extension which people of Tibetan race once inhabited exclusively and where they are still in the majority. In that wider area, "political" Tibet exercised jurisdiction only in certain places and at irregular intervals; for the most part, local lay or monastic chiefs were in control of districts of varying size. From the 18th century onwards the region was subject to sporadic Chinese infiltration.[11]

The modern Sino-Tibetan border in these two regions was generally established during the mid-eighteenth century when Manchu China took control over most of the areas of ethnographic Tibet. While the Tibetan government has never accepted the loss of these regions as permanent or de jure—for example, it claimed all of Kham and Amdo in the Simla Convention of 1913–14—most of these areas in fact were not a part of its polity for the two centuries preceding the rise to power of the communists in China in 1949.[12]

The political separation of ethnic Tibetans into those living in the Dalai Lama's polity and those in ethnographic Tibet was bridged in part by religion. Tibetans from all over ethnographic Tibet made religious pilgrimages to Lhasa and other holy sites in political Tibet, and large numbers of monks from the borderlands continuously came to study at the great monastic seats in Central Tibet. Many of the greatest scholar-monks and abbots in political Tibet's monastic seats, in fact, came from ethnographic Tibet—Kham and Amdo.[13] Consequently, religion was a unifying force that to a degree reintegrated on the ideological level the millions of Tibetans politically divided between ethnographic and political Tibet (as well as between those living in disparate native states within ethnographic Tibet). Thus, while understanding the divergent historical and political experiences of ethnographic and political Tibet is essential for any examination of Tibetans in China, in the religious and cultural spheres the commonalities seem equally significant. In this volume, both areas are examined. The chapters by Goldstein and Kapstein discuss cases from political Tibet, while those of Epstein and Peng and Germano deal with religious revival in ethnographic Tibet (Qinghai and Sichuan).

BUDDHISM IN TIBETAN SOCIETY

Buddhism has played a central role in Tibetan society, defining morality and the fundamental meaning of existence through its core notions of karma, rebirth, and enlightenment. At the same time, it punctuated the daily rhythm of life by engaging individuals in concrete religious practices such as counting rosaries, turning prayer wheels, doing circumambulations, and maintaining altars in homes. Individual Tibetans also made religious pilgrimages to temples, monasteries, and distant sacred locations (see chapter 4 in this volume), and they sent their sons to become lifelong monks in astonishing numbers. Roughly 10 to 15 percent of Tibet's males were monks, and virtually all Tibetans in the traditional society knew a monk or nun personally as a relative, a friend, or a neighbor (see chapters 2 and 3).

Tibetan Buddhism in its popular dimension also played a major role in the problems of daily life since it incorporated a plethora of autochthonous deities and spirits. These local gods were easily offended and caused illness and misfortune when angered, so avoiding, counteracting, or placating their potential negative power was a core concern (see chapter 5). In times of illness or uncertainty, therefore, Tibetans typically consulted religious specialists for advice on how to proceed, for example, asking monks to perform sacred divination or asking shamans to summon a god and serve as a medium so that they could consult directly with the god. Tibetan Buddhism was thus a dominant ideological framework for both day-to-day life and the ultimate questions dealing with the meaning of existence and life.

Buddhism in political Tibet also had profound meaning as the raison d'être of the Tibetan state, and it was the main source of Tibetans' pride in their culture and country. Tibetans traditionally considered their country unique because of its "theocratic" form of governance in which politics was intimately intertwined with religion. The Tibetan state was headed by a ruler, the Dalai Lama, who was believed to be a bodhisattva who repeatedly returned to earth to help humankind in general and Tibet in particular. Half of the government's officials were monks,[14] and the government actively sought to foster the practice of Buddhism. Tibetans, in fact, referred to their political system as *chösi nyindre* (*chos-srid gnyis-'brel*), religion and politics joined together, and in the great monasteries around Lhasa the powerful religious role of the government was often described by the saying, "[The government is] the ruler who is the patron of the dharma."[15]

Moreover, unlike other minorities who were the *object* of a Manchu/Chinese "civilizing project,"[16] Tibetans considered themselves the *agents* of their own Buddhist civilizing project with regard to the spiritual life of the Mongols and Manchus, including the Manchu emperors of China. The Dalai Lamas, for example, regularly sent monks and incarnate lamas to Beijing to instruct the royal family in the Tibetan language so that they could read prayers in the language of the scriptures.[17] Tibetans were the only minority with an advanced civilization whom the emperors of China actually sought to learn from. Religious sophistication and greatness, therefore, were at the heart of Tibetans' identity and self-image. This religious-national pride was conveyed simply in a letter the Tibetan government sent to Chiang Kaishek in 1946: "There are many great nations on this earth who have achieved unprecedented wealth and might, but there is only one nation which is dedicated to the well-being of humanity in the world and that is the religious land of Tibet which cherishes a joint spiritual and temporal system."[18]

Tibetan Buddhism, therefore, exemplified for Tibetans the value and worth of their culture and way of life and the essence of their national identity. It is what they felt made their society unique and without equal.

THE DESTRUCTION AND REVIVAL OF TIBETAN BUDDHISM

To experience a revival, there first has to be a decline. This occurred in Tibet, as in the rest of China, not by spontaneous changes in the attitudes of the populace regarding the value and efficacy of religion, but rather by the conscious, hostile intervention of the Chinese communist state. The timing of this intervention in political Tibet diverged somewhat from other parts of China, but ultimately it followed a similar course. We can distinguish four main phases through which Tibetan Buddhism passed after creation of the PRC in October 1949.

The first phase covers the period from the liberation of China in 1949 to the uprising that began in ethnographic Tibet in 1956 and then spread to political Tibet. This culminated in 1959 with the Lhasa uprising and flight of the Dalai Lama to India. China's Tibet policy in the early years was characterized by a strategy of "gradualism" in both political and ethnographic Tibet. Traditional institutions, including religion and monasticism, were at first allowed to function unchanged, the government employing a top-down strategy in which Tibetan society would ultimately be transformed not by direct force but by gradually convincing the lay and religious elites of its desirability and then, through them, the masses.

In political Tibet the gradualist strategy was employed to a degree not seen in any other nationality region because of its unique political and international status. In 1949 after the CCP conquered China and established the PRC, it still faced a Tibet that was operating as a de facto independent government and was strongly opposed to becoming part of China. Tibet also had an international status of sorts, engaging in diplomatic relations directly with its neighbors as well as with Britain and the United States. Consequently, although Beijing certainly had the capacity to "liberate" Tibet militarily, because its ultimate goal was to legitimize its claim of sovereignty over Tibet internationally, it did not do so. Instead it made a major effort to induce Tibet's leaders to formally accept a political settlement that made Tibet an integral part of the PRC. To this end it used a carrot-and-stick approach. On the stick side, it sent units of the People's Liberation Army into Tibet's eastern province in October 1950 to show the Dalai Lama it was ready and able to conquer the entire country. It achieved its military object in a two-week campaign. At this point the carrot part of the strategy came into play. The army stopped its advance and sent new overtures to the Dalai Lama calling for negotiations and proposing relatively liberal terms.

Receiving no external support for its urgent appeals for help, the Lhasa government reluctantly accepted these terms and signed the 17-Point Agreement for the Liberation of Tibet.[19] By this agreement China gained the Tibetan government's acceptance of Chinese sovereignty but in turn offered the Dalai Lama terms that allowed his government and the traditional economic system, resembling a feudal system, to continue virtually unchanged for the foreseeable future. Between 1951 and 1959 the estates of the great landlords in political Tibet were not expropriated, and no effort was made to foment class struggle by prodding the masses to rise against their masters. And, most important, the Dalai Lama continued to rule internally.

The 17-Point Agreement was particularly explicit about protecting religion, stating in point 7, "The policy of religious freedom laid down in the Common Programme of the Chinese People's Political Consultative Conference shall be carried out. The religious beliefs, customs, and habits of the Tibetan People shall be respected, and lama monasteries shall be protected. The central authorities will not effect a change in the income of the monasteries."[20] Chinese officials in Tibet, moreover, were careful to show respect for religious customs and institutions, and on a number of occasions actually gave alms to all the monks in Lhasa and the surrounding monasteries. Thus, during this early period, not only did religion and monasticism continue, but so too did the socioeconomic system of estates and bound peasants that underpinned it.[21] Throughout most of the 1950s China's Tibet policy sought to win over Tibet's political and religious elite, and through them to persuade Tibetans to embrace socialism voluntarily. Religion, therefore, was almost totally unaffected by Tibet's becoming part of socialist China.

Nevertheless, a start was made to integrate Tibet's Buddhism into the incipient national system of religious organizations. In 1953 an eleven-person Tibetan delegation went to Beijing to participate in the inauguration of the Chinese Buddhist Association (CBA), which spanned the entire country and served as an intermediary between the Buddhism community and the government. It helped to elect 29 Tibetans to the 93-member CBA council.[22] The key governmental office involved with the actual administration of religion, the Religious Affairs Bureau (RAB), was set up in Tibet in 1956, its first head being the highly respected incarnate lama Trijang Rimpoche, the Junior Tutor of the Dalai Lama.[23] A year later a branch of the CBA, the Tibetan Buddhist Association, was also begun in Lhasa. These offices, however, had no authority over Tibetan monasteries or popular religion.

The parallel experiences of political and ethnographic Tibet with regard to religion began to diverge in 1955–56 as a consequence of the "Socialist Transformation" campaign launched by Mao in the middle of 1955. This called for a speeding up of the collectivization of rural China and set local officials in most areas scurrying to create new collectives. Although the gradualist policy for Tibetans was still in effect, the provincial leaders of Sichuan decided that the time was appropriate for collectivization all over the province. Consequently, they began to implement the socialist transformation campaign in Tibetan as well as Han Chinese areas even though "democratic reforms" (expropriation of land from the aristocratic and monastic landlords) had not yet been conducted in the Tibetan areas. The Tibetan religious and lay elites opposed these reforms and responded by launching a series of bloody uprisings that involved monks of several of the most prominent Gelugpa monasteries such as those in Litang and Batang. The separation between religion and politics was now breached and the Chinese army responded vigorously, bombing and shelling both of these monasteries. Socialist political and economic reforms now began in earnest.[24]

The frustration of those seeking to finesse a modus vivendi between Tibetan Buddhism and the socialist ideology of the state is seen somewhat poignantly in two speeches made by Geshe Sherap Gyatso, a learned "progressive" monk who was a ranking PRC cadre in Qinghai Province. In the first, Sherap Gyatso criticized Tibetans who use Buddhism to further political ends hostile to the CCP, articulating the view that this will lead to the destruction of Buddhism, not its advancement: "Purging the enemy who hides under the cloak of religion is a righteous struggle entirely in keeping with the freedom of religious belief provided for in the Constitution. If they are not purged or if they are believed and allowed to influence people, then freedom of belief will be lost."[25]

In a second speech delivered at the National People's Congress on 22 June 1956, Sherap Gyatso criticized officials of the Chinese Communist party for trying to constrain Tibetan monasticism in ways that are incompatible with its foundational norms.

> It is, of course, an undisputable truth that cooperation is the only way to improve minority people's agriculture and animal husbandry so as to follow Socialism, but owing to their different standards, the methods of following socialism should not be the same. The key point is to pay quick attention to the religious problem of minority nationalities. Our State policy of freedom of religion is a policy which is very satisfactory to religious people, but in carrying it out, various authorities have to be careful at all times. The Tibetan lamas have the Buddhist rule and custom whereby they cannot take part in farm work—a tradition which can not easily be

changed. . . . [T]he lamas cannot obtain remuneration by labor after these farms and animals are transferred to farm cooperatives. Therefore, the remuneration for their farmlands and cattle and sheep should still be paid to them to solve their difficulties and relieve their uneasy feelings. . . .

The expenses for certain religious activities of lamaseries and monasteries had always been borne by a certain tribe, or several villages, or a single village or several families as a matter of custom. After all of them were organized into higher cooperatives, it has become difficult to find benefactors. In future, adequate arrangements should be made so that expenses for this kind of religious activities will not be affected.[26]

In the end the rapprochement experiment of the 1950s failed and the 1959 uprising in Lhasa resulted in the Dalai Lama fleeing to exile in India and denouncing the validity of the 17-Point Agreement, that is, Chinese sovereignty over Tibet. Following the suppression of this rebellion, Beijing also renounced the agreement and incorporated political Tibet directly into the PRC's administrative system, launching its program of democratic reforms. All religious estates were confiscated and the political, economic, and ideological dominance of the religious and aristocratic elites was totally destroyed.

The five years between the 1959 uprising and the onset of the Cultural Revolution comprise the second period. With the old socioeconomic system ended, the funding of monasteries and monks also, and monastic life disintegrated rapidly. Though folk rituals and ceremonies continued, monastic life became moribund. Monasteries were seen as intrinsically disloyal and hostile to the CCP, and with only a few exceptions, their power and influence were crushed.[27] The leaders of Tibet's great monasteries were incarcerated along with many scores of monks involved in the uprising, and most other monks were sent home or to other work units since the government did not organize a system of funding monks qua monks as Sherap Gyatso had urged. As chapter 2 on Drepung Monastery describes, monasteries ceased to function as centers of study and prayer. The policy of gradualism was over. In fact, among Chinese cadres there was a backlash to the gradualist strategy that led to many excesses and concomitant hardship and suffering.[28] Individuals, however, were still permitted to practice religion, and Tibetans continued to recite prayers and maintain altars to deities in their homes.

The third religious period began with the onset of the Cultural Revolution in 1966. A hallmark of the Cultural Revolution was the view that China must eliminate traditional values carried over from the old society.[29] Religion was one of the key targets of the Red Guards, and within two years *all* remaining vestiges of religion in China were eliminated. Tibet was shown no special consideration because of either its minority status or the central role of religion in the people's way of life. All practice of Buddhism and popular religion was prohibited and effectively eliminated, Tibetans being told over and over that their religion—their gods, lamas, and monks—were primitive and false. Private religious activities, including altars, were forbidden; religious structures such as temples, monasteries, and prayer walls were torn down; and thousands of religious texts and icons were burned or desecrated.[30] Tibetans, therefore, were forced to abandon deeply held values and customs. Although this policy was implemented all over China, because Tibetans' national and cultural identity was so closely associated with Buddhism, the attacks on these struck squarely at Tibetans' core ethnic identity in a way that the destruction of Chinese Buddhism or Christianity did not do for Han Chinese. Thus, while many Tibetans became Red Guards and enthusiastically attacked traditional culture,[31] for the majority of Tibetans the Cultural Revolution was a tremendous shock that led many to feel they had been lied to by the Party and the State during the gradualist era. A black joke that became popular during this period captures the essence of this feeling. "Chinese policies are like a leather hat," the joke goes. "At first when moist it fits very comfortably, but after a while, it dries out and becomes more and more constrictive." This period, therefore, created a broad-based community memory of hatred and distrust that continues to the present.

The fourth, or current, "revival" period began with the Eleventh Party Plenum's decisions in 1978. With regard specifically to Tibet, the reform policy represented Beijing's attempt to redress the wrongs that had been done to Tibetans within the framework that Tibet was an inalienable part of China. It had a number of salient dimensions, such as quickly improving the living standard of individual Tibetans, developing the economic infrastructure of Tibet to enable sustained growth in the years ahead, and most critically, allowing more cultural autonomy for Tibetans in the realm of religion, customs, and language and education.

Although many Tibetans initially feared this was a trick to expose those still harboring old thoughts and ideas, very quickly it was understood that the policy had really changed. Over the past two decades, Tibetans have actively availed themselves of the new opportunities, and Tibet today is alive with religion and religious activities.

This outpouring of religious activity has been interpreted as a spontaneous resurrection of beliefs that continued to exist in the minds and hearts of Tibetans during the period when their expression had been prohibited by state decree and sanctions. Israel Epstein expresses this view, arguing that the revival was not a "new surge of faith but an unworried coming into the open of what had been there all along." In the previous period, he says, a believer who did not take his prayer wheel outdoors might have fingered a rosary, instead, within his sleeve. And a circuit pilgrim would walk around the Bargor (the market route surrounding the sacred temple in the center of Lhasa) as though "taking a stroll."[32] In other words, although the state was able to suppress all overt practice of Buddhism in Tibet during the decade of the Cultural Revolution, it could not obliterate such practice on a cognitive and emotional level. A new people's proletarian culture was widely hailed but not genuinely created in the sense of being felt and believed. Most Tibetans maintained their belief and faith in Buddhism unshaken. Consequently, as soon as the State revoked its legal prohibitions and persecution of religion, Tibetans spontaneously began to practice the religion that had continued to exist in their minds during the ten dark years. Like pent-up air in a balloon whose opening is tied, the religious practices rushed forward when the binds were removed.

This interpretation accurately conveys an important dimension of the revival but also oversimplifies it by ignoring its dynamic and adaptive dimensions. As the chapters in this volume reveal, the matrix of beliefs and practices that comprise Tibetan Buddhism have not been restored to their original state like frozen vegetables defrosted in a microwave oven. Some individual cultural traits have reemerged identical with the past, but others have reappeared somewhat changed, and still others have not reemerged at all. In still other cases, views held by a minority in the old society have now gained prominence. And this process has not been homogeneous throughout the areas where Tibetan Buddhism was practiced. Not only were there historical differences between political and ethnographic Tibet (cf. chapters 2 and 3), but differing local sociopolitical conditions have also fostered variant adaptations and new complexes of beliefs and practices. Tibetan religion, therefore, has not simply reappeared. Rather, a dynamic process of adaptation has occurred and is still occurring.

One of the key issues affecting this process of adaptation is the Tibet Question, that is to say, the conflict over what should be the political status of Tibet vis-à-vis China. Beijing's leaders in 1978–79 appear to have been eager to put the Tibet Question behind them and set out to achieve rapprochement with the Dalai Lama. They saw themselves as reformers committed to a policy of improving conditions in Tibet and rightly considered normalization of relations with the Dalai Lama to be in their long-term interests. Not only would it silence one of China's most vocal critics abroad and end all doubts about the legitimacy of Chinese sovereignty over Tibet, but it would also send a positive signal to Hong Kong and Taiwan. Informal talks took place in Hong Kong in 1978 between representatives of the Chinese government and the Dalai Lama's elder brother (Gyalo Thundrup) at which both sides expressed an interest in reconciling the Tibet Question. Soon after this, in 1982, Deng Xiaoping invited the Dalai Lama to send representatives for face-to-face negotiations in Beijing.

The problem facing the Dalai Lama and Dharamsala's leaders was how to respond to the Chinese at these meetings. Should he and his officials indicate willingness to accept less than independence, and if so, how much less? Although they felt strongly that history clearly supported their contention that Tibet had been independent, at least from the fall of the Qing Dynasty in 1911, they understood that China had physical control of Tibet and was a powerful nation that Tibetans could not defeat on the battlefield. The focal decision, therefore, was whether they should take a hard-line approach that held out for their regaining political control in Tibet because time was on their side, or whether they should adopt a more conciliatory posture in the belief that this was a unique moment for them to secure the best deal they could to preserve an ethnically "Tibetan" Tibet. These very difficult choices prompted months of in-depth discussions in Dharamsala.

On top of this, the exile government was deeply committed to the re-creation of a "Greater" Tibet, that is to say a Tibet that included traditional political Tibet and ethnographic Tibet. This had been a goal of previous Tibetan governments, but it was especially important in exile because of the presence of large numbers of Tibetan refugees from those ethnic areas. The Dalai Lama had worked hard since 1959 to meld the disparate refugees into a unified community by including them in the exile government as equals and by setting as a fundamental political objective the inclusion of their areas in a future free Tibet. However, Tibet had not ruled most of these areas for a century or more, and it is difficult to see how China could have handed over large areas in Sichuan, Qinghai, Gansu, and Yunnan, many of which included Chinese and Chinese Muslim populations that had migrated there well before the communists came to power in 1949. However, if Dharamsala decided not to pursue a demand for a Greater Tibet and this leaked out, it would be breaking the faith with the eastern Tibetans in exile. Like forsaking independence, this issue was highly contentious and could easily split the unity of the exile community if handled wrongly.

In the end, therefore, not only was there no consensus in Dharamsala as to what the Dalai Lama's bottom line should be regarding political and territorial concession, but there was pressure *not* to create one for the negotiations in Beijing. Dharamsala, consequently, sent its high-level representatives to Beijing with a brief to talk only in general terms, for example, to present historical arguments about Tibet and Sino-Tibetan relations. The discussions, therefore, did not get down to substantive issues about the Dalai Lama's return. The Tibetans made only a single comment about their political position, stating *in passing* that if China was willing to offer Taiwan the "one country, two systems" option, Tibet should receive far more.

The Chinese were disappointed by the Tibetans' attitude. They had hoped the exiles would arrive ready to discuss specifics about their return in a friendly and forthcoming manner, and were frustrated when they persisted in talking about general issues and past history in a way that indicated they were not ready to accept a Tibet that was under the "unified leadership" of the CCP. Beijing wanted rapprochement but did not want to enter into a genuine give-and-take with the exiles over the issue of changes in the political control of the Tibet Autonomous Region. In the end, therefore, this historic meeting not only produced no new movement toward solving the Tibet Question but also raised serious questions in Beijing about the feasibility of rapprochement with the Dalai Lama. In the aftermath of the 1982 meeting, the exile leadership showed some goodwill by refraining from commenting on the meetings but at the same time continued to attack Chinese policies and human rights violations in Tibet,[33] often actually going beyond what the actual situation warranted, for example, with charges of Chinese genocide. Dharamsala still felt more comfortable pursuing an adversarial model of interaction than one that emphasized friendship and harmony.

On the Chinese side, opponents of the "moderation" policy toward Tibetans interpreted the Dalai Lama's unwillingness to get down to substantive issues and his officials' continuation of attacks as a sign of their insincerity. In fact, some explicitly saw this as déja vu—as a replay of what they considered the duplicitous behavior of the Dalai Lama and his government in the 1950s when the Dalai Lama talked to Mao and others in Beijing with the voice of a "progressive" but did not act as one after returning to Tibet. Beijing, therefore, moved to intensify a strategy of trying to win the approval and loyalty of Tibetans in Tibet by allocating increased funds for development. This policy was finalized at the Second Tibet Work Conference held in Beijing in 1984. It approved forty-two major construction projects in Tibet and extended China's Open Door policy to Tibet, despite the concerns of some leaders and experts that this would draw more non-Tibetans to Tibet and would therefore exacerbate Tibetan hostility toward China and the Chinese. In a sense, since Beijing could not solve the Tibet Question by inducing the Dalai Lama to return to solidify its control of Tibet, it sought to do so without him by quickly modernizing and developing Tibet while allowing Tibetans the freedom to express their culture and practice their religion.

Another face-to-face meeting in Beijing in 1984 between representatives of the Dalai Lama and the Chinese government yielded no results. At this meeting the Tibetans made a substantive proposal that included creation of a demilitarized Greater Tibet that would have a political status in excess of the "one country, two systems" proposal for Taiwan.[34] It was, of course, futile from the start. Beijing was not willing to discuss real political autonomy for Tibet. It was looking to enhance its stability and security in Tibet, not lessen it by turning over political control of Tibet to its "enemies" in Dharamsala, let alone give up control over a Greater Tibet. Dharamsala's leaders, in one sense, had misjudged both their own leverage and Beijing's desire for an agreement, but, in another sense, they simply could not bring themselves to contemplate accepting anything less. They were angry and frustrated by Chinese intransigence. In this strained atmosphere, a proposed visit of the Dalai Lama to China/Tibet fell by the wayside.

Dharamsala thus found itself in an awkward situation. It was clear that Beijing had no intention of allowing them to rule Tibet with a different political system, let alone independence, and it was also clear that Beijing was pursuing, with some success, their worst-case scenario in that its new economic reforms in Tibet might win, if not the hearts of Tibetans, at least their stomachs. Material life had improved tremendously in both Lhasa and the countryside where communes had been disbanded. At the same time, China's economic power and international prestige were increasing, and a major goal of U.S. policy in Asia was to strengthen its strategic relationship with China. Thus there was now a real danger that the exile's role in the Tibet Question would be marginalized.

Dharamsala and the Dalai Lama responded in 1986–87 by launching a new political offensive—what is described as their "international campaign."[35] It sought, on the one hand, to secure new Western political and economic leverage to force Beijing to offer the concessions they wanted and, on the other, to give Tibetans in Tibet hope that the Dalai Lama was on the verge of securing U.S. and

Western assistance to settle the Tibet Question, that is, shifting their attention from their stomachs to their ethnic hearts. As discussed in chapter 2, this initiative brought the Dalai Lama to the United States in 1987 to address the Congressional Human Rights Caucus, and this in turn sparked a demonstration by monks in Lhasa that quickly produced a major riot. Over the next two years three more large riots occurred, and in 1989 Beijing finally decided to declare martial law in Tibet to regain control.

Since 1990 Beijing's relations with the Dalai Lama have worsened demonstrably, and today the Chinese government is engaged in a campaign that vilifies the Dalai Lama as the main enemy of Tibet and the Tibetan people. Along with this has come a substantial hardening of Beijing's attitude toward Tibetan culture, religion, and language. Beijing's current approach to its "problem" in Tibet is to reduce the influence of the Dalai Lama and the exiles while also fostering Tibet's cultural, economic, and demographic integration with the rest of China. The monasteries have been a focus of this new approach, the government insisting that the monks abide by the nation's laws. In 1996 it launched a major campaign aimed at cleansing the monasteries of political dissidents. (How this played out in Drepung Monastery is discussed in chapter 2). Consequently, the political jockeying of the leaders of China and the Dalai Lama over the past two decades has directly influenced the revival of Buddhism, and Tibetan monks (and nuns) have assumed a prominent role in antigovernment political dissidence.

This volume examines the process of revival in four localities. The aim of the chapters is not to assess quantitatively the extent of Tibetan revival, for example, by calculating the number of monasteries, monks, and so forth, but rather to explore key elements in the nature of the revival process, in particular, the forces that have interacted to propel and mold the form this revival has taken. Each of these studies was conducted through firsthand fieldwork by a scholar who speaks and reads Tibetan and is an expert in either Tibetan anthropology/ethnology (Epstein and Peng and Goldstein) or Buddhism (Germano and Kapstein). Two of the chapters (Goldstein, Germano) deal with monasticism and learning, and two (Epstein and Peng, Kapstein) with the ritual side of religion. All deal with the interface between Buddhism, modernity, and nationalism. In the end, we hope this volume provides objective new data on Buddhism in contemporary Tibet as well as insights into the successes and difficulties that Tibetans throughout China have encountered in reviving Buddhism.

TWO

The Revival of Monastic Life in Drepung Monastery

Melvyn C. Goldstein

Religion in Tibet played a role that went beyond its universal functions as an explanation of suffering and a template for salvation. Tibetans saw religion as a symbol of their country's identity and of the superiority of their civilization.

At the heart of Tibetan Buddhism in the traditional society was the monastery and the institution of the monk. Monasteries were (ideally) collectivities of individuals who had renounced attachments to materialism and family and had made a commitment to devote their lives to the pursuit of Buddhist teachings, including a vow of celibacy. Their presence was both the concrete manifestation and the validation of Tibetans' belief in their society's religiosity. In this chapter I examine the revival of Drepung, Tibet's largest monastery in the precommunist period.

Tibetan monasticism shared many features with its Buddhist counterparts in South, Southeast, and East Asia but also differed in several important ways. First, the overwhelming majority of monks were placed in monasteries by their parents as young children, generally between the ages of six and twelve. They were chosen without particular regard to their inclination or personality and were expected to remain celibate monks for their entire lives.[1] Tibetans articulate a straightforward rationale for a system of child enrollment: it is better to enroll candidates at a young age before they have had much exposure to secular life (in particular, to girls).

Second, monasticism in Tibet was pursued with an implicit ideology of "mass monasticism" in that it enrolled as many monks as sought entrance and expelled very few. Size rather than quality became the objective measure of the success of monasticism (and Buddhism) in Tibet, and there were a staggering number of monks. In 1951, at the time of the Lhasa uprising, there were approximately 2,500 monasteries and 115,000 monks in Tibet proper, comprising roughly 10 to 15 percent of Tibet's male population.[2] The magnitude of this can be appreciated by comparing it with Thailand, another prominent Buddhist society, where only 1 to

Figure 2.1. Drepung Monastery.

2 percent of the total number of males were monks.[3] Monasticism in Tibet, therefore, was not the otherworldly domain of a minute elite but a mass phenomenon.

There were many reasons why parents sent their sons to become monks in traditional Tibet. For many, it was a deep religious belief that this bestowed a great privilege on the child and brought good merit and esteem to the parents. For oth-

Figure 2.2. A senior monk and his young monk ward.

ers, it was a culturally valued way to reduce the number of mouths to feed while also ensuring that the child would avoid the hardships of village life. Parents sometimes also committed a son to monkhood to fulfill a solemn promise to a deity to dedicate a sick boy to a religious life if the deity spared the boy. Occasionally, an older monk asked a brother or a sister to send a son to the monastery to live with him, and in yet other cases, recruitment was simply the result of a corvée tax obligation (*grwa-khral*) that some monasteries were entitled to collect from their subjects.

Parents occasionally broached the topic with the child before making him a monk but usually simply told him of their decision. In theory the monastery asked the young candidates whether they wanted to join, but in reality this was pro forma. For example, if a new child monk ran away from the monastery, he was inevitably returned by his parents and welcomed by the monastic administration. There was no thought of dismissing him on the grounds that he obviously did not want to be a monk. Tibetans feel that young boys cannot comprehend the value of being a monk and that it is up to their elders to see to it that they have the right opportunities.

In addition to the high prestige of being a monk, the emphasis on mass monasticism can be seen in the manner in which monasteries made it easy for monks to find a niche within the monastic community by allowing all sorts of personalities to coexist. The monastery did not place severe restrictions on comportment, nor did it require rigorous educational or spiritual achievement. New monks had no exams

Figure 2.3. A young Drepung monk memorizing a text.

to pass in order to remain in the monastery, and monks who had no interest in studying or meditating were as welcome as the dedicated scholar monks. Even illiterate monks were accommodated and could remain part of the monastic community. In fact, rather than diligently weed out young monks who seemed temperamentally unsuited for a rigorous life of prayer, study, and meditation, the Tibetan monastic system allowed all sorts of deviance to exist, including a type of "punk monk" (*ldab-ldob*) who fought, engaged in sports competition, and was notorious for stealing young boys for use as homosexual partners.[4] Monks were expelled only if they committed murder or major theft or engaged in heterosexual intercourse.

The lofty status of monasteries was reflected in their position as semiautonomous units within the Tibetan state. Drepung, for example, had the right to judge and discipline its monks for all crimes except murder and treason and to own land and peasants. The three great monastic seats around Lhasa, Drepung, Ganden, and Sera, moreover, exercised an almost vetolike power over major government policy. They believed that the political and economic system in Tibet existed to further Buddhism and that they, not the government, could best judge what was in religion's short- and long-term interests. Thus, although they were not involved in the day-to-day ruling process, when the monastic leadership felt strongly on some issue, their views could not easily be ignored by the Dalai Lama's government. The 20,000 monks resident in Drepung and its two sister monastic seats dwarfed numerically the small military contingent maintained by the government in Lhasa and represented a genuine physical threat that on occasion has been used. For example, in 1947 Sera Monastery's Che College rebelled against the Regent, and in 1912–13 Drepung's Loseling College together with (Lhasa's) Tengyeling Monastery supported the Chinese Amban against the Dalai Lama.[5] Drepung and its two sister monastic seats also had an important political role by virtue of the presence of their abbots (and former abbots) in Tibet's National Assembly where they had an often-pivotal say on major issues.

The power and influence of monasteries like Drepung also extended to the economic sphere. Economic support for monasteries in the "old society"[6] was extensive, and many owned large tracts of productive land in the form of estates that had been obtained from the state and individual donors. Between 37 and 50 percent of the arable land in Tibet, in fact, was held by monasteries and incarnate lamas. By contrast, only 25 percent of the land was in the hands of the lay aristocracy and about the same was held by the government. The state also provided generous subsidies to select monasteries, funding religious rites such as the annual Great Prayer Festival in Lhasa and the daily morning prayer chanting assemblies in the three monastic seats.

Monasteries and monks, therefore, were integral to Tibetan Buddhism and to Tibetans' perception of the glory of their civilization and state. And as a result of the ideology of mass monasticism, Tibet contained thousands of monasteries and monks. These monasteries, however, varied considerably in size and scope. Some held only five or ten village monks; others contained thousands of monks from all over Tibet as well as Mongolia and India. The focus of this chapter, Drepung, exemplifies the latter category.

DREPUNG IN TRADITIONAL TIBETAN SOCIETY: OVERVIEW

The largest monastic institution in traditional Tibet was Drepung. Founded in 1416 by Jamyang Chöje and located about five miles west of Lhasa, it was a virtual town housing about ten thousand monks at the time of the Chinese invasion in 1950–51. It epitomized the institutionalization of mass monasticism in Tibet and was at that time the world's largest monastery.

Drepung was organized in a manner that resembled the segmentary structure of classic British universities like Oxford in that the overall entity, the monastery, was a combination of semiautonomous subunits known as *tratsang*. These are conventionally called "colleges" in the English literature, although there were no schools (with teaching faculties) in the Western sense. In 1959 Drepung consisted of four functioning colleges: Loseling, Gomang, Deyang, and Ngagba.[7] Each was a mini-monastery with thousands of monks, an administrative structure headed by an abbot, and its own rules and traditions. Each was a corporate entity in the sense that it had an identity (a name), owned property and wealth, and had its own internal organization and leadership. The monks came and went over the decades, but the entity and its property endured.[8] A monk's loyalties, in fact, were primarily rooted in his college.

The highest official of a college was the abbot. He held his office for a term of six years and could be renewed for another six-year term. He was appointed by the ruler (the Dalai Lama or in his minority, the regent) from a list containing six or seven ranked nominees submitted by the college in question. The ruler had the final authority over the appointment and could select someone not on the list, although this was rarely done. Nevertheless, power to choose the administrative leadership of colleges was one of the main ways that the Tibetan government maintained control over powerful and potentially unruly monasteries like Drepung. Under the abbot, various officials such as the *gegö* (disciplinary officer) and *nyerba* (economic manager) oversaw specific aspects of monastic life. Also, an "assembly" of the more senior monks periodically met to discuss collegewide issues.

Large monastic colleges were normally subdivided into smaller, named residential units known as *khamtsen,* or residence halls as I shall refer to them. These units, similar to the colleges in terms of administrative structure, consisted of one or more buildings divided into apartments (*shag*) where the monks lived. Residence halls had a strong regional flavor since each khamtsen held rights to recruit monks from a specific geographic area or areas. Because great monasteries like Drepung recruited monks from all over the Tibetan cultural world as well as from non-Tibetan areas such as Mongolia, this system helped to facilitate the initial period of acculturation by situating a new monk in a residence together with others who spoke his dialect or language.

Drepung as a whole functioned as an alliance of colleges. There was no single abbot at the helm. Instead, monasterywide issues were decided by a council made up sometimes by the abbots of the different colleges and sometimes by the current and the former abbots. The monastery as a whole also owned property, and there were several important monasterywide monk stewards whose responsibility was to manage these. There were also monasterywide disciplinary officers.

At the level of the individual monk, Drepung's ten thousand members were divided into two broad categories—those who studied a formal curriculum of Buddhist theology and philosophy and those who did not. The former, known as *pechawa*, or bookish ones, were a small minority, amounting to only about 10 percent of the total monk population. These "scholar monks," as I shall refer to them, pursued a fixed curriculum that involved approximately fifteen classes or levels (*'dzin-grwa*), each of which took a year to complete (Anon. 1986). This curriculum emphasized learning Buddhist theology by means of extensive formal debating. Like much else in Drepung Monastery, the theological study program was conducted at the college rather than the monastic level. Three of Drepung's four colleges offered such a curriculum (Gomang, Loseling, and Deyang); the other, Ngagba, taught tantric rituals. The scholar monks in Gomang, Loseling, and Deyang met three times a day to practice debating in their respective college's outdoor walled park called a *chöra*, or dharma grove. The curriculum in each college used a slightly different set of texts, although in the end they all covered the same material. Monks pursuing this trajectory started in the lowest class and worked their way up until they were awarded one of several titles or degrees of *geshe* by their college's abbot.[9] The title of geshe was sought by both monks and incarnate lamas of the Dalai Lama's Gelugpa sect, including the Dalai Lama himself.[10] Monks came to Drepung from all over the Tibetan Buddhist world to see if they could master the difficult curriculum and obtain the degree of geshe. The intellectual greatness of the Gelugpa sect's monastic tradition was measured by the brilliance of these scholar monks.

The overwhelming majority of common monks—the *tramang* or *tragyü*—however, did not pursue this arduous course and were not involved in formal study. Many could not read much more than one or two prayer books, and some, in fact, were functionally illiterate, having memorized only a few basic prayers. These monks had some intermittent monastic work obligations in their early years but otherwise were free to do what they liked. However, because Drepung did not provide its monks with either meals via a communal kitchen or payments in kind and money sufficient to satisfy their needs, they had to spend a considerable amount of time in income-producing activities. Some monks, therefore, practiced trades like tailoring and medicine, some worked as servants for other monks, some engaged in trade, and still others left the monastery at peak agricultural times to work for farmers.

The reason for the monastery's financial shortfall was not a lack of resources. Drepung, for example, owned 151 agricultural estates and 540 pastoral areas,[11] each of which had a population of hereditarily bound peasant families who worked the monastery's (or college's) land without wages as a corvée obligation. Drepung also was heavily involved in money- and grain lending and had huge capital funds with thousands of loans outstanding at any given time. The monastery's inability to fund its monks, therefore, derived primarily from its decisions on how to utilize its income vis-à-vis its monks. On the one hand, Drepung allocated a substantial portion of monastic income to rituals and prayer chanting assemblies rather than to monks' salaries; on the other, it did not attempt to restrict the number of monks to the income it had available. Rather, it allowed all to join. Despite a traditional government-set ceiling of 7,700 monks, monasteries like Drepung made no attempt to determine how many monks they could realistically support and then admit only that many. How monks financed their monastic status was, by and large, their own problem.

The monks most affected by the insufficient funding were those who had made a commitment to study Buddhist theology full-time, that is, the scholar monks. They were sorely disadvantaged since they had no time to engage in trade or other income-producing activities because of their heavy academic burdens. Consequently, they typically were forced to lead extremely frugal lives unless they were able to find wealthy patrons to supplement their income or were themselves wealthy, as in the case of the incarnate lamas. Tales abound in Drepung of famous scholar monks so poor that they had to eat the staple food—*tsamba* (parched barley flour)—with water rather than tea, or worse, who had to eat the leftover dough from ritual offerings (*torma*).

Consequently, in the traditional society monasteries like Drepung (and Sera and Ganden) were full of monks who spent a large part of their time engaged in moneymaking activities. Periodically, some monastic leaders sought to reform this situation and return the monastery to a more otherworldly orientation, but this was not the dominant point of view. The karma-grounded ideology of Tibetan Buddhism saw the enforcement of morality and values as an individual rather than an institutional responsibility. Individuals, monks or otherwise, were responsible for their actions. Depending on the morality of their behavior, actors reaped quantities of "merit" or "demerit," which in the end interacted to determine the nature of their future rebirths. Monks, by virtue of their commitment to monastic life, especially their forsaking of the binding "this-world" attachment to sex and family life, had elevated themselves to a higher moral-spiritual plane than laymen, and the need of many to engage in secular work to secure subsistence was viewed as secondary in comparison to the extraordinary merit-producing behavioral commitment they had made. Thus it was only in the most serious cases such as heterosexual intercourse that the monastery as an institution felt the need to enforce morality and eliminate those who lapsed.

Consequently, at the time Mao Zedong incorporated Tibet into the new Chinese state in 1951, the ideology and practice of mass monasticism were in full play in Drepung.

INCORPORATION INTO THE PEOPLE'S REPUBLIC OF CHINA

During the first phase of the new Sino-Tibetan relationship—the years from 1951 until the abortive Tibetan uprising of 1959—China's strategy in political Tibet, today's Tibet Autonomous Region (TAR), focused on gradually winning over the majority of the Tibetan elite rather than on immediately trying to implement socialist reforms.

Instructions sent by the Central Committee of the Chinese Communist Party (CCP) to the Chinese leaders in Lhasa in mid-1952 regarding the Three Monastic Seats convey the gist of this gradualist policy:

> The united front work of the three main monasteries is like other united front work in Tibet. The emphasis should be on the upper hierarchy. We should try to win any of those close to the top of the hierarchy, provided that they are not stubborn running dogs of imperialists, or even bigger bandits and spies. Therefore, you should try patiently to win support among those upper level lamas whom you referred to as those full of hatred to the Hans and to our government. *Our present policy is not to organize people at the bottom level to isolate those at the top.* We should try to work on the top, get their support, and achieve the purpose of building harmony between the masses and us.[12]

The arrival of the Chinese communists in Tibet, therefore, did not change monastic life or the monastery's ownership of estates and peasants/serfs during the initial period. The abortive uprising in 1959 ended Beijing's gradualist policy in Tibet, changing overnight all facets of monastic life in Drepung. Beijing now moved to destroy the political, economic, and ideological dominance of the estate-holding elite, including the monasteries.[13]

The overwhelming majority of Drepung monks were not active participants in the Lhasa uprising, although certainly all had great faith in and support for the Dalai Lama. However, a number of monks from Drepung had defended the Dalai Lama's summer palace and fought in Lhasa. Because of that, Drepung was classified as a rebellious monastery and had all its estates and granaries confiscated without compensation.[14] Similarly, all the loans it had made which were still outstanding were canceled. Chinese accounts state that Drepung at this time had 140,000 tons of grain and 10 million yuan in cash (equal then to U.S. $5 million) outstanding in such loans.[15] The flow of income to Drepung (in kind and cash) totally ceased.

Monastic life and monastic administrative structure were also fundamentally altered. In the initial months following the uprising, a group of officials called a work team (*las-don ru-khag*) was sent from Lhasa to take charge of the monastery. They ended up staying continuously in the monastery until the onset of the Cultural Revolution in 1966. These officials immediately terminated the power and authority of the traditional leadership and appointed a new administrative committee selected from among the poorer and "progressive" monks in a manner analogous to what was done in the rest of China years earlier. The new administration was called the Democratic Management Committee (*dmangs-gtso bdag-gnyer u-yon lhan-khang*, henceforth DMC).[16] It has continued to the present.

One of the main initial tasks of the work team (and the new DMC) was determining how monks should be grouped into the various class categories used by the state. Monks involved in the uprising and virtually all the monastery administrators/leaders were classified as "exploiters" and imprisoned or sent to labor camps. The rest of the monks were given several months of "education" in the new socialist ideology, including the need to engage in productive labor. At this time all the monks, and especially the young ones, were encouraged to leave the monastery—to return to their home areas or to join nonmonk work units. The number of monks in Drepung decreased sharply, and by the end of 1959 there were only about four thousand remaining. A Drepung monk described this period: "At first, at this time there was [political] education all day. We were taught things we never heard before like the 'three antis' and the 'two exemptions' and the 'three great mountains.' . . . [How we got food] depended on the wealth of the monks. The poor monks ate together using the food the monastery had amassed in its storerooms, while the better off monks ate in their apartments using their own food supplies. I was among the latter."[17] After a few months of this political reeducation and reorganization, the remaining monks began to engage in manual labor projects, initially as "volunteers" and then as part of work units. Another monk recalled,

> At first we ate the monastery's food in our own residence halls, but then after many monks were sent off and the total number of monks became much less, the remaining monks gathered together in Loseling College where we ate food together. After about 5–6 months, the monastery's food stores ran out. However, by then we were all engaged in productive labor so we got food through that work. At this time only the old monks were [regularly] left in the monastery. All the younger monks were out working on projects. How often we returned to the monastery varied; some returned once a week, some daily. These jobs weren't permanent postings.
>
> After communal dining at Loseling broke up, we divided into smaller production units that worked and ate together; for example, there was a sewing unit, a masonry unit, a construction unit, a carpentry unit and a firewood collecting unit. Later some of these were again divided into two units. Each unit, therefore, had its own livelihood [i.e., was organized as a collective] and ate together. The tsamba was divided among the monks, and the butter was kept jointly and used to make tea for all. The monks ate their tsamba separately and took tea together. The older monks who couldn't work and wouldn't go home were organized as an "old people's unit" (gensogang) and lived off subsidies from the government.[18]

In 1965, six years after the uprising, one foreign visitor to Drepung reported that only 715 of the 10,000 monks present in Drepung in 1959 remained.[19] The physical shell of Drepung stood and those monks who remained had vows and prayed in their rooms when not working, but the defining institutional religious activities—joint prayer chanting sessions and the dharma grove theology curriculum—had ended. The monastery ceased to function as an institution where religious study, debate, and ritual were practiced. But the worst was still to come.

The third, and most devastating, period for Drepung began with the onset of the Cultural Revolution in 1966. It brought an end to the religion practiced by individual laypersons and monks alike. Drepung remained "open" in the sense that monks continued to live there, but the monks were no longer allowed to wear their robes or maintain private altars in their rooms, and all religious acts were now prohibited. At the same time, political struggle sessions attacked religious beliefs and practices as well as former leaders. Lay and monk Tibetans were encouraged and pressured to ridicule and deride religious laws and gods as well as despoil sacred sites. And although Drepung was fortunate in that most of its building were not destroyed during this period (as were so many other Tibetan monasteries), it was no longer a monastery: those who remained were simply former monks living and working in what used to be a monastery. By the end of the Cultural Revolution in 1976, the number of monks in Drepung had decreased to only 306, and a number of these were married.[20]

The fourth, or current, period began with the liberalizing decisions made in Beijing in 1978 at the Eleventh Party Plenum (see chapter 1). In Lhasa the new policy quickly resulted in the reemergence of "individual" religion, that is, the religious practices performed by individuals. At the same time, a number of temples and shrine rooms were reopened so the public could make religious visits and offerings to deities as in the past.[21] Tibetans responded enthusiastically to the new opportunities and began a host of traditional practices such as circumambulating holy sites. By 1980–81 the shrine rooms in Drepung Monastery were receiving religious visitors from Central Tibet as well as from the ethnic Tibetan areas in Qinghai, Gansu, and Sichuan provinces daily. However, the revival of monasticism per se did not progress as rapidly as did that of individual religion.

The first changes in Drepung began in 1979–80 and paralleled those of the lay society. "Monks," although still engaged full-time in manual labor, began openly to practice religion as individuals, setting up altars in their rooms, using rosaries to count prayers, and reading religious prayer books in their free time. At the same time, the number of monks in Drepung increased slightly after a small number of former monks returned to take up residence in the monastery.[22] Some Drepung monks also were again able to engage in full-time religious work when monk caretakers (*gönye*) were recruited to look after Drepung's newly opened shrine rooms. These monks performed the necessary propitiatory rites to the shrine's deities, collected donations given by pilgrims, and guarded against theft.

However, collective monastic activities did not immediately reemerge in Drepung. A 1995 leader in the DMC explained this as follows:

> The official document [of the Eleventh Plenary Session] stating the new proclamations of Deng Xiaoping reached us in the monastery later than others in Lhasa, . . . but it was still earlier than other remote areas in Tibet where class struggle was still

in progress as late as 1982 and 1983. . . . No one at this time came to us and told us that now we could do religious activities and do the joint prayer chanting sessions, but gradually as we read the document and thought about it, we concluded that the religious freedom it expounded meant we could return to practicing religion in Drepung.[23]

Another current DMC official in Drepung recalled this period in a similar vein: "With the new liberalized nationality and religious policies, we and the people thought that the monastery can't continue to remain empty as it then was [i.e., without religion]. At the very least, we should revive the joint prayer chanting sessions."[24]

When Drepung's DMC finally decided in 1981 that the time was right to revive monastic life in an active sense, they also understood that this would be neither easy nor straightforward. It would need the agreement of the government of the TAR. Many officials in Tibet were hostile to this, believing that Tibetan monasteries were an anachronism, that they were unnecessary or even worse, a threat to socialism and the domination of the Communist party. Nothing should be done, they felt, to allow monasteries and lamas to once again function as unifying institutions for the Tibetan masses since this would inevitably give new hope to those most reactionary and hostile to Beijing and foster nationalistic, pro-independence dissidence.

Moreover, the laws governing religious freedom included a number of important limitations to which a "new" Drepung would have to conform. For example, the 1982 Chinese constitution's definition of religious freedom specifies, "In our country, citizens may believe in religion or disbelieve, but politically they have one thing in common, that is, they are all patriotic and support socialism. . . . The State protects legitimate religious activities, but no one may use religion to carry out counter-revolutionary activities or activities that disrupt public order, harm the health of citizens, or obstruct the educational system of the State . . . [and] no religious affairs may be controlled by any foreign power."[25] And there were other important caveats. Because religious freedom was part of the more basic freedom to believe or *not to believe,* the state sought to create a level playing field by prohibiting religious education and recruitment of individuals into the priesthood who were under the age of eighteen.

Religious freedom in China, therefore, was predicated on religious practitioners and organizations accepting the principle of the unity of the nation, eschewing any activities that foster separatism, remaining completely free from foreign control, and not engaging in activities the government deemed "exploitive." However, whether Tibetan monasteries would actually abide by these rules was uncertain and, given the history of the monks' opposition to communism and their likely sympathy with the exiled Dalai Lama, entailed a considerable risk.

Despite such dangers, China's new policy toward Tibet compelled it to permit the process of revival to begin. In 1978–79 Beijing had set out to improve conditions in Tibet and if possible induce the Dalai Lama to return from exile. In particular, it sought to reverse the cultural assimilationist policies of the Cultural Revolution period. This new policy was orchestrated by Hu Yaobang and the Central Committee of the Communist party over the strong opposition of virtually all the leading Han and Tibetan officials in Tibet. Beijing did so because it believed that this strategy would be welcomed by Tibetans and would enhance their confidence in, and loyalty to, the state. In mid-1980 Hu Yaobang made an unprecedented visit to Tibet where he announced the new policy.[26] His public statement on Tibet conveys the tone of the Central Committee's new "conciliatory" policy:

> So long as the socialist orientation is upheld, vigorous efforts must be made to revive and develop Tibetan culture, education and science. The Tibetan people have a long history and a rich culture. The world renowned ancient Tibetan culture included fine Buddhism, graceful music and dance as well as medicine and opera, all of which are worthy of serious study and development. All ideas that ignore and weaken Tibetan culture are wrong. It is necessary to do a good job in inheriting and developing Tibetan culture.
>
> Education has not progressed well in Tibet. Taking Tibet's special characteristics into consideration, efforts should be made to set up universities and middle and primary schools in the region. Some cultural relics and Buddhist scriptures in temples have been damaged, and conscientious efforts should be made to protect, sort and study them. Cadres of Han nationality working in Tibet should learn the spoken and written language. It should be a required subject; otherwise they will be divorced from the masses. Cherishing the people of minority nationalities is not empty talk. The Tibetan people's habits, customs, history and culture must be respected.[27]

The new Chinese policy made a revival of monastic life feasible but, as mentioned above, did not eliminate the need for the monastery's leaders (the DMC) to proceed carefully. Drepung's DMC, as they contemplated how to transform the new Chinese policy into practice, had to make difficult decisions regarding what functioning as a monastery meant in the context of the ideology and values of both the old and the new society. They had to prioritize and structure the revival so as to restore an institution that would both be accepted by Tibetans as authentic and at the same time fall within the purview of China's definition of religious freedom, that is, would avoid precipitating a government crackdown and renewed suppression. Drepung's leaders focused initially on two essential aspects of the monastic way of life: collective prayer assemblies and the recruitment and education of new monks.

Unlike tightly structured Christian monasteries, Drepung traditionally had no activities that required the participation of all monks. Whether a monk spent his time praying or studying or sitting in the sun was his own decision. In Tibetan Buddhism, as indicated earlier, individuals were responsible for their own religious behavior and, via karmic cause and effect, reaped rewards or punishments in their next life based on their decisions in this one. Nevertheless, there were large-scale joint activities that symbolized the monastery as a collectivity. The most important of these were the meetings at which large numbers of monks assembled to chant

Figure 2.4. Monastic official reading the names of patrons at the monks' collective prayer chanting session.

prayers for the benefit of all sentient beings. Collective chanting sessions lasted several hours, including a break during which the monks were served tea (and sometimes food).[28] These prayer assembly meetings also had direct economic importance traditionally because they were the time when patrons distributed alms to the assembled monks.

In 1980–81, the DMC sought and received permission from the Lhasa Religious Affairs Bureau to begin to hold these prayer chanting sessions on a regular basis.[29] One old monk recalled the first assembly meeting in 1982:

> When we got permission, we immediately tried to get the stoves in the monastic kitchen back in shape so we could have the first prayer chanting assembly on the 30th of the fifth lunar month. However, we couldn't manage this so we had to be satisfied with a "dry" assembly [i.e., a prayer assembly at which tea was not served]. We kept on working and quickly got the kitchen operating again so on the festival that commemorates the first sermon of the Buddha on the 4th of the sixth lunar month (Trugpa tsheshi), we held our first full prayer assembly with tea. On that day the DMC sponsored [financed] the tea and gave each of us a small torma religious offering made from tsamba.[30]

From then on, Drepung held prayer chanting assemblies regularly, at first three times a month and then five times a month.[31] In addition, special sessions were held on holidays such as the Great Prayer Festival of the first lunar month.

Figure 2.5. Monks in the kitchen making tea to serve at the prayer chanting session.

While this was going on, Drepung sought and received permission to revive a second critical monastic activity—enrolling new (young) monks. It is not surprising, given the energetic revival of individual religion in 1979–81, that there was a revival of interest among some parents, their motives involving the old mix of economic and religious reasons but also a strong new religionationalistic belief that Tibetan religion, the basis of the greatness of the Tibetan nationality, should be revived to its former greatness. Demographically, this was not problematic since the Chinese government's "one-child policy" had not been implemented in Tibet and rural Tibetans had large families.

Parents seeking to make a son a monk went about this in accordance with the customs of the old society; they sought an older monk (usually a relative or family friend) to serve as the boy's sponsor-guardian (*kegya gegen*) and take the boy in to live with him. Since a foundation of traditional Tibetan monasticism was that monkhood should be available to as many people as possible, it was difficult for older monks to refuse such requests, especially since parents assured them they would provide all the food and clothes their boys needed. Consequently, by 1981 a number of the older monks in Drepung had young boys living in their monastic apartments. These boys took monastic vows. But they were monks without a monastery, for although they were living in Drepung, they were not officially accepted in its monastic rolls.

Figure 2.6. A lay Tibetan patron distributing alms to the monks at a prayer chanting session.

In the old society, when a guardian monk took a young ward to the abbot of his college, he was invariably admitted and immediately became a "legal" monk in the monastery. In the new society, the situation was different. The DMC, like the college's abbot in the old society, had the authority to select applicants, but now this decision was not final. It had to seek approval from the government, which was reluctant to permit the reemergence of monasteries housing many thousands of monks and thus did not readily give such approval. While the government wanted to try to meet the religious aspirations of Tibetans by permitting Drepung and other formerly great monasteries to reopen, it did not want them to become too large or powerful. Consequently, the young boys who went to live with guardian monks in Drepung did not immediately obtain official status and thus were not eligible to participate in prayer assemblies or to receive alms from patrons. Only official monks could partake of these. They were, therefore, novice monks living in Drepung waiting to be formally admitted.[32]

In 1982 the government gave approval to officially enroll the first such monks and fifteen to twenty of those who were already in residence were entered into the monastic roll. This occurred at the same time that Drepung received permission to begin regular prayer chanting sessions. The "new" Drepung, therefore, emerged at this time.[33]

These successes raised the question of what sort of rules should be established for the new monks. Should all monks be forced either to work for the monastery or to study religious theology, or should monks be permitted to work or not work according to their own wishes? And should monks be allowed to engage in private business as in the old society, or must they only work for the monastery? Basic to such questions was the underlying issue of whether the focus of the monastery should be quantity or quality. Was it better for Drepung to try to maximize the number of monks even if most of these would primarily be engaged in manual labor or business, or should Drepung support fewer monks, most of whom would be engaged in the rigorous study of Buddhist theology?

In the traditional society, the answer to this question was clearly quantity. The ideology of mass monasticism dominated. In the new society, Drepung, as I shall show below, had difficulty supporting even a small number of monks financially, and the new political and social climate opposed allowing monasteries to fill up with monks who neither studied nor worked, or worse, became private businessmen as was typical of pre-1959 Tibet. The issue of shifting the monastic emphasis from quantity to quality, however, was not merely a response to the values of the new society or financial constraints. It also had deep roots in the old society and, as the following example illustrates, it was a contentious issue.

THE GOMANG COLLEGE DISPUTE OF 1958–59

In the 1950s in Drepung monks did not have to pass examinations to remain part of the monastic community, and even in the large monastic seats like Drepung only about 10 percent of the monks were actively engaged in the Buddhist study curriculum that led to the title of geshe. This became a problem for Drepung's Gomang College when the number of monks annually receiving the geshe title became so low that it embarrassed the abbot of the college. As the Gomang College prayer chant master (*umdze*) of the time explained,

> During the six-year term of each abbot, it was expected that 60 geshes would be produced. But in recent years in Gomang College, only two, three, or four were graduating each year. Because of this, the government asked Drepung why there were so few geshes now whereas in the past there had been so many. When we looked into this, we found . . . that the number of geshes produced was declining because in general only 100 to 200 of Gomang College's over 4,000 monks were engaged in active study. So we decided that we had to do something to reverse this trend.[34]

Part of the reason for this dearth was Drepung's policy of not providing special financial support for monks engaged in full-time theological studies. Since these monks had no time to engage in income-producing work like ordinary monks, they faced lives of hardship and poverty unless they had some other source of support. This manner of allocating monastic wealth, therefore, functioned as a disincentive for producing substantial numbers of scholar monks.

Nevertheless, there was very little support in the monastery for providing extra income to scholar monks or, alternatively, for forcing all monks to study and pass exams. Most of the monks, particularly the common monks and monk administrators, in fact, felt that the scholar monks were studying for their own benefit, not for the welfare of the monastery, so deserved nothing special. Consequently, the Gomang College reformers decided that the best way to proceed was indirectly. They convinced the abbot to make a new rule shifting the site of the salary payments the college made to all monks to the dharma grove where the scholar monks debated. The logic behind this move was explained by one of the leaders of the reform faction: "We thought that if we distributed salaries in the dharma grove, more monks would come to it, and if we did this continually, then some of these monks would get used to the dharma grove [and come even when there was no salary distribution]."[35]

The abbot's new order meant that all monks, even administrators, had to go to the dharma grove and sit through the prayers that began a debating session before collecting their salaries. Although they did not have to study, or participate in the debates, or attend the dharma grove during the rest of the year, this order produced an outcry of protest from the monk officials who handled the college's administrative work. At their instigation, the mass of common monks became involved, insisting that the rules of the monastery were sacred and could not be changed.

This controversy polarized Gomang College's monks and eventually led to violence when a mob of angry monks broke into a meeting on this issue and

Figure 2.7. The Drepung dharma grove.

dragged three of the reform leaders outside where they tied them to pillars, beat them, and then locked them up as prisoners. Ultimately, the Dalai Lama's government intervened and freed the monks, but while it expelled the leaders of both factions, it did not force the monks to go to the dharma grove to collect their salaries. The reform program had failed. At this point the Tibetan uprising of 1959 occurred and the traditional monastic system ended.

Consequently, as the DMC and older monks contemplated how to re-create a monastic community in the early 1980s, there were both historical and contemporary reasons for deviating from past tradition, and the leaders opted for a monastery that would emphasize quality over quantity. Monks in the new Drepung would either have to pursue the full-time study curriculum in Buddhist theology or engage in productive work on behalf of the monastery. The formal Buddhist studies curriculum would be revived and monastic life would be structured so that as many monks as possible could devote themselves to the study of Buddhist theology. Thus, as Drepung began to function again as a monastic community, it set out to recruit a new generation of monks, socialize them into the monastic alternative culture, and educate and support the brightest to pursue the theological study program that would eventually result in their attaining the geshe title.

Theological study in Drepung traditionally centered on the dharma grove where a college's scholar monks met three times a day (during semester periods) to

Figure 2.8. Monks debating in the dharma grove.

engage in formal debate on issues of Buddhist theology. Rather than attend formal classes in the Western sense, students studied with private teachers in the
monastery. Monks pursuing this trajectory started in the lowest class and worked
their way up until they were awarded one of the geshe titles by their college's
abbot. The curriculum was arduous. It required memorizing thousands of pages
of Buddhist texts and their commentaries, understanding their meaning and significance, and being able to use these to engage in high-level formal debates with
other scholar monks and teachers. The scholar monks devoted the overwhelming
preponderance of their time to their studies, often debating in the dharma grove
until late at night. As mentioned above, they traditionally received no special
salary or alms for doing this. In the new Drepung, this changed. In 1984, when
Drepung revived the dharma grove debating system (with permission of the government), it did so with a major innovation: the monastery would now provide
financial support for all monks opting to study full-time.[36]

Securing government permission for prayer assemblies and dharma groves,
however, did not imply government willingness to provide financial support for
these activities. On the contrary, the state was adamant that monasteries had to be
totally self-sufficient. Consequently, the expanding revival of monastic life placed
new economic responsibilities on Drepung. How Drepung handled this is an important dimension of the revival of institutional Buddhism in Tibet.

THE FINANCING OF TODAY'S DREPUNG

In the old society, Drepung's income primarily came from the monastery's own re-sources—its manorial estates and its moneylending operations—and from the government. For the individual monks, alms from donors were also an important source. In the new society, with no estates, the inability to engage in private moneylending, and no financial support from the government, Drepung faced a formidable challenge, especially since it had opted for quality in its approach to monastic organization. Not only could its monks' subsistence no longer simply be left to their own resourcefulness, but a large number of monks—the scholar monks—now had to be subsidized.

Hypothetically, let us say that each monk should receive as income 150 yuan per month.[37] In 1992–93 this would have been a decent, but not high, wage. Lhasans working in the education sphere, by comparison, earned 281 yuan per month in 1992, those working in factories earned on the average 258 yuan per month (per capita), and those in trade earned 237 yuan per month.[38] To support monks at this modest level, Drepung needed to generate an astounding amount of income. If it were to again house ten thousand monks as it did in 1959, the monastery would have to generate a net annual income of 18 million yuan just to cover those salaries, and more when upkeep, renovation, and other such nonsalary expenses were factored in. And even if we consider only the 437 monks who were actually present in 1993, the annual income needed was 787,000 yuan—about 1 million yuan if repairs and other costs are included. How daunting a challenge this is be-comes evident when we examine the income Drepung generated by its monk-staffed ("co-op") economic units and enterprises.

In the agriculture sphere, the monastery owns a large apple orchard that pro-duced a gross income of about 66,000 yuan in 1993.[39] That income represents just 8 percent of the 787,000 yuan needed for monks' salaries. The monastery also owns and operates a herd of several hundred milch yaks (and calves) and sells some of the yogurt and butter produced by them. The gross income from this was only 11,000 yuan for the year.[40]

Drepung also engages in nonagricultural economic activities. It operates a gro-cery store and a restaurant, both just outside its entrance. The latter services the tens of thousands of pilgrims and tourists who come to visit the monastery every year. In 1993, they grossed 43,000 and 64,000 yuan, respectively. Drepung also owns and operates two trucks that it hires out for transportation and operates con-struction and tailoring work units staffed by monks. Together these earned about 45,000 and 46,000 yuan, respectively, in 1993. Finally, monks engage in a number of smaller activities (on behalf of the monastery) such as selling tree branches for prayer flags, consecrating new statues, and making ceremonial items. And the monastery sells ceremonial scarves to pilgrims who use them to make offerings in the various shrine rooms in the monastery. These activities generated another 29,000 yuan.

As impressive as this array of activities seems, the monastery's total gross income in 1993 was only 294,000 yuan. After deducting expenses, the net profit was only 138,000 yuan, that is, only 17 percent of the 787,000 yuan Drepung's 437 monks needed. Put in another way, the 138,000-yuan profit would have supported only 76 monks at the 150-yuan-per-month level. Traditional Tibetan mass monasticism, therefore, represents an economic hurdle that Drepung and other monasteries cannot easily meet through their own business operations.

Drepung, however, actually fared better economically than the above figures suggest because it had other sources of income. One of these was the yield from the entrance fees it charges visitors (foreign and Chinese). These fees generated as much income as everything else mentioned above: in 1993, 247,000 yuan.[41] In addition to this, the monastery charged each car or bus that used the road leading from the main highway to the monastery a fee of 1 yuan per round-trip. That yielded another 17,000 yuan in 1993, bringing the total for these two activities to 264,000 yuan. When this is added to the 138,000-yuan net income mentioned above, the new total net income for Drepung came to 402,000 yuan in 1993.[42]

This income was not distributed equally. As Drepung is organized economically as a co-op, the income produced by monks on all these enterprises goes into the general coffer, with each working monk receiving income based on the amount of work he does. The latter is calculated via a system of work points (*skar-ma*). In this system, each task or job receives from 1 to 10 points per workday. Every six months the total number of work points accumulated by all monks is totaled, and this amount is divided into the total net income produced during the period.[43] This produces the cash value of a single work point.[44] On this basis, each monk is paid in accordance with the total number of work points he earned during the accounting period. In 1993, 333 of Drepung's 437 monks (76%) engaged in activities that earned at least one work point and the average compensation received by each monk was 93 yuan per month. However, averages are misleading, and many elderly monks in fact worked very little. For example, 38 percent of the above-mentioned monks with work points actually earned less than 50 yuan per month (the lowest being only 1 yuan per month). Thus, in reality, more than half of the monastery's monks either did not work at all or worked only part-time and thus earned nothing or very little. These included the 115 elderly monks and the 137 monks who were studying full-time in the dharma grove program. These non-worker monks secured their subsistence in a variety of ways.

Part of the income of Drepung's elderly monks comes from welfare paid by the government under a nationwide "safety net" program that provides aid to elders living alone (the "five guarantee household" program). However, because this subsidy is small—only 35 yuan per month—the monastery supplements it, in 1993 allocating 25,000 yuan or roughly 18 yuan extra per month in welfare for each elder. These two payments, however, raised the average monthly income of the old monks to only 53 yuan per month.

The other group of nonworking monks, the scholar monks, received no income from the government. Instead, a major portion of their income came from the scholarship money Drepung paid them: 4.75 yuan by the monastery for every day they attended the dharma grove.[45] Figures for the second half of 1993 reveal that the average payment per month for these monks was 91 yuan and the highest payment was 104 yuan per month.[46] Although this is better than the income of the elderly, it still does not meet the 150-yuan standard.

However, the income of these and all other Drepung monks is greatly enhanced by donations from outside the monastery—from the alms (*'gyed*) individuals give to the monks. The most common form this alms-giving takes is a distribution made to each monk during a prayer chanting session. Such payments were a traditional Tibetan custom that reemerged when Drepung revived the collective prayer chanting sessions.

In Drepung, these alms are funneled through the *rikshung*,[47] a monk work unit that was specially created for this purpose. It collects the money individuals donate for the prayer chanting sessions and the monks' alms and organizes the sessions, including the preparation of tea (or food) in the monastery's kitchen. Individuals wishing to sponsor (fund) all or part of a prayer session and/or give aims to the monks go directly to the monastic kitchen where the rikshung officials are located. The rikshung is headed by the gegö, traditionally the head disciplinary officer of a college. He, along with the other rikshung members, are appointed by the DMC and are therefore subordinate to it, but they have financial autonomy (the donations they receive are not added to the rest of Drepung's income). It remains in their hands and is used entirely for alms and prayer sessions. The amount of donation money the rikshung receives is substantial. It covers the expenses of all of the tea (and food) served in the prayer chanting assemblies and provides important income to the individual monks. According to 1991 figures, the rikshung distributed 225,000 yuan in alms to the monks, or 43 yuan per month for each monk.

A second similar source of outside income also comes as alms, but here via the semiannual public religious teaching (*sungjö*) held in Drepung's prayer assembly hall by one of its lamas, Gen Lamrim. These teachings last several weeks and are attended by thousands of Tibetans from the TAR and other parts of ethnographic Tibet, virtually all of whom give an alms offering to Gen Lamrim.[48] They are important to the monks' finances because Gen Lamrim donates *all* the alms he personally receives during this period to the rikshung for redistribution to the monks. In 1991 this amounted to roughly 200,000 yuan.[49]

These two sources of alms, therefore, totaled roughly 425,000 yuan per year, an amount greater than the 402,000 yuan generated by all of the monastery's productive activities and fees. They added about 81 yuan per month to each monk's income and brought the total monthly income of most monks to at least the 150-yuan-per-month level. Ironically, although most Drepung monks were critical of the government for not supporting the monastery financially, objectively their income was good, and most older monks I talked with agreed that economically

Figure 2.9. Pilgrims on the way to a religious teaching being given by a Drepung lama.

they were better off than in the old society. Even the monks at the bottom of the monastic income hierarchy—the old monks on welfare—received an average of 134 yuan per month.[50] By contrast, the average monthly income of all citizens of the TAR in 1992 was only 105 yuan, and farmers and herders earned only 41 yuan.[51]

These figures, moreover, do not take into account the fact that some of Drepung's monks also receive direct food transfers from parents and relatives. The older guardian monks regularly receive such transfers from the parents of the boy monks living with them, and since roughly 20 percent of Drepung's official monk population are serving as guardian monks, the impact of this source is not trivial.[52]

The monks in today's Drepung, therefore, receive excellent income, although it is clear that this is not so much a result of the success of Drepung's revenue-producing endeavors as a consequence of the enormous supplemental income provided by the alms donated by thousands of individual Tibetans. Without these alms, the monastery would not have been able to support the 437 monks it housed in 1993 without reverting to monks having to fend for themselves economically. These alms donations accounted for roughly 50 percent of the monks' total income, excluding the direct food transfers.[53]

Economic anemia, however, is clearly not the main reason for the small number of monks at Drepung: only 437 monks in 1993 (547 in 1995) instead of the 10,000 that were present in 1959. Even if Drepung were able to increase its income exponentially by developing new businesses or by doubling or tripling donations, it could not increase the number of monks it houses because of restrictions imposed by the state. Drepung's current ceiling is 600 monks.

DREPUNG AND POLITICAL DISSIDENCE

Like much else in contemporary Tibet, it is difficult to divorce the revival of Buddhism and monasticism from the struggle over the political status of Tibet vis-à-vis China, that is, from what is often referred to as the Tibet Question. This nationalistic conflict is being played out in two major arenas. Abroad, there is the vocal and active independence movement led by the Dalai Lama and his exile government. In Tibet, the center of Tibetan political consciousness is Lhasa (and its environs), the capital of the traditional Tibetan state. There, monks and nuns launched a very visible campaign of active political dissidence beginning in 1987. From Drepung alone, ninety-two monks were arrested for participating in ten antigovernment political demonstrations between 1987 and 1993.

However, at the time the Chinese government liberalized its policy on religion in 1978–80, resolution of the Tibet conflict seemed promising. Beijing had invited the Dalai Lama to send fact-finding delegations to visit Tibet, and the exiles had begun discussions with China aimed at reaching a mutually acceptable solution to the Tibet Question. But this was not to be. The talks stalemated when the gap between the Chinese position emphasizing enhanced cultural autonomy and the exile's position emphasizing real political autonomy could not be bridged. By the mid-1980s, therefore, the momentum for reconciliation had collapsed and both sides unilaterally pursued policies aimed at improving their position relative to the other.[54]

For the Dalai Lama and his government-in-exile, this meant launching a new political offensive that sought to persuade the United States and Europe to use their economic and political leverage to force concessions from Beijing. At the same time, they sought to counter China's policies aimed at winning over Tibetans within Tibet by conveying to Tibetans there not only that the Dalai Lama was actively working on their behalf in the West but also that his endeavors were successful—that he represented a realistic hope for securing Western assistance to settle the Tibet Question in Tibet's favor.

The key innovation in this strategy was having the Dalai Lama himself carry the exile's political message to the United States and Europe. Prior to this, the Dalai Lama traveled as a religious leader and did not make overtly political speeches. In 1987 there were several important breakthroughs. In June the U.S. House of Representatives adopted a bill that condemned human rights abuses in Tibet, instructed the president to express sympathy for Tibet, and urged China to establish a constructive dialogue with the Dalai Lama.[55] Then, in September, the Dalai Lama made a major visit to the United States during which he presented his first political speech to the Congressional Human Rights Caucus (on 21 September). It was a carefully crafted talk arguing that Tibet had been independent when China invaded it. Specifically, he said, "though Tibetans lost their freedom, under international law Tibet today is still an independent state under illegal occupation." The speech also raised serious human rights charges, referring twice to a "holocaust" inflicted by the Chinese on the Tibetan people.[56]

The Dalai Lama's activities in the United States were widely known and eagerly followed in Lhasa where Tibetans regularly listen to the Chinese-language broadcasts of the Voice of America and the BBC. The Chinese government's media also covered this trip on radio and television, making vitriolic attacks on his visit and views. Among Tibetans in Lhasa the visit was widely taken as confirmation that the tide of history was shifting in Tibet's favor and that the Dalai Lama was on the verge of achieving victory.

At this juncture, a group of about twenty Drepung monks staged an overt political demonstration in Lhasa—the first political demonstration of its type. They did not demonstrate to protest any particular problem Drepung was facing at the time but rather to show Beijing and the West that Tibetans in Tibet support the Dalai Lama and independence. On the morning of 27 September, while the Dalai Lama was still in the United States, they met in Lhasa's central marketplace, the Bargor, unfurled signs that included a handmade Tibetan national flag, and walked around the circular "Bargor" road three times. When nothing happened to them, they marched about a mile down one of the main east-west streets and continued their protest in front of the headquarters of the Tibet Autonomous Region government. At this point they were detained by security forces. Their arrest made news throughout the Western world.

A few days later, on the morning of 1 October, a group of monks from several other monasteries in the area staged a demonstration to show support for the Dalai Lama and the previous monk demonstrators and to demand the latter's release from jail. Police quickly took them into custody in the Bargor and allegedly started beating them. A crowd of Tibetans demanded the release of these monks, and before long this escalated into a full-scale riot. In the end, a number of vehicles and buildings were burned, and anywhere from six to twenty Tibetans were killed when police (including ethnic Tibetan police) fired at the rioters.

Over the next year and a half scores of monk- and nun-led demonstrations occurred, three more of which ended in bloody riots. Martial law was finally declared in 1989 and was not lifted until 1990. In the eight years since then, monk and nun demonstrations have continued, although tight security measures have prevented them from turning into riots. The political atmosphere is volatile, however, and the danger that some monk- or nun-led incident or protest will precipitate a new riot remains ever-present.

These events rocked Drepung, creating a serious crisis that threatens its viability and future. One of the key negative consequences of the political activism was its inadvertent decimation of Drepung's nascent theological study program. Not only were many of the young monk demonstrators part of the dharma grove program, but the most gifted of Drepung's young scholar monks were involved, arrested, and thus lost to the monastery. Still other young monks have fled to India to join the Dalai Lama and the exile community. For a time, Drepung's dharma grove actually ceased to be used.

The political conflict also negatively affected the government's attitude toward Drepung and other similarly involved monasteries. The risk Beijing took in allowing a monastic revival in Tibet has turned out poorly as monks have become, as many hard-liners in China predicted at the outset of the liberalization, leaders in the nationalistic opposition to Chinese rule in Tibet. Although the principle of religious freedom continued to be espoused, with, of course, the inherent caveats mentioned earlier, and although the government claims it does not hold the monastery responsible for the political protests of individual monks, in reality the government's attitude toward Drepung hardened demonstrably. Monastic requests from Drepung's DMC on a range of issues, such as assistance in renovating the main prayer assembly hall, payments for teachers, and, critically, permission to increase the number of monks, were denied or approved only on a limited basis. At the same time, the government instituted much closer security scrutiny and supervision over Drepung. Moreover, with regard to Tibet in general, these dissident activities have led Beijing to implement a more hard-line policy that minimizes the importance of meeting Tibetans' cultural and religious expectations and maximizes Tibet's economic and political integration with the rest of China.

Equally significant is the negative effect the political activism has had on the morale and purpose of the monks themselves. As the monastery's revitalization gained momentum in the early 1980s there was hope among the older monks that a serious monastic community could be restored, despite Tibet's presence as part of communist China. There was even hope that regular contact with the Drepung Monastery in exile (in India) would ultimately be possible and that lamas from India could participate in Drepung's revival.[57] The initial focus of their attention, therefore, was on how to operationalize a high-quality revitalization—i.e., how to structure finances, education, recruitment, discipline, and so forth—not politics or nationalism. The major escalation of political activity in the mid-1980s challenged this orientation by thrusting nationalistic and political issues onto center stage where they competed head to head with solely religious interests.

Traditionally a monk's primary loyalty was to his monastery/college and Buddhism rather than the state and nation, and great monasteries like Drepung (or even colleges within them) were not reluctant to oppose the Tibetan government. As mentioned earlier, Tengyeling Monastery and Drepung's Loseling College gave support to the Manchu/Chinese Ambans and troops in Lhasa after the fall of the Manchu dynasty in 1911–12.

The Chinese invasion and incorporation of Tibet into the People's Republic of China in 1951 changed this in important ways. It created a heightened sense of national identity and political purpose among Tibetans, including the monks. Tibetans, whether rich or poor, monk or layman, Easterner or Westerner, now more than ever before defined their identity primarily in terms of political nationalism, as Tibetan vis-à-vis the Han Chinese. Defending the religious interests of one's monastery (and religion in general) now was projected to a larger arena where defending Tibet as a nation-state was seen as synonymous with defending and preserving Buddhism against an atheistic enemy. Such feelings intensified after the abortive Tibetan uprising of 1959 when the Chinese government devastated Tibet's proud monastic tradition. Communism and the Chinese state became a hated enemy for all monks.

But history does not stand still, and China's dramatic shift in policy in 1978 ushered in a new chapter in the relations between Tibetan Buddhism and the Chinese state. In Drepung this revival process started in the early 1980s and had begun to gain momentum by the middle of the decade when political issues exploded on the scene. Once some Drepung monks began political dissidence in 1987, all monks were forced to reassess whether their primary loyalty was to Buddhism and their monastery as in the past or to their nationality and the Dalai Lama. The question facing monks, in essence, was whether the restoration of monasticism and the study of Buddhist theology took precedence over the political struggle to wrest Tibet from Chinese control, and in particular, to support the Dalai Lama.

Every Drepung monk believes in the sanctity of the Dalai Lama and wants him to return to Tibet, and virtually all support his efforts to secure Tibetan independence. Nevertheless, some monks believe these efforts are not only unrealistic but also harmful to the monastery and the revival of religion. The DMC,[58] for example, has repeatedly tried to persuade the monks that Drepung's interests are best served by focusing their efforts on religious study and eschewing political activism. Some senior monks have similarly tried to persuade their young wards to reject political activism because of the personal and monastic dangers. However, by and large, such efforts were not successful. Most Drepung monks believed that the Dalai Lama was moving to free Tibet with U.S. assistance, and there was a broad consensus that this was a time for monks—who have no wives and children to worry about—to sacrifice themselves for the good of the Dalai Lama, religion, and Tibet. The intense distrust of the motives of the atheistic communist state toward Buddhism and the caveats and constraints Drepung operates under made it easy for some monks to conclude that Buddhism cannot flourish in China despite the new liberalism. Accepting the risks entailed in openly demonstrating against the Chinese state, therefore, for some monks became not only a nationalistic-political activity but also, by extrapolation, a religious one. Moreover, for the young monk activists, the traditional notion of acceptable political action to defend religion was infused with new meanings from the West in the form of the incorporation of notions of universal human rights.[59] Such new constructs, however, were not shared by all monks, some of whom, as mentioned above, value the efflorescence of Buddhism in Tibet above abstract universal values such as democracy and human rights, neither of which, of course, existed in the traditional society.

In any case, Beijing has chosen not to close the monastery, and monastic life goes on with the leaders of Drepung trying to make the best of the situation, despite deep-seated frustration at their inability to control the events in which they are mired. They are focusing their attention on two related problem areas.

One of the most serious issues Drepung's DMC faced in the years immediately following martial law was what to do about the hundreds of unofficial young monks waiting to gain official admittance. The DMC was able to persuade the government to admit some of these in 1992 and 1993, but this still left a backlog of several hundred, and more were coming all the time. Given the continuing monk-led political tensions in Lhasa, it was reasonable to assume that Beijing would not permit many more new monks since these obviously would provide a pool of potential new political recruits for the activists in the monastery. It was likely, therefore, that some of these unofficial youths would never become official Drepung monks.

This posed an ethical problem for the DMC. If some of these youths ultimately had to leave Drepung and return to the secular world, the leaders felt that many would have difficulty adjusting since they had missed out on school while "waiting" in Drepung. Not having been educated to function in secular society, their lives might be ruined. The DMC decided this was unacceptable and concluded they had an obligation to provide these boys with decent schooling, at least with regard to reading and writing.

The traditional system of education in Drepung provided no model for how to do this. In the old society there were no formal schools in Drepung. Monks sought out knowledgeable scholar monks to study with on their own and honed their analytic abilities in the debating sessions in the dharma grove. Drepung monks, moreover, were taught to read Tibetan visually without learning how to write in the beautiful cursive script used in all governmental writing.[60] The rationale for this was that monks unable to write with good calligraphy were less likely to leave the monastery for secular jobs. This orientation, of course, fit the traditional ideology of mass monasticism—keeping as many monks as possible.

In the new Drepung, however, a formal school seemed necessary. A leader in the DMC explained the committee's thinking:

> We started the school so that the future generation of monks would be capable. We wanted them to be able to be good in reading religious texts, and also in writing and calculating. This was our desire. If we could accomplish this, the monks who stayed in the monastery would benefit, and those who went into the [secular] society would also benefit. . . .
>
> The main thing was that we had about 200 young boys [in 1991] who were not in the official monk register. The older monks were taking 2 to 3 of these boys each, so that's how we got so many of them. All these were not getting permission to join the monastery, so we worried that they would get ruined unless we acted. So to prevent them from being ruined, we established this school. In the old society, we admitted as many monks as came. Now it's not like this. Now there are only a little over 400

monks in the register. So we felt if we didn't do something these kids would end up beggars.

We discussed this problem in the DMC. We felt that since we are all monks, it is not proper to tell monks and the larger society they can't bring in new boys to be monks. This goes against our religious rules [*chos-khrims-nas 'gal*]. So we didn't say anything [at first] and loads of boys came and started causing us . . . problems. . . . We told their guardian monks to look after them and see they study, etc., but the guardians couldn't control these kids. For example, some guardians went to prayer assemblies, some worked, and so the kids were left alone in the apartments a lot. Some of these fooled around, some stole, etc. So we in the DMC discussed this and said it's best if we started a school for them. We decided to establish this in [what used to be] Kongpo kamtsen, and asked the RAB for permission to do this. They approved, saying this was a good idea. . . . We thought we would get some expenses from the government to help us since they fund other schools in the society, but on this count we were wrong. We got nothing.[61]

Drepung used its own funds to build and open this school, which in 1995 contained almost 400 young students and 7 full-time monk teachers. Three of these teachers were themselves new monks who had graduated from lower middle school before joining Drepung. They taught written Tibetan and some basic arith-

Figure 2.10. The school set up by the monastery for young monks waiting to gain official admittance.

metic. The other four teachers were older monks who taught elementary religion via the religious texts traditionally used in Drepung.[62]

The founding of this formal school, however, was a palliative response to a problem, not a long-term solution. Maintaining hundreds of "waiting" monks for years on end was not in the best interests of either the youths or the monastery. Consequently, Drepung's DMC (together with those at Sera and Ganden monasteries) pressed the government to establish a clear numerical size limit so that everyone would know more or less where they stand with regard to the likelihood of ultimate admission. This has involved repeated discussions on the utility of a formal commitment to a fixed number of monks for each monastery and arguments over what that number should be.

Drepung has been partially successful in this endeavor in the sense that the government has given its verbal commitment to allow it a maximum of 600 monks, but this is still not formal law, and the DMC would like to see the final number set at between 700 and 750 monks. However, even the larger number would be too low since in 1995 there were actually 934 monks living in Drepung (540 official and 396 nonofficial), plus another 100 or so from other provinces outside of the TAR.[63]

The DMC is also trying to restrict the flow of new unofficial monks to prevent the current impasse from being further exacerbated. It has registered all the current "waiting" monks and has instructed senior monks to cease accepting new "wards" without permission. There is, in effect, a moratorium on taking in new wards. However, it is not clear whether this "order" will be enforceable. Drepung's new commitment to quality over quantity means that today's Drepung monks have to be productive: they have to either study theology or work on behalf of the monastery. No longer can monks loaf around or do their own private business. However, this new attitude does not negate the traditional value of the monastery being open to all males who seek to renounce the material world. So long as boys are willing to be "quality" monks, the overwhelming feeling in the monastery is that they should be admitted. It is thus likely that more boy monks will arrive in Drepung in the future, despite the DMC's current moratorium.

Finally, Drepung faces a major problem concerning the theological study program. On the positive side, the DMC was able to revive the dharma grove after martial law was lifted in 1990, and it has subsequently grown to include 240 full-time monks. Moreover, the traditional winter "debating" semester called Jayan Günjö was recently revived.[64] More than 400 scholar monks attended it in 1995. But on the negative side, Drepung has not yet produced a single new geshe, and the ten to fifteen nearest scholar monks are still years away. Since political conflict precludes free exchange of monks from the exile Drepung Monastery in India, many older monks fear that a new generation of geshe scholars will not be ready to take over the educational activities in Drepung when the last of the old society monks die off. In their view, therefore, Drepung is locked in a race against time, and there is pessimism about whether it will be able to succeed given the volatile politicization of religion in Lhasa.

CONCLUSION

The central place of monks and monasteries in Tibetan society made it inevitable that the new era of religious freedom in China would produce powerful pressures to revive Tibet's monastic tradition. The freedom to practice religion as individuals was clearly not enough for Tibetans, and local communities throughout Tibet have rebuilt or repaired traditional monasteries, usually without government financial help. In Lhasa the desire to restore famous monastic centers like Drepung to their former greatness was especially strong. By representing the sophistication of Tibetan culture, monasteries like Drepung bolstered Tibetans' cultural identity and fostered ethnic pride vis-à-vis that of the politically dominant Chinese. And so, as the changes implicit in China's new rules became understood and believed in Drepung, a slow monastic revival commenced. The first major step in this process occurred in 1982 when new youths were admitted and regular collective prayer chanting assemblies started.

The five years following those events were characterized by a period of "institutional revival." The DMC and senior monks set out to operationalize a new monastic community and culture, making difficult decisions about how to finance, educate, and discipline the new monks. Through a delicate, and not entirely conscious, process of adaptation, traditional values, customs, and beliefs were restored, in some cases intact and in other cases with modifications and innovations. The result was an emergent monastic social matrix that was sociopolitically compatible with the realities of the current socialist society yet culturally authentic. From a baseline of zero religion at the end of the Cultural Revolution in 1976, Drepung was able to revive a practicing monastic community with new young monks, regular prayer chanting sessions, and a large theological study program.

This process of institutional reconstruction changed dramatically in the fall of 1987 when open political demonstrations by monks ushered in a new era—the period of "religiopolitical confrontation." Monks (and nuns) suddenly leaped to the forefront of active political opposition and received worldwide attention and plaudits. The monastic revival had become politicized, at least in the regions in and around Lhasa.

This new religious militancy challenged all monks and nuns, confronting them with an emotionally powerful alternative to quietly (apolitically) working within China to rebuild their monastic tradition; that is, it presented them the emotionally compelling alternative of participating in the nationalistic struggle to free Tibet from Chinese rule. Feelings of anger and hatred toward the Communist party and the Chinese, of course, were present before the first demonstration, but after it, Drepung's monks consciously had to choose between conflicting loyalties—Buddhism or the Tibetan nation—or, as some who chose the latter course did, to eliminate the cognitive dissonance by trying to redefine the interests of Buddhism as being best served by political activism.

All of this has placed Beijing in a very difficult situation. Although it is still committed to a policy of religious freedom in Tibet (so long as its political caveats are adhered to) and does not officially hold Drepung responsible for the acts of individual monks, it is also committed to stop monks from continuing to fan the flames of political dissidence. Since intensified "political education" in Drepung has heretofore not succeeded in stopping activism, how Beijing will move to ensure this without simply closing down the monastery is not at all clear. It is reasonable to assume that the government's tolerance of monasteries like Drepung will decrease in the coming years if monastic leaders do not work out some way to stop the political protests of the monks.

This scenario is understood by Drepung's leaders and is creating an underlying atmosphere of frustration and depression. Despite the laudatory objective gains in reviving their monastic community, most of Drepung's leaders are disheartened about the future. Cut off from fellow monks and lamas in India, under scrutiny from a government they consider hostile (or at best unfriendly), unable to convince current monks to eschew political militancy (or prevent them from doing so), they find themselves embroiled in constant political tension and conflict they cannot control. And some, undoubtedly, have doubts whether they should be trying to control this. Their successes, no matter how impressive, are always just a demonstration away from disaster. There is a gnawing fear, moreover, that the continued involvement of monks in demonstrations is setting the stage for the worst of all outcomes—that the Tibet Question will not be settled in Tibet's favor and the monastery will be destroyed.

The revival of Drepung Monastery seventeen years after liberalization, therefore, has been somewhat mixed. On one level, the progress has been impressive; yet on another, the gains seem very unstable. At the heart of this contradiction, like so much else in contemporary Tibet, is the Tibet Question.

The older monks love their monastery and want to see it thrive again as a great center of Tibetan religion. Most laypersons feel the same. Consequently, despite their pessimism and apprehension, the monastery's leaders will certainly continue to work to adapt the basic elements of the monastic way of life to whatever obstacles the unpredictable national and international sociopolitical environments throw in its way. But, whatever happens, Drepung's leaders are unlikely to be able to return to the more placid times of the period of institutional revival unless some major breakthrough in the struggle over the Tibet Question occurs. With the monks, especially the younger monks, torn between nationalistic and religious ideals and loyalties, the future of Drepung is uncertain and unpredictable. Only time will tell whether Drepung will move into a third, more positive phase of revival in which it regains most of its former greatness, or whether monk-led confrontations will escalate and the state will decide to crack down harshly on the monastery and reverse most of the gains of the past decade and a half. The leaders of Drepung, therefore, find themselves trapped between two forces they cannot control, and while they hope that Drepung can weather the storm, they are far from optimistic.

EPILOGUE[65]

The political fears mentioned above materialized in the summer of 1996 when Beijing launched a major new "patriotism education"[66] campaign aimed at enhancing its control over the most visible source of opposition—the monasteries. As part of its general "get tough" policy in Tibet, this campaign sought not merely to educate monks on the "proper," apolitical, role of religion in China (see chapter 1), but more important, to demonstrate to monks that if they did not adhere to these rules they could not remain in the monastery. The campaign sought to take steps to reduce the danger that monasteries like Drepung would continue to function as breeding grounds for political opposition.[67] The vehicle for enforcement was what is known in China as a "work team,"[68] that is, a group of officials pulled together from various government offices and sent to carry out a political campaign. In Drepung's case, more than a hundred officials arrived there in summer 1996 and remained in residence until roughly the end of that year.[69]

The ideological brief of the work team is illustrated by a document handed out to the monks of Drepung's sister monastery, Sera, at the start of the parallel campaign there:

> The time has arrived for patriotic education to take place in Sera monastery by means of Comprehensive Propaganda Education [*gcig sdud kyis dril bsgrags slob gso*]. The purpose of carrying out this education session is to implement the Party's policy on religion totally and correctly, to stress the management of religious affairs according to law, and to initiate efforts for the harmonious coexistence between the religious and socialist societies. It is also aimed at creating the thought of patriotism and implanting in the masses of the monks the view of the government, the political view and the legal view. The campaign is also for the purpose of educating [monks] to oppose completely any activities aimed at splitting the motherland.[70]

Work teams had been sent to Drepung on a number of occasions in the past so the presence of this one in Drepung itself was not exceptional. However, the task of the 1996 work team differed from previous ones in that its brief included vetting each monk with respect to his political views and his future acceptability as a monk.

The work team sent to Drepung interviewed monks and led sessions on topics such as Chinese law, Tibetan history, patriotism, and the government's view that the Dalai Lama and his Western supporters were playing a negative role in trying to split Tibet from China. All monks were required to study political education materials that spelled out these views, attend classes that went over the official positions, and convey their attitudes about these issues verbally and in writing.

In keeping with the strident rhetoric of the new hard-line policy in Tibet, the work team directly attacked the Dalai Lama, removing his photographs from the monastery's chapels and temples (and other public venues) while asserting that the monks must denounce the Dalai Lama as a duplicitous "splittist." The harsh personal attacks on the Dalai Lama, however, assaulted Tibetan ethnic and religious sensibilities and precipitated a major test of wills in Drepung (and in many other monasteries).

Faced with the necessity of attacking the Dalai Lama by name and agreeing to historical views and "facts" they considered untrue, many monks dug in their heels and, in a variety of ways, refused to participate in what was commonly perceived as a throwback to the mass political campaigns of the 1960s and 1970s, even if this stance meant having to leave the monastery. A few monks expressed their protest by openly challenging the veracity of the work team's facts at public sessions. Four such monks, it is said, ultimately were sent to reform-though-labor camps when they repeatedly refused to recant. A larger number of Drepung monks—about sixty—adopted a less confrontational method to protest. They chose to leave the monastery on their own accord rather than accept the campaign's demands. Some of these quietly fled to India, producing the first reports of the campaign abroad.[71] One very old monk, it is said, became so distraught by the thought of either leaving the monastery or denouncing the Dalai Lama that he committed suicide.

Most monks, however, were willing to accept—at least on the surface—the basic ideological "points" of the campaign to remain in the monastery, but they drew a line with regard to the demand that they comment negatively about the Dalai Lama's political persona. A meeting of work team members with Drepung's elderly monks illustrates the depth of this opposition. At this meeting, three or four monks rose and said emotionally, tears in their eyes, that as simple monks they knew nothing of the Dalai Lama's politics but only his religious stature, and this they could not oppose. Consequently, if the work team insisted that they speak against the Dalai Lama, they would have to leave Drepung and go begging in the streets of Lhasa.[72] Comments like this coming from monks who were basically nonpolitical and had lived most of their lives in the monastery had a powerful impact on the work team's thinking, leading to a reconsideration of the campaign's anti–Dalai Lama component. The campaign had sought to cleanse the monastery of politically unreliable monks and convince the rest that it was in their and their monastery's best interests to dissociate themselves from political dissidence, not purge Drepung of virtually all senior monks. Consequently, it was decided that trying to force monks to criticize the Dalai Lama directly would be counterproductive, and this was removed from the list of "conditions" the monks had to accept publicly, leaving only the following items: to cherish the nation and cherish religion; to oppose separatism/splittism; to accept the correct ideology of the Chinese Communist party; to respect the motherland's unity; to work to continue the socialist system and to obey the orders of one's superior officials. Monks who "passed" the political education program by stating their acceptance of these conditions were reaffirmed as official Drepung monks and issued a new registration document (in the form of a red handbook with their name, photo, birthdate, etc.).

Although it is easy to dismiss the rhetorical "parroting" the Socialist Education campaign generated as a kind of political charade that changed no one's views, the 1996 campaign was not limited to rhetoric. It also initiated a number of real structural changes. One such "reform" was the addition of a new criterion for official membership as a Drepung monk—proper age. As mentioned earlier (and in chapter 1), the laws of the People's Republic of China prohibited the recruitment of monks and priests under the age of eighteen. Religious freedom in Chinese law meant the freedom to believe or not to believe, and the party from early on felt it was important to prevent young children from being indoctrinated into a religious life before they had the maturity to make an informed judgment. Nevertheless, exceptions were made, most notably in Tibet where the great emphasis Tibetans placed on child recruitment was tacitly respected by not enforcing the minimum age rule. The 1996 campaign reversed that policy, the government announcing that Tibetan monks must now be at least eighteen. And it implemented this standard, albeit with a few concessions, the most important of which were that for the duration of the campaign the minimum age for the monks already present in Drepung would be reduced to fifteen, and even younger monks were admitted in a few hardship cases involving those who were orphans with no home to return to or child monks whose coresident guardian monk was so old or infirm that he depended on the young monk.[73] In the future, however, the government decreed that new monks would have to be at least eighteen years of age.

The work team also eliminated the hundreds of unofficial monks who had been residing in Drepung at the start of the campaign "waiting" to be admitted officially. These youths, frustrated and angry at the government's refusal to allow them to become official Drepung monks, were clearly a fertile breeding ground for political dissent. They were eliminated in two ways. The underage monks (numbering between 80 and 100) were sent home with no political prejudice or stigma attached to this expulsion. They were told to enter secular schools and reapply for admission if they wished when they reached the age of eighteen. The remainder of the older "waiting" monks (numbering more than 160) were officially admitted into the monastery, increasing Drepung's size by about 30 percent to 706 official monks.[74] This number constituted Drepung's new official maximum size, although the number of resident monks was actually higher since about eighty unofficial "visiting" monks from outside the TAR continued to live and study in Drepung as in the past.[75] To prevent the reemergence of a new cohort of "waiting" monks, older monks were warned not to allow nonofficial monks to live with them regardless of their age.[76]

Equally significant were changes made in the administration of Drepung. The government tightened its supervision over the monks by replacing the monk-staffed Democratic Management Committee with a new committee called the "Management Committee" (*do dam u yon lhan khang*), which included secular cadres who lived in the monastery along with monks.[77] The presence of these lay cadres in the monastery has given the government important firsthand control over the monastery's day-to-day operational decisions.[78] Some changes were also made in monk administrative personnel; the former monk head of the Democratic Management Committee, for example, was replaced with another monk, as was the former disciplinary official, the *gegö*.[79]

The 1996 campaign also brought about a series of lesser changes in the life of Drepung. A number of the major monastic economic enterprises were converted to the "responsibility" system, the monks working for these having to guarantee the monastery a fixed annual "lease fee." For example, the monastery's store has to guarantee to pay 90,000¥ a year to the monastery, and the restaurant, 80,000¥. Anything these enterprises earn above this they can keep, but it is interesting to note that the monks operating these have pledged that they will only take a salary equal to the salary of other working monks (regardless of how much profit they generate) since as monks they have no desire to become rich.[80]

From another direction, Drepung's income suffered a severe blow in 1997 when its most revered spiritual leader, Gen Lamrim, died. Overnight the monks lost the several hundred thousand yuan that his biannual public religious teachings generated, as well as his spiritual leadership. The increases in income from implementing the "responsibility" system will not make up for this loss.

Changes were also made in Drepung's school for younger monks. In 1996 the curriculum was expanded to include Chinese and English, and the school was established as a full six-year primary school. In July 1997 the school enrolled 178 monks. The content of the dharma grove educational program was not altered, but a formal ceiling was set at 230 full-time monks (i.e., 33% of the total number of Drepung monks). These scholar monks continued to receive salaries to support themselves while they studied; the advanced scholar monks receive 7¥ per day, the middle level 5¥ per day, and the newer ones (those admitted in 1996) 2.5¥ per day. Monks from outside the TAR were still permitted to study in the dharma grove, although they did not receive salaries from the monastery.[81]

The 1996 monastery rectification campaign reflects the government's new hard-line strategy in Tibet, one characteristic of which is less conciliation toward ethnic culture, as well as its frustration with the monks' hostility and political activism. However, although the campaign was launched with a torrent of tough rhetoric and initially seemed likely to marginalize monasteries like Drepung, in the end its results were somewhat equivocal. Rather than drastically scale back the number of monks, the government again offered up its standard religious compromise—if you concentrate on religion and eschew political dissidence, we will permit you to stay as monks and allow monasticism to develop—and it actually allowed Drepung to increase by more than 30 percent despite the fact that the monks would not denounce the Dalai Lama. However, the campaign also revealed clearly to the monks that the government will no longer tolerate monasteries like Drepung functioning as centers of political and nationalistic opposition and that this was more than empty rhetoric—it was now ready to intervene and forcibly alter elements of monastic life to prevent this.

The future of monasteries like Drepung, therefore, more than ever depends on the monks' acceptance of the government's separation of religion and political dissidence, that is, the government's demand that monks devote themselves to their religion and eschew all antigovernment political activity. So while Drepung can continue to try to train a new generation of scholar monks, the government has made it clear that it will not tolerate the monastery being used as a breeding ground for political dissidence and, of course, that resistance is futile and counterproductive.

Drepung's future, therefore, remains uncertain and precarious since it is impossible to predict how its monks will respond to future vagaries of the Tibet Question, in particular, to events outside of China.[82] The Chinese government's attempt to persuade (and/or intimidate) Drepung's monks to delink religion from nationalistic politics reached a new plateau of intensity in 1996 but did not truly resolve the fundamental conflict of many at Drepung between their political aspirations and their religious loyalties.

THREE

Re-membering the Dismembered Body of Tibet

Contemporary Tibetan Visionary Movements in the People's Republic of China

David Germano

BODIES, BURIAL, AND RENEWAL

We now know that religious Tibet experienced devastating material losses during the period of Chinese control from 1959 onward, a process that gradually intensified until the culminating orgy of violence that constituted the Cultural Revolution (1966–76). In addition to the many bodies of Tibetans sacrificed to the revolution's chaotic agenda, the body of Tibet herself was stripped of its web of stūpas, temples, and other architectural markers, and even the memories of her sacred caves, groves, and mountains were at times eradicated through the human loss.[1] Wooden and metallic bodies of Buddhas, bodhisattvas, and lamas situated within these residences were destroyed or shipped off in amazing quantities to the illicit markets of Hong Kong and elsewhere, often to reappear in museum and private collections in Europe and America in a deanimated form as art dealers emptied their interiors of the sacred contents that give them life. Finally, the immense corpus of religious texts constituting the teaching bodies not only of the Buddha[2] but also of the myriad Indian and Tibetan masters who followed in his footsteps was devastated. Thus the bodies of religious Tibet were sacrificed and resacrificed on multiple fronts for a three-decade period which resulted in the literal deconstruction of an entire civilization. The sacrifice was not total, however, for not only were the essential elements of Tibetan religiosity preserved in memories and emotions buried within the individual bodies of Tibetans—and even partially in hidden valleys where Tibetans continued to practice Buddhism throughout the period—but Tibetans also concealed in the earth of Tibet an unknown quantity of Buddha bodies in statuary and painting, associated ritual items, and, most important, the literary corpus of Buddhism. With the end of the Cultural Revolution in 1976 and the gradual easing of restrictions on religious expression, these buried realities of Tibetan culture have slowly been reexcavated and brought into the light of day. These excavations have played an important role in the explosion of temple building and scripture printing that has ensued in Tibet since the end of the Cultural Revolution, as well as in the equally explosive growth in the often-illicit international art trafficking that has thrived there.[3] It is this phenomenon that I would like to examine, particularly in light of how Tibetans and Tibet have been slowly trying to heal their multiple damaged bodies and reconstitute some semblance of health, despite continuing oppressive realities.

There is in fact an ancient Tibetan precedent for burying religious artifacts in the earth in the face of persecution and later reexcavating these concealed items amid a landscape of ruined temples and resurgent hope. The great Tibetan empire (seventh to ninth century), which created Buddhism as a national religion, began to disintegrate in the mid-ninth century when the emperor Langdarma (817–42) instituted a persecution of institutional Buddhism, traditionally said to culminate in his assassination by a Buddhist monk. During the ensuing dark period of institutional and material decay, it appears that religious artifacts such as texts and artwork were purposely concealed to ensure survival through the chaos; others were presumably lost or forgotten in caches scattered among the neglected network of temples. The following economic and cultural renaissance (beginning in the late tenth century) produced a widespread interest in reexcavating these items from the imperial past out of the Tibetan earth, particularly among the traditionalists who preferred to continue dynastic period traditions rather than adopt newly imported Indic lineages.[4] Among these groups, the excavations included a distinctive continuation of Indian Buddhist revelatory practices that produced a wide variety of scriptures said to have been concealed by famous dynastic period saints in the consciousness of their reincarnating disciples through paranormal means. Thus these myriad new scriptures known as Ter, or treasures, were understood to have been concealed, physically *and* mystically, during the imperial period in Tibetans' bodies and the body of Tibet herself for the sake of future generations.[5] Within the Nyingma tradition, the key figure in the Ter cult came to be an eighth-century Indian master named Padmasambhava who played an important role in bringing Buddhism to the Tibetan empire. As a distinctive mythos began to crystallize around him, from at least the twelfth century onward Padmasambhava was understood to be the main concealer of Ter in Tibet and, as such, the central devotional figure in the Nyingma Ter cult.[6] The treasure finders themselves, or Terton, were generally understood to be mystically appointed reincarnations of his main dynastic period disciples. While initially primarily a Central Tibetan phenomenon, after the sixteenth century its force largely shifted to eastern Tibet (Kham) where it became the heart of the ecumenical movement (*ris-med*) of the nineteenth century.[7]

This dyadic structure of a period of persecution-impelled decay of Buddhism followed by its renaissance obviously parallels events in Tibet over the past four decades; I will argue that these parallels have resulted in intersections of memories among Tibetans.[8] In fact, one of the most interesting phenomena in the post-1978 religious renaissance in Tibet has been that in addition to the widespread excavation of vast amounts of artwork and texts secretly buried just a few decades ago in response to Chinese-initiated repression of Buddhism, in eastern Tibet the treasure movement revealing sacred scriptures and material items from the seemingly distant imperial past has been dramatically revitalized.[9] I discuss this contemporary treasure movement in eastern Tibet by means of the story of its most prominent proponent, Khenpo Jikphun, who represents one of the most amazing stories of Tibetan endurance and survival through the Cultural Revolution, and compare its contemporary manifestations with the treasure tradition's initial parameters in eleventh- to thirteenth-century Tibet. In doing so, I highlight ways in which contemporary Tibetans *have* been able to manipulate their Buddhist past in its conflict with modernity so as to be capable of generating innovation and renewal.

THE CENTRIPETAL NATURE OF RELIGIOUS IDENTITY IN GOLOK

After 1978 government prohibitions against practicing religion were relaxed in the People's Republic of China, resulting in the gradual renewal of Buddhism in the areas of cultural Tibet fragmented between the contemporary provinces of the Tibetan Autonomous Region, Sichuan, and Qinghai, among others. Despite the renewal of Tibetan culture and Buddhism in particular, there remains a deep, abiding cultural depression among Tibetans, from the educated youth and religious elite to nomads and villagers. In particular, one constantly encounters feelings of alienation and inadequacy among religious practitioners and communities. There is a pervasive feeling articulated by young people with serious religious or intellectual interests, such as lay scholars educated at the Dawu Nationalities Institute in Kham, that their religious and intellectual as well as political situation is hopeless, given the continuing Chinese cultural and political onslaught. This depression often results in self-imposed exile in India; in one famous case, a prominent young scholar committed suicide, leaving behind a note that is rumored to have explicitly linked his death to the besieging of Tibetan culture by Han Chinese.[10] Among the monks, this expresses itself in the feeling that it is impossible to gain a decent religious education in Tibet today.[11] Reasons for this situation are fairly obvious: the loss of several generations of scholars (from those who would now be in their forties to those who would be in their seventies) to death, exile, or the absence of opportunity; the consequent absence of decent study programs, even where bodies and buildings are available; the escape into exile of many of the most prominent religious figures in all traditions; the material devastation of the vast network of temples, monasteries, stūpas, and other sites that constituted the infrastructure of Tibet's extended religious body, often including even the culturally transmitted memory of the location of key sites, inferiority complexes created by the racism and material superiority of recent Chinese immigrants, and a host of other associated realities of modern Tibetan life. Tibet's inherent centrifugal tendencies, caused by a small population inhabiting a vast landscape with immense geographic barriers, were thus reinforced to the point of disintegration by the Cultural Revolution. This decentering of religious identity often results, at present, in emotional energy being diverted outwardly in two directions in particular, if not surrendered altogether to Chinese-approved outlets: the nostalgically remembered past or the escapist dream of refugee communities in South Asia.

Against this backdrop, before proceeding deeper into the phenomenon of Ter, we will begin by looking briefly at a particular case of religious revival of Nyingma traditions in contemporary Tibet. My comments are based on observations during extended stays in 1990–92 in Kham and Central Tibet, now politically classified as Sichuan and the Tibetan Autonomous Region respectively, as well as on contemporary hagiographies. For most of this time I was researching textual and contemplative traditions of the Great Perfection (rdzogs-chen) in a variety of religious communities belonging to the Nyingma sect of Tibetan Buddhism. My own experience suggests that Tibetan religious communities in Sichuan are somewhat less coercively controlled by Chinese political authorities than are their counterparts in the Tibetan Autonomous Region, particularly the monasteries and nunneries within five to six hours by road from the main urban centers of Lhasa and Shigatse. In fact, the Nyingma tradition in particular has undergone a major institutional revival in a very short time to produce an extensive network of large and small monastic communities throughout eastern Tibet. In part fueled by the general linkage of nationalistic sentiment and religious institutions along with the economic surplus recently generated in some areas, the Nyingmas' growth seems to lie in their traditional focus on nationalistic literature such as the Gesar of Ling epic and dynastic period mythology and the relative prevalence of charismatic teachers whose appeal exceeds their monastic boundaries.

The most interesting of these new communities are a religious institute and a nunnery in Golok Serta headed by Khenpo Jikphun, who is at the heart of the resurgent Nyingma tradition in eastern Tibet. I first heard of Khenpo Jikphun in the summer of 1989 when I was staying in South India at the monastery of Penor Rinpoche, the current titular head of the Nyingma sect. Khenpo Namdrol, now president of its academic college (bshad grwa), was Khenpo Jikphun's student, having recently traveled to Kham to study with him. Two things immediately stood out from Khenpo Namdrol's description of his teacher: he was unusually learned in the Great Perfection tradition of tantric Buddhism and he was a prolific Terton. The latter assertion particularly struck me, since the Ter movement had not for the most part been successfully transplanted in refugee Tibet, not surprising given the vast changes in the cultural and geographic landscape on which Ter was so dependent. In addition, Ter was widely rumored among refugee communities to be drastically limited in scope within Tibet itself in comparison to its exalted pre-1950 status as a visionary process of renewal that revealed massive collections of new texts interwoven with a bizarre collection of material items and esoteric tendrel, or interdependent supports of talismanic value.

The following year I briefly met Khenpo Jikphun for the first time in Lhasa, where he was resting with Khenpo Namdrol on his way to India for his first trip outside of the People's Republic of China. Subsequently during that year, I heard a number of vague accounts of Khenpo Jikphun while staying in Kham which generally reflected a mix of respect, awe, and jealousy. However, it was not until the following year in Dartsedo (Kangding) that I was able to talk with Khenpo and his students at greater length during a weeklong series of teachings he gave there. Khenpo Namdrol's initial descriptions of him were borne out in observations of his charisma among Chinese and Tibetans as well as the miraculous nature of many of the stories told about him, which even by Tibetan standards seemed to stretch one's imagination. In particular, they centered around his status as a Terton, a revealer of treasures or new scriptures from Tibet's ancient past. It also became clear that Khenpo's community was extraordinary in terms of the propagation of Great Perfection tantric traditions, which ultimately brought me there in connection with my own research. I thus arranged for a two-month stay that summer (1990) in Golok Serta at Khenpo's institute.

What I found there proved to be in many ways startlingly different from what I had encountered in other parts of Tibet. Here the sacred landscape of Tibet was being revived in the radical way that only Ter can, and religious energy thus appeared centripetal in marked contrast to the alienated state in which institutionalized Buddhism finds itself in many parts of Tibet. Khenpo Jikphun has created a significant countermovement reestablishing the center of gravity within Tibet herself, thereby stemming the flow of authority and value toward Chinese modernity, on the one hand, and refugee Tibetan communities, on the other. Not only has he created an academic environment that in some ways surpasses what is available in refugee monasteries, but he has also managed to project an intellectual, mythic, and charismatic presence capable of competing with any of the great Nyingma lamas now living or recently deceased in exile.[12] He has constellated Tibet's fragmented cultural energy around him, reinvested it in the Tibetan physical and imaginal landscape, directly relinked the contemporary situation with Tibet's past, and thus in a major way reconstituted Tibetan identity within the realities of life in the contemporary People's Republic of China, thus reinvigorating Tibetan pride, self-confidence, and sense of purpose. He has done so in a uniquely Tibetan, and in particular Nyingma, fashion. The strategies he has employed have revolved around the identification of present figures with strings of reincarnations stretching back to the eighth-century Tibetan empire; the reconfiguration and reanimation of the body of Tibetan sacred geography through rituals, dreams, miraculous events, and actual physical discoveries linked to that web of reincarnations; rebuilding the intellectual and material substructure of Tibetan intellectual culture within that landscape by founding temples, stūpas, monasteries, and retreat centers; and, above all else, his assumption of the mantle of the Terton, the treasure finder who is able to establish a visceral link to Tibet's glorious past and to bring discrete products of that link into the present. In these ways, Khenpo has helped to reverse the centrifugal flow of Tibetan identity into contemporary Chinese urban culture, refugee centers in South Asia, depression, nostalgia, or even the far-off alien dream of the West, and instead revitalize a profoundly Tibetan sense of identity within a uniquely Tibetan landscape.

BEYOND THE CULTURAL REVOLUTION

Before discussing the Ter movement and how it has functioned to create a centripetal religious force in contemporary eastern Tibet, I would like briefly to highlight some of the details of Khenpo's life. As related by himself, his biographers, and various scattered oral accounts, his life has all of the miraculous elements so standard in traditional Tibetan hagiographies, particularly for a celebrated Terton.[13] He was born in 1933 to nomadic parents. It is said that he was born with consummate ease with his feet first and head unbent, with the placenta sac draped around his left shoulder like a monastic robe. He then sat up by his own power, opened his eyes, and said Mañjuśrī's personal mantra, *Oṃ a ra pa tsa na dhīḥ*, seven or eight times. These extraordinary events were detailed by his biographers from the eyewitness accounts of the midwife Drontshe and a man named Tsenseng, both of whom were still living in Amdo in 1990. Khenpo later recollected experiencing an intense light on emerging from the womb, which he thought was perhaps the light of a butter lamp, and feeling a strong sense of compassion. He was given the name Kelzang Namgyel, which translates as "Victorious Good Fortune."

During his teens he was recognized as the reincarnation of the famed Terton Lerab Lingpa (1856–1926), who was an important Nyingma teacher of the thirteenth Dalai Lama. Khenpo was quite well known in his early years both for psychic powers and intellectual achievements but at his prime became trapped within the chaotic *bardo* of the Chinese occupation culminating in the Cultural Revolution.[14] It is here that the modern legend of his life began to unfold, since he was neither imprisoned nor tortured during this tumultuous period but actually continued religious activities unabated. During the early phases of the Cultural Revolution Khenpo was at one point summoned to an organized "struggle session" where religious figures and other "class enemies" were routinely physically and verbally abused, often leaving permanent physical damage. The night before the session he performed offering rituals with intense prayer directed to the great warrior deity Gesar of Ling, the hero of the Tibetan national epic that has been particularly important in eastern Tibet. Over the course of the night, his face unexpectedly swelled up and became hideously distorted, according to his later account of events. In the morning when people saw his disfiguration, they were convinced Khenpo had contracted a dangerous infectious disease and thus banished him from the town. At other key junctures when he was threatened by authorities, he said he was able to repeat the feat through the blessings of Gesar of Ling and thus remained in isolated spots throughout the long political and social turmoil. Other accounts speak of a miraculous disappearance of his encampment when search parties were sent out, as well as the abrupt rescinding of orders for his arrest, which may indicate a less than paranormal complicity on the part of local political authorities. Most of his time during this period was thus spent herding goats and sheep in the mountains with his sister and her daughter while he continued to give empowerments, teach texts, and transmit practices to a limited circle of disciples.

Khenpo Jikphun's past-life memories also play a critical role in his relationship to Tibetan epic literature, since he has said he clearly remembers a previous incarnation as the son of a famous general associated with King Gesar named Danma (famous for his archery and bravery).[15] King Gesar is famed for his prowess as a warrior and reputed to be an incarnation of Tibet's patron bodhisattva, Avalokiteśvara. Because a vast cycle of epic poetry and mythology has been woven around King Gesar over the intervening centuries, he has assumed a mythic status perhaps analogous to England's King Arthur, and in eastern Tibet he has also assumed an importance in normative religious traditions as prominent lamas have composed rituals and meditations centering on him.[16] Such rituals draw on King Gesar's warrior status for the invocation of fierce energy that may be needed to subdue internal or external obstacles, and thus he became a "warrior deity" frequently invoked in times of turmoil. At critical junctures in his life, and especially during the Cultural Revolution, Khenpo Jikphun has thus relied on contemplative supplications to this warrior deity for assistance, both in his internal purification of his own being and to overcome external obstacles posed by others. During the Cultural Revolution he also had a number of visions of Ling Gesar, including one on the twenty-fifth day of the seventh lunar month in 1969. After practicing an "Attunement with the Spiritual Master" (Guru yoga) meditation (in this case a ritual composed by Mipham Rinpoche oriented toward Ling Gesar as the master), for seven days he had a vision at dawn in which his dreams seemed to be integrated with radiant light. In Khenpo's own words:

> In this vision I arrived in front of the door of a beautiful castle made of diverse precious materials, where I met a gorgeous teenaged girl wearing a variety of jewelry in the fashion of the southern Amdo region, such as a long necklace of zi stones and coral.[17] She took hold of my hand, and said, "I'm delighted that you, my faithful heart-friend of many lifetimes, have come to join me here. Do you recognize me, 'Young One' (*Ne'u chung*), your intimate devotee? Let's go to my father!" With these words she led me inside the castle's courtyard and into her father's presence. There we found a youthful adult wearing a black cloak with lambskin lining, whose physical presence was so majestic that I couldn't help but look down in awe, for he seemed to have the authority and dignity of an older man. On the right and left side of his body were a sheathed bow and sheathed arrows respectively, and as I watched him he sat there polishing a razor sharp sword radiating sparks of fire which he held in his hands. When I saw him thus, I became convinced he was no other than King Gesar's famous general Danma, and felt intense exhilaration and faith well up from within. I thus put my head to his chest and wept, at which point he said, "My dear

son, now we should go to the Great Lion of the World, King Gesar who epitomizes the Body of all the Buddhas throughout the three times."

We then proceeded to a house constructed of red crystal called the Palace Treasury of Jewels, whose interior was adorned with all sorts of wealth and luxury, a profusion of scriptural volumes and statues. When we went inside it, sitting atop a bed of many piled soft brocade silk cushions was a great individual with a white body adorned by a red glow, his right hand brandishing in the sky a five tipped vajra adorned with multicolored strips of silk, while his left hand held a blue jewel radiating with light. He wore a large mantle of red silk brocade around his body, while I can no longer recall his other ornaments. Upon meeting him I felt boundless faith and respect for him, such that I touched my head to the knees of this great man and beseeched him, "Oh great one! I implore you to bless me by transferring the immeasurable splendid qualities of your Body, Speech and Mind into my own inner being, such that great benefit to the Buddhist teachings and living beings may be brought about!"

Then as Gesar flourished the multicolored vajra in the sky with his right hand, he said the famous seven-line supplication to Guru Padmasambhava and the words of a ritual invoking the Enlightened Spirit of Padmasambhava.[18] After placing the vajra on my head, I put my palms together and sat in front of him. At this time all ordinary appearances and experiences dissolved within reality's expanse, and the great radiant light of empty awareness became vividly manifest to me. Minister Danma sat down on a square carpet-seat beside King Gesar's main shrine and a variety of offering substances spontaneously and naturally emerged. We were then all delighted by a vajra-song sung by the gnostic Ḍākiṇī Young One,[19] after which my father Danma said we should take our leave and go. As he prepared to lead me away, I awoke from my dream-vision.

Also later on the night of the fourth day in the ninth lunar month of 1970, I dreamed I met a Terton who I thought must be Ratna Lingpa [1403–1478]. He told me, "Previously during a radiant light-dream you encountered King Gesar and his Minister Danma, at which time Young One sang a song. The song has extremely potent blessings for whomever recites it now."

Visions such as these—generally bound up with past-life memories, encounters with great cultural heroes of Tibet's past, revelations of potent teachings, artwork, and songs, and often closely connected with Tibet's sacred landscape and history—have been central to Khenpo Jikphun's reputation as a great spiritual master deeply grounded in the still vibrant matrix of Tibetan traditions, and they have been the basis of many of his actions. It should be noted that not only was Gesar centrally emphasized in the nineteenth-century ecumenical movement, but he has also been a mythic paradigm historically operative in the constitution of a distinctively Tibetan sense of community or "protonationalism."[20] As such, an incipient millenarian cult called the Heroes of Ling developed in 1981 around a Tibetan claiming to be Gesar's incarnation. It offered to initiate others into a cult centering around possession, healing, and prophecy but was quickly suppressed by Chinese authorities for its political implications.[21] As I will argue below, Khenpo's skillful invocation of such "mnemonic" icons has allowed him to surreptitiously assert Tibetan national identity and symbolic community while simultaneously engaging in institutional renewal without Chinese prohibition.[22]

When the liberalization following the Cultural Revolution finally penetrated to these remote areas of the People's Republic of China, in 1980 at the age of forty-seven Khenpo immediately set about establishing a Buddhist monastic center and nunnery linked to various visions and prophecies. Prophecies play an important role in general within Tibetan Buddhism but particularly within the Ter cult, in which they are understood not just as predictions of the future but as "words of truth" of an enlightened figure that have the intrinsic power of bringing events into being.[23] A key prophecy used to authorize the school's founding was drawn from the prophecies of Dodrub Kunzang Zhenphen (1745–1821), the first of a famous line of Nyingma incarnate lamas based in Golok itself:

In the La valley by the Ser-nga-dam deity,
There will be an emanation of the glorious Padmasambhava named "Jikme"
    (jigs med);
He will make the exoteric and tantric teachings as radiant as the sun
For a collection of Bodhisattvas of the fourfold entourage,
While with perfect stability he reaches the summit of living beings' welfare,
Thus pervading the ten directions with the disciples in his pure retinue
And placing all connected to him in the place of great bliss.

Khenpo Jikphun's full name is Jikme Phuntshok, and accordingly he interpreted the second line as referring to him by name, so that lines three through five were taken as general references to the extensive nature of his teachings, disciples, and enlightened activities. The first line, however, he interpreted syllable by syllable as having a very specific reference to the site at which he should found his new religious center: La(ma)rung valley (literally, "suitable [rung] for spiritual masters [lama]"), a power spot said to be inhabited by a tree goddess (deity) and located in the "golden horse" district (Serta) of Golok between Ngalataktse and Damcan, two sacred mountains located to its east and west respectively. This special spot was said to have been the chief residence for thirteen religious practitioners in the past who had attained the "rainbow body," a synonym for enlightenment in the Great Perfection tradition, and to have never been defiled by practitioners who broke their tantric vows. In addition, its importance as a sacred site had been prophesied by its resident wrathful tree spirit in a visionary encounter with a famous nineteenth-century treasure finder related to Khenpo named Thrakthung Dudjom Dorje.[24] At the age of five, on the twenty-fifth of the fourth lunar month at the head of the Yarchen valley, the spirit appeared to him, gave him a ritual arrow wrapped in a white ceremonial silk scarf, and said, "This red tamarisk arrow is an initiatory item and with its five colored silk strips, the fourfold enlightened activities will be actualized.[25] If in a future hare year it is planted at the upland of yonder valley, its merit, fame and glory will flourish far and wide." Later in life the Terton thus built a personal hermitage at the site, though no community or institution ever developed there.

In fulfillment of that prophecy, Khenpo Jikphun went to the desolate Larung valley, located off the main road about ten minutes drive from Golok Serta, and founded his present academy there on the tenth day of the seventh lunar month in 1980 (the iron-monkey year) for the express purpose of reviving Buddhist scholarship and meditation. It was named Hermitage of Freedom within the Great Esoteric Light-Body (*gSang chen 'od skur grol ba'i dben khrod*), and Khenpo had his own personal residence constructed on the location of Thrakthung Dudjom Dorje's former hermitage. In neighboring areas people came to refer to the center simply as Larung gar, while in more distant areas it is often referred to as Khenpo gar—literally, Khenpo's military or trading "encampment," the term "*gar*" (*sgar*) referring to a religious center that is not explicitly monastic in constitution. Before this, Khenpo lived elsewhere in Golok as the site itself was totally devoid of any human constructions, or much else for that matter, for this traditionally nomadic region is above the tree line, such that it is barren in the winter and filled with flowering grasses in the spring and summer. However, in 1968 (an earth-monkey year), Khenpo Jikphun had transmitted the *Nucleus of Mystery* (Guhyagarbha) empowerment ritual to a few disciples in this same spot, after which he said to Khenpo Gakdor in a seemingly joking manner, "In the monkey year twelve years from now I will found a large monastic academy in this spot. At that time this area, from the shadowy north of the valley to its sunny southern parts, will become filled with study, critical analysis, and meditation. Will you go in for study and analysis, or meditation?" Thus unlike many large monasteries or nunneries now found in cultural Tibet, Khenpo's religious center is not the revived form of a previous establishment located at its original site. Although there are prophetic associations tied to the Larung valley, the main force behind the establishment's development is found in the charismatic presence of Khenpo.[26]

Although I do not have access to detailed records of the events that governed these initial years, and particularly of the extent to which the government may have been aware or disapproved of the community's initial growth, it appears that the founding of the community began in an informal, and typically Tibetan, manner: a charismatic lama simply built a small personal home and an initial small circle of close disciples took up residence nearby. The community then grew as word of mouth attracted other religious practitioners, who in a very haphazard fashion built one-room residences in accordance with their means, ranging from the rare wood cabin and the more common stone and dirt huts to simple crude residences built from stacked squares of turf.[27] Individuals were free to come and go without any formal membership process, as long as they adhered to the monastic behavioral norms that Khenpo insisted on. As these newcomers' residences began to sprawl over the hillside, the evolving community rapidly expanded during its first decade to a total resident population of one thousand monks and nuns, divided between the academy and a nunnery just down the stream. While Khenpo reportedly experienced initial problems from governmental authorities, a key turning point occurred when the Panchen Lama certified the institute as an academy

Figure 3.1. Khenpo's home institution. Most of the buildings are the simple residences that sprawl over the mountainside.

in 1987. In the late 1980s the community was granted special local government funding for electricity. Private funding with donated labor and materials resulted in the building of a huge stone assembly hall in 1991 so that the entire congregation of monks and nuns could assemble for special events.[28] A few years later Khenpo had a large lay complex with its own temple built farther downstream where formerly a "mortician" practicing the Tibetan art of sky burial—cutting corpses up and offering them to wild birds—lived with his family.

As Khenpo has declined any annual subsidies from the government and decided against his academy becoming a formal monastery, he has largely avoided the need to engage in periodic political lectures, and the atmosphere is mainly religious with few political overtones. In addition, there appear to be few, if any, restrictions in the way of government permits or authorization governing disciples from distant areas joining the academy, or traveling back and forth, beyond permission from their home monasteries. In 1991 Khenpo had a midlevel political position in a Tibetan research office in Beijing and in Serta headed a staff of five at the Buddhist Association (*nang bstan*) that oversees monasteries in conjunction with the country's Religious Affairs Bureau (*chos lugs las khungs*). He also has a political position in Ganzi, but he has requested that there be no promotion of that position since it would require trips to Chengdu and responsibilities that would distract him from his primary task at the academy. Relations between Khenpo and the district government

Figure 3.2. Khenpo's home institution. The building to the left is Khenpo's own residence; the massive building under construction is the assembly hall.

at Serta are close, and in fact he has performed the traditional lama's role of mediator in some political disputes. In the summer of 1991 a potentially explosive dispute erupted over the boundaries between Serta County in the Ganzi region and the Padma district in the Tshongon region, evidently with economic implications since the area is a rather dense forest. After failing to resolve their differences, both sides were preparing for armed battle when the second-ranking political figure of Serta came to Khenpo to ask for help. Khenpo wrote a series of letters to people on both sides suggesting a compromise and eventually defused the situation. However, in the mid-nineties Khenpo became the object of political suspicion after he was one of the very few Tibetan religious leaders who refused to sign a certification of the government's candidate in the Panchen Lama reincarnation controversy. This was compounded by the arrest and reported torture of an associate in Golok for reportedly possessing literature concerning Tibetan independence. As a result, I have been told that as of 1996 he has been limited in the ability to engage in religious activity outside his own institute.[29]

Although the vast majority of its residents are monks governed by monastic rules of conduct and following a strict scholastic program, and although Khenpo Jikphun himself has maintained monastic vows throughout his life, he has self-consciously termed the academy a mountain hermitage (*ri khrod*) rather than an actual monastery that would establish and maintain his own distinctive traditions in line with the characteristic Tibetan emphasis on sectarian continuity and lineage (*brgyud pa*). For this reason all the monks have separate home monasteries, to which many often return when Khenpo Jikphun is not teaching or in residence; in addition they do not perform certain monastic communal activities such as masked dances (*'cham*).[30] Aside from the obvious benefit of avoiding the excessive regulations and state supervision associated with being classified as a monastery in the People's Republic of China, Khenpo's frequently stated reason for not forming a monastery is that he sees the most pressing contemporary need to be the renewal of scholarship and meditation all over Tibet, a task that in his view a new monastery with its inevitable sectarian tendencies could never accomplish.

Individuals thus come to the academy for an indefinite period without changing previous monastic affiliations or continually travel back and forth between their home monasteries and Larung. Generally the population is divided among all the major sects of Tibetan Buddhism, though a majority are affiliated with the Nyingma sect. Roughly 65 percent of the resident population are Nyingma, 20 percent Kagyü, 10 percent Sakya, 5 percent Geluk, with a few from the Bon and Jonang lineages. During major initiatory rituals representatives of all sects tend to congregate temporarily in great numbers. The center has thus functioned to inculcate a sense of the ecumenical movement, since in addition to Khenpo's eclectic teachings drawing from all Buddhist sectarian traditions, monks from different areas, traditions, and sects spend lengthy periods together in a shared environment. While there is a large contingent from surrounding areas, the academy and nunnery also draw considerable numbers from throughout the Tibetan districts of Sichuan and Qinghai provinces, especially from Serta, Golok, Tshongon, Aba, Repgong near Labrang, and Minyak; there are some from the Tibetan Autonomous Region (which includes western and Central Tibet), though most are from its eastern areas such as Chamdo and Gonjo.[31] One notable problem for many who come to the academy is the prevalence of the Golok nomads' dialect, which is extremely difficult for other Tibetans to understand; it is quite distinct from neighboring Amdo and Kham dialects and, of course, Central Tibetan. Monks from Gyelrong are particularly hard pressed, since their language is distant from other forms of Tibetan (to the degree it is even classified as Tibetan). Generally it takes new residents up to a year to begin to understand the Golok dialect with some facility, and it is not an uncommon experience for a bright scholar to find even religious lectures incomprehensible at first. The open door policy allowing any monk to come and stay for any length of time—only people known to have broken major religious vows, such as those who physically abused their teachers during the Cultural Revolution, are refused—has resulted in a revolving population of about 2,000 in winter and 1,400 in summer, with an expanded population of up to 10,000 during major initiatory rituals.[32]

Within this constantly changing community Khenpo Jikphun has also founded a rigorous multiyear curriculum of traditional academic study designed to culminate in the attainment of a "khenpo" degree, which is analogous to the "geshe" degree in the Geluk sect and a doctorate in Western universities. The program involves systematic study of a large body of texts in diverse genres, critical analysis, and evaluative procedures, with the exception that composition is of considerably less importance than in Western academic programs. Its standard requirements for Tibetan monks include painting, medicine, grammar, poetry, history, epistemology, the Indian Buddhist Mahāyāna philosophical systems of Madhyamaka and Cittamātra, the classic tantras, and the Great Perfection. Recipients of these degrees have traditionally been accorded great religious prestige in Tibet and have become important teachers, scholars, and authorities in Nyingma and Kagyü monasteries. However, it is precisely such products of long-term, rigorously structured programs who were in short supply in all sects following the long chaos of the Cultural Revolution. Thus the development of rigorous scholastic training programs at Larung, as well as at the other teaching academies (*bshad grwa*) in eastern Tibet that he founded during the 1980s, has been a top priority for Khenpo Jikphun. In the first decade roughly one hundred khenpos graduated from his academies, most of them young men in their twenties or thirties. Requirements for a khenpo degree have been somewhat relaxed in light of the pressing need for qualified teaching scholars, so that top students can complete the program in five years. Some of these new khenpos ultimately return to their own monasteries to teach, some stay at the center to become advanced teachers in their own right or engage in further studies, and some are sent by Khenpo Jikphun to monasteries with especially critical needs for teaching assistance.

Khenpo Jikphun has established other schools, such as the one in Nyarong at the site of his previous incarnation's residence (two hundred monks) and one in Minyak (one hundred monks). He also routinely makes visits to other monasteries, schools, and retreat centers to give teachings and empowerments. Since his academy trains many new khenpos who are sent to teach elsewhere, his links to other monastic centers are unusually close. Given his explicit desire for the academy to serve as a center for the renewal of Buddhism all over Tibet without requiring that individuals change their monastic affiliation, these relationships are of a different order than those typically enjoyed by traditional hierarchs of monasteries with strong intralineal concerns; in fact, he has founded scholastic academies and meditation academies (*bsgrub grwa*) in a number of the monasteries that have reemerged since the Cultural Revolution's end. Throughout he has stressed the exposition of the scriptures concerned with monastic discipline and the rituals of the bimonthly monastic confessional, the summer retreat and strict observance of its regulations. However, unlike similar religious institutions affiliated with the Nyingma sect in the refugee communities of Indian and Nepal, which have become concerned above all else with maintaining sūtra-based exoteric traditions to the detriment of esoteric traditions, Khenpo has consistently given teachings to entire monastic assemblies on the supreme esoteric traditions of the Great Perfection; he has also guided a great number of monastic and lay individuals currently practicing its contemplative precepts known as breakthrough and direct transcendence.[33]

This unusual blend of monastic discipline and the Great Perfection's appeal of tantric freedom would seem to be driven by two overarching motivations: the Great Perfection's traditional role in the type of ecumenism that Khenpo has so strongly advocated and its highly experiential yet streamlined contemplative system, which offers a direct and easily implementable mode of practice not reliant on structured communities, complicated ritual expertise, or extensive academic learning.

Though the resident monks are thus not actually part of a monastery, the nuns located just ten minutes down the valley are forming a true nunnery headed by Khenpo's young niece, Ani Muntsho (b. 1966 in the fire-horse year), the need for which Khenpo explains as being due to the relative poverty of religious institutions for women. There are four older male khenpos who have been assigned to teach the nuns; in 1991 there were also four female khenpos. Initially, nuns did not often receive Khenpo Jikphun's teachings, though they did receive empowerments, but in 1991 the assembly hall was constructed expressly so nuns and monks could receive these teachings simultaneously. In this new hall a line of flowers splits monks and nuns and there are different doors for entry and exit so as to prevent interaction that could lead to breaches of the code of celibacy. For general study, however, the nuns continue to use their own building facilities.

Figure 3.3. A ritual procession of nuns colorfully dressed in wigs and silk costumes. The nuns are from the nunnery headed by Khenpo's niece and the site is the area located between the institute and the nunnery.

Khenpo Jikphun also has a number of Han Chinese disciples, and two Tibetan monks in their early thirties specialize in teaching Chinese and translating Khenpo's teachings into Chinese.[34] In 1991 thirty to forty Chinese monks and nuns were in semipermanent residence, two of whom knew Tibetan and the rest of whom studied in Chinese within the organized program run by the bilingual Tibetan instructors. In fact, Khenpo pays the Chinese monks and nuns a special allowance of seventy yuan per month because they have come from so far; this allowance covers the cost of tsampa, butter, yak dung (for fuel), and other basic necessities. While there are examples of Chinese monks who have wholeheartedly assimilated the Tibetan lifestyle, many seem to maintain an attitude of cultural superiority and separation, evidently thinking of the association as something they will subsequently use to legitimate their own status as teachers. Despite the overtly racist attitudes displayed by many Chinese toward Tibetans, there remains a potent belief in the spiritual power of Tibetan Buddhism. I also witnessed periodic visits from devoted Chinese disciples who made the long trek from their homeland to visit Khenpo in his residence; some of them are considered to be very advanced students. In 1988 Khenpo spent two months in Beijing at the Buddhist Higher Academy at the Panchen Lama's invitation, during which time many Chinese were said to have arrived from other provinces in the PRC to receive teachings.

Monastic Visions

The creation of a large monastic center is part of the lifelong trajectory of Khenpo's career. He himself took novice vows at the age of fourteen and became a fully ordained monk at the age of twenty-two. His life has been characterized throughout by a constant emphasis on strict monastic discipline (including celibacy), especially manifest in his advocacy of monastic renewal and strict ethical standards as the key to revitalizing Buddhism in Tibet following the Chinese destruction of existing institutions after the mid-1950s. Given his credentials as a visionary Terton, this makes him an unusual figure in the Nyingma tradition. A large number of major lamas thought to integrate both scholarship and yogic realization in the current Nyingma tradition are married or have been, especially those who are also Terton, and Khenpo Jikphun is in this way one of the few exceptions who has remained devoted to the monastic tradition. His strict monastic lifestyle is thus in stark contrast to most other treasure revealers, who generally take consorts prior to their main revelations in order to practice sexual yoga, often with reports of stormy relationships ensuing.[35]

The critical juncture in Khenpo's monastic orientation occurred in his twenties, when he encountered a young woman whom he recognized as his karmically destined consort yet declined to unite with her in favor of a lifelong commitment to monasticism. On this occasion, when he first met her, she said to him, "Since we two are intimately connected by Padmasambhava's blessing-prayers and I am thus karmically destined to be your consort, I have come here." In Tibetan tantric

Buddhist lineages, women are often said to be of crucial importance as consorts for male visionaries, since it is believed that it is possible to traverse the transcendent path swiftly in reliance on the tantric techniques of sexual yoga; in addition, it is believed that sexual yoga contributes in some essential way to a Terton's ability to reveal treasures.[36] Though Khenpo Jikphun accordingly felt that the signs, circumstances, and karmic connections all indicated that the time had come to engage in sexual yoga to enhance his realization, he chose not to act on them.[37] Echoing earlier figures such as the founder of the Geluk tradition, Tsongkhapa (1357–1419), Khenpo later explained his feeling that most contemporary "yogis" were not superior to ordinary individuals and used the claim of a "tantric lifestyle" to legitimize doing as they pleased under the spell of sexual desire. He thus felt it important to set an example to preserve the teachings' integrity and refused to accept his consort despite their karmic connections, as well as the positive advantages he would have derived from their practice of sexual yoga. Shortly afterward, he related these events to a well-known master named Lodrö, who became upset and exclaimed, "Nowadays Tibetans have such slight virtuous merit! What can be done?! Because this has transpired, from now on you must perform the recitation and evocation rites for the Sky Dancers (*mkha'-'gro, ḍākiṇī*) and praise the merits of sexual yoga amidst large gatherings. Since later in your life your gathering of disciples will greatly increase, at that time you must propagate the sūtra and tantra teachings with an emphasis above all on the eloquent writings of Longchenpa and Mipham.[38] In this way vast benefit will accrue impartially to the teachings and to living beings." Thus, despite being destined to take up a consort as a necessary support for his discovery of Ter, Khenpo felt forced to decline the opportunity because he perceived the need for strict ethical examples during a time of moral decay (expressed by Lodrö in the traditional terminology of Tibetans' "merits," or overall accumulation of virtuous acts and positive karmic energy).

It is not surprising, then, that a key element of Khenpo's public mission following the end of the Cultural Revolution has been to express the need for a thorough purification and ethical reform of Buddhism in Tibet as a corrective to the many corruptions he felt had developed during the preceding three decades. Monastic discipline—that is, celibacy—and serious study of classic Buddhist texts figure prominently in Khenpo's vision of Tibet's Buddhist path and future, in addition to such traditional Tibetan religious values as loyalty to one's guru. While "corruptions" in the sense of noncelibate monks, illiterate monks, disrespect to gurus, and so on, clearly predate recent Chinese influence, it seems reasonable to conclude that the close of the Cultural Revolution found the traditional ideals of Tibetan religious culture in a far worse condition than in the preceding centuries. Khenpo put forward explicit standards as to which tendencies and conduct should be encouraged and which should be rejected. Above all, in line with a resolute belief in ethical discipline as the foundation of all positive qualities, he emphasized the need for dedicated practitioners to become monks and nuns, with the exception of those special few who had already mastered tantric contemplation and were thus beyond any need for conventional morality and discipline. He also disseminated a widely read circular advising that Tibetan monks and nuns in particular needed to act in strict accordance with the Buddha's ethical teachings on monastic discipline and the tantric corpus. For those practitioners who broke their monastic and tantric vows during the Cultural Revolution (such as vows of celibacy, respect for religious structures, and reverence for one's teachers), if the corruption was not so severe as to be beyond restoration, he instructed the performance of appropriate rituals for renewing vows; for others whose actions had severely damaged their vows beyond any possibility of ritual renewal, he insisted on expulsion from monastic assemblies. He also exhorted serious religious practitioners in general—whether ordained as monks and nuns or lay tantric practitioners—to exert themselves in techniques for purifying their negative acts and transgressions and to forsake other secular activities such as agriculture which they were forced to engage in during the Cultural Revolution. He felt that people who had broken their commitments (*dam tshig, samaya*) by such acts as beating lamas should now be permitted to visit the monasteries but not to take part in empowerments, rituals, and so on, even if formerly they were high reincarnate lamas. Though he was only able to insist on adherence to the circular's prescriptions within his own centers, he actively encouraged other monasteries in eastern Tibet to commit themselves publicly to supporting his agenda. This forceful assertion of the primacy of strict monastic values and traditional standards in the post–Cultural Revolution environment has led to consistent tension with those who engaged in anti-Buddhist activities during the Cultural Revolution, since Khenpo Jikphun has advocated a hard line against such individuals. This has been the source of considerable tension with local political leaders, who argued that the Cultural Revolution constituted a special situation and thus did not involve a breach of monastic or tantric vows. However, the Panchen Lama also advocated withholding tantric teachings from those with broken commitments, suggesting that instead they be given exoteric sūtra teachings.

In this way Khenpo felt that monastic communities could purify themselves and again become worthy fields of merit for lay people to honor, offer alms, and go to for refuge. It cannot be overemphasized how central this ethical issue is in terms of the relationships between lay individuals and monks, since ethical purity (especially celibacy) is what qualifies the monks as recipients of offerings from the lay community. Even if this "purity" is always of a relative sort, when infractions are very public and extensive it can lead to lay people questioning the entire institution, at least in its local manifestation. It also guarantees in turn that such offerings constitute "religious merit making," with merit understood as positive karma that will lead to mundane benefits, better rebirths, and eventually spiritual growth. As Ronald D. Schwartz has shown, this relationship between benefactors (*sbyin bdag*) and monks as a key element of Tibetan society has been repeatedly attacked by Chinese religious policies for its political implications.[39] While Khenpo has conjoined his strong educational and ethical standards with a strict emphasis on monasticism and insistence on exposing Tibetan religious hypocrisy, even while avoiding direct complicity with Chinese rule, he has distanced his movement from any involvement with overt political protests. This contrasts sharply with Schwartz's portrayal of the conjoining of ethical aspects of Buddhism with political protest that has dominated the ongoing demonstrations in Lhasa.[40] Khenpo's brand of nationalism has not involved confrontational resistance to governmental authorities, whether in his stress on systematic education in traditional Tibetan learning as an antidote to colonialist-intensified embarrassment over Tibet's seemingly backward past or in his revival of the traditional merit-making institution of interaction between monastic and lay communities. However, Khenpo Jikphun's ethical agenda, as well as his unusually open teaching of the esoteric tantric teachings (particularly the Great Perfection), has been the source of a considerable degree of controversy among *Tibetans*, though not with Chinese authorities. At one point, Khenpo Jikphun explained his motivations to a huge monastic assembly:

> Before I began this purification and reform of the teachings, there was not even one person displeased with me among all the monks, nuns and lay people. However by force of my undertaking this purification, many people high and low have begun to consider me as almost an enemy. Even so my own motivation in doing so has been devoid of even the slightest self-interest, other than the hope that in these extreme times when the Buddhist teachings have become a setting sun by virtue of the five corruptions' pervasive spread,[41] there might emerge the means for the pure teachings to remain, even if just for a day. With the three jewels as my witness,[42] I can sincerely say that I don't feel the slightest shame for my actions, and thus even if I had to sacrifice my own life for the sake of these teachings, it is certain that I would joyfully do so without the slightest regret. My feeling is identical to that expressed by the great Bodhisattva Śāntideva in the following verse:[43]

> Although many beings may kick and stamp upon my head,
> Even at the risk of dying may I delight the Protectors of the World [by not retaliating].

Another outcome has been conflict with some lay tantric practitioners (*sngagspa*) over Khenpo's criticism of their conduct, which has been linked to his advocation of strict monastic standards and conventional ethical norms as the best path to revitalization of Buddhist culture. This has been compounded by his own unusual status as a monastic hierarch deeply involved with the visionary Ter movement and the unusually tantric cast of the monastic teaching curriculum.[44] Ngakpa are often-hereditary lay practitioners of Buddhist tantra found throughout Tibetan cultural areas who have historically had a particularly close relationship to the Nyingma tradition; they at times possess considerable religious stature on the basis of the mystique of their spiritually potent family "lineage" (*brgyud-pa*) and personal achievements or charisma.[45] Although the extent of this tension is not clear to me, since a number of such figures are Khenpo's personal disciples, it appears that it derives from Khenpo's consistent criticism of supposed ethical lapses disguised in a tantric rhetoric of antinomianism and transcendence among many in their rank and file. Ngakpa have families and reside within ordinary lay communities, and I have found that it is not uncommon that entirely mundane concerns for power, sex, and money are at times masked by such figures with references to the classic tantric paradigms of the spiritual transformation of negative emotions and the violent subjugation of demonic forces. Khenpo's criticism has been particularly aggravating to some because it has been conjoined with a strong privileging of celibate clergy as the paramount ideal to which all Buddhists should aspire, with the clear implication that material and social resources should be channeled to the support of celibate monastic institutions. This criticism goes hand in hand with his criticism of married "monks," a phenomenon that apparently has traditional and recent roots.[46] This tension was reflected, for instance, in 1993 when the lay Nyingma lama Kusum Lingpa visited the United States from Golok and reportedly criticized Khenpo on several occasions, asserting that only his own "treasures" were valid.

Resuscitating the Tibetan Body

Khenpo's revival of the devastated Tibetan Buddhist systems of educational training (the Tibetan mind) has been nothing short of remarkable, and his ecumenical emphasis on monastic-centered ethics separated from political activism has offered a powerful Tibetan religious paradigm for survival in the People's Republic of China that contrasts sharply with the political activism of monks and nuns in Central Tibet. Khenpo Jikphun's most striking activity, however, has been his resuscitation of sacred pilgrimage networks in conjunction with a series of revelations of physical and literary items considered as Ter, or treasure. This contrasts, again, with the politicized brand of Buddhism Schwartz finds in Lhasa, which emphasizes "the ethical aspects of Buddhism as a religion—rather than its magical elements."[47] This treasure-driven resuscitation has been intertwined with dreams and visions of his own past lives that have governed his actions following his return to mainstream life after the Cultural Revolution. It has involved the revelation of historically important but currently forgotten or neglected geographic sites such as sacred caves, describing the forgotten significance of rooms within temples, leaving footprints and handprints in rock to create new sacred sites, and extracting treasures from the earth, all linked to his own memories of Tibetan history in the immediate fashion of recollection of previous lives. Often just his *visits* to crucial sacred spots are vital events in reestablishing this lost body of Tibetan religion for local residents, and are always marked by careful attention to the appropriate offering and ablution rituals directed to the sacred mountains considered to be the residences of Buddhist deities. Activities by lamas such as Khenpo Jikphun are thus literally reconstituting and reconnecting the extended cultural body of Tibet in its geographic landscape. The sheer density of memories evoked and personal identification with them envelop the present within a healing terrain of sacred sanctuaries, tantric deities, saints of the past, and potent Buddhas adequate even to the contemporary and seemingly implacable version of the host of demons that have afflicted Tibetan lives from time immemorial.

To adequately understand these contemporary manifestations of Ter, we need first to look back into the historical context of its origins. Buddhism was first imported into Tibet on a massive, government-sponsored scale during the period of the Tibetan empire, a time when Tibet controlled much of the Asian continent with successful military incursions even into the heart of China. This state-sanctioned importation focused on the development of monastic institutions and scholastic literature yet was intertwined with an unsanctioned diffusion of less orthodox tantric forms of Buddhist lifestyles, rhetoric, and practices. Following the gradual collapse of political centralization after the assassination of the emperor Langdarma in 842, Tibet underwent a dark period (mid-ninth to late tenth century) during which state-sponsored Buddhism largely collapsed while lay tantric movements continued to flourish. When economic revival began to generate surplus wealth such that political centralization and concomitant large-scale cultural projects reemerged in Tibet (late tenth century onward),[48] the glorious imperial past and its Buddhist associations became a key site of rhetorical contestation among the various groups attempting to take control of the future of Tibet. In brief, a dominant strategy for groups linked to the new centers of wealth and political power was to import current Indic traditions of Buddhism and deploy them in the Tibetan cultural field with a supporting rhetoric of purity and modernity, in the face of the supposed corruption and antiquity of previous Tibetan lineages. Thus the age of the "great translators" was born in the eleventh century under the aegis of "modernism" (gsar-ma, literally "new-ist") with Tibetans and Indians who traversed the Himalayas in search of teachings, fame, money, and enlightenment. This movement gradually began to dominate the Tibetan cultural arena with its powerful rhetoric and mythos centered on the grand project of the translation of Indian Buddhist scriptures into Tibetan, as well as its astute links to political and economic centers in conjunction with a monastic reinstitutionalization. This was successfully linked in reality, and in imagination, to the contemporaneous reawakening of Tibetan economic and political vitality, such that the "renaissance" of Tibetan civilization came to be linked to the modernists' "reform" of Tibetan religion. Both employed a rhetoric of the taming or control of a barbaric indigenous reality with structured language, community, practices, and belief systems derived from a more civilized India.[49]

Modernist Tibetan rhetoric tended polemically to paint Buddhist groups that resisted their agenda—who came to be known as the "ancients" (Nyingma)—as passive traditionalists continuing an antinomian form of mysticism stemming from the dark period, thereby attempting socially, religiously, and intellectually to disenfranchise those groups maintaining the "old" Buddhist traditions without becoming actively engaged in the reform movement. In fact, those groups loosely organized under the rubric of the "ancients" embarked on an equally complex religious and intellectual renaissance during the same period (late tenth to fourteenth

century) which continued pre-eleventh-century Tibetan traditions while revitalizing them via creative appropriation of the wealth of material flowing into Tibet
through the modernist translation project. One of their most successful rhetorical
weapons was the innovative adaptation of Indian Buddhist models for scriptural
authentication that became known as the treasure (Ter) movement.[50] The Tibetan
Ter movement thus began in earnest in the eleventh and twelfth centuries with the
cultural revival that followed the dark period. As the new Buddhist groups im-
porting teachings and authority from India put older Tibetan Buddhist lineages
on the defensive, the latter, the Nyingma, developed the Ter movement as a response. Ter involved the visionary notion that during the dynastic period the literary jewels of Indian Buddhism had been embedded in the subtle bodies of Tibetans as well as the geographic body of Tibet herself,[51] so that after the dark
period their only location (the fragile esoteric traditions having since disappeared
in India) was this latent enfolding within the Tibetan body. In other words, many
teachings hitherto unknown were said to have been brought to Tibet in the eighth
century by Padmasambhava and Vimalamitra but concealed for the sake of future
generations instead of being publicly disseminated at that time. These teachings
were now being gradually recovered by reincarnations, particularly of Padmasambhava's and Vimalamitra's eighth-century Tibetan disciples who had been
appointed as the predestined revealers of the treasures, the Terton. Thus once the
darkness lifted, these treasures were said to be gradually revealed or excavated by
reincarnations of these key dynastic period players. From an external perspective,
it appears that the treasure cult involved innovations and adaptations of doctrinal
as well as contemplative systems that creatively synthesized indigenous lineages
with the new modernist material. Its historical mythos provided a legitimizing
force that combated the modernist manipulation of contemporary Indic authority and lineal purity.[52]

   While complex classificatory schemes developed concerning the nature and
content of such rediscoveries, it is sufficient to consider two dichotomies: (1) texts
versus nontexts (statues, ritual implements, etc.) and (2) texts revealed in visions
without material support versus texts uncovered from the earth as physical manuscripts, though often in special encoded form known as Ḍākinī script. The latter
distinction can be summarized in terms of earth treasures (sa gter) and treasures of
"intention" or "wisdom" (dgongs gter),[53] one physically buried in the body of Tibet
and the other mystically concealed in the transmigrating, embodied psyches of
Tibetans. While we may readily understand the latter in terms of spontaneous
composition, which by firsthand reports is accompanied by iconic flashes of past-
life memories as well as intense and unusual bodily sensations, the earth treasures
involve complicated searches based on visions and prophecies, discoveries of
strange material items, and an often fragile process of decoding that can fail if any
of the tendrel, or supporting circumstances, are disrupted. In either case, whether
the texts were buried within the depths of the Tibetan earth or the depths of a Tibetan body,[54] the agent of concealment is most often Padmasambhava or Vi-

malamitra, while the agent of discovery is the reincarnation of one of their principal Tibetan disciples.

The functions of the early Ter movement during cultural turmoil were thus threefold:[55] (1) in the face of modernist attacks, to authorize and authenticate the Nyingmas' religious traditions by invoking a competing power structure located in culturally powerful memories of the dynastic period, headed by a reinvented Padmasambhava; (2) to appropriate and transform for a self-consciously autochthonous tradition the new intellectual and religious materials stemming from India without acknowledging them as such; and (3) to develop uniquely Tibetan theories, practices, and systems in an environment often dominated by a sense of cultural inferiority. In terms of the third point, the Ter ideology gave these traditions an Indic guise for legitimation while also creating a space in which they could transform Indic influences in Tibetan terms without simply reproducing them. Thus Ter had an important buffer function that prevented indigenous Tibetan concerns, practices, and beliefs from being overwhelmed by the immense power and authority that imported classical Indian Buddhist systems assumed in the eleventh and twelfth centuries. It was intimately concerned with formulating and sustaining Tibetan self-identity in the face of an influx of foreign culture, and thus with the value of Tibetan autonomy. Even in its invoking of Indic authority with Padmasambhava and Vimalamitra, it was precisely their presence and actions *in Tibet* that was of crucial significance, and thus this invocation simultaneously functioned to reiterate the significance of Tibetan culture in and of itself.

Finally, I would like to emphasize the role of the Great Perfection in the treasure cult: not only was it one of the most important bodies of early Ter as well as arguably the key doctrinal system in the nineteenth-century ecumenical movement that Khenpo Jikphun is heir to, but it also has been the most important Buddhist tradition in Khenpo's corpus, oral teachings, and community. The Great Perfection was central to the Ter movement as it underwent momentous transformations that clearly reflected the appropriation of the modernist importations into a characteristically Nyingma space, while its rhetorical directions offered the most sustained and clearly articulated inversions of the dominant modernist rhetorical strategies: naturalness is emphasized instead of regulated refinement, indigenous resources instead of imported civilization, advocacy of inaction instead of massive projects, spontaneous patterning instead of contrived intentional ordering, lay life instead of monasticism. What made the Great Perfection so uniquely suited to the task of interpretive assimilation was precisely its strong rhetoric of denial, which was infamous in Tibet for its apparent negation of key Buddhist beliefs and values. As I have argued elsewhere,[56] one of the key functions of this deconstructive language was to destructure the imposing intellectual coherence and authority of a given Indic system of thought and practice, thereby enabling its elements to be reconfigured within a distinctively Tibetan vision. The end result was a genuinely Tibetan transformation of Buddhist tantra that innovatively appropriated and thoroughly revised it in the cauldron of Tibetan ideolo-

Figure 3.4. Murals representing the visions of Great Perfection contemplation from the Lukhang (*Klu-khang*) temple located in Lhasa. The figures to the left are the classic maṇḍala of the five male and female Buddhas, which the maṇḍala to the right represents in nonanthropomorphic fashion.

gies, culture, and language. The Great Perfection's rhetorical negation thus functioned to create and sustain a bounded *Tibetan* discourse that resisted the pressure of domination from the new Indic materials flowing into Tibet and yet performed the alchemy of cultural assimilation. This process was hampered in modernist circles by the immense drains of faithfully translating primary materials from an alien culture and language (i.e., Indian Buddhist scriptures), the need to appear faithful to the transplanted paradigms, and their general rejection of the production of new canonical literature and paradigms through Tibetan authors speaking in the anonymously creative voice of a Buddha (as was frequent in Ter). Ter, the Great Perfection, and the modernists' own diligent Indology were thus the three main factors that enabled the Nyingmas to create literary and intellectual works of enduring value that were as rooted in Indic forms as they were in the Tibetan soil.

Revealing Treasure in the Twentieth Century

We return now to Khenpo Jikphun's redeployment of this ancient Ter strategy of legitimation and innovation against the backdrop of the transformed landscape of the twentieth century. Some of the more remarkable accounts of these later

Figure 3.5. A selection of Ter items that Khenpo Jikphun has uncovered. Most of them are the treasure chests, the third from the right being the dark green globe said to have fallen from the sky during one of the described treasure revelations. They also include a yellow scroll, two statues, and the ritual implement known as a vajra (*rdo rje*).

post–Cultural Revolution events of revelation are as follows. In 1990 he identified a site in northeastern Tibet as being the location of the palace of the legendary King Gesar and directed an archaeological dig that turned up ancient building stones as well as several treasure chests (*sgrom bu*).[57] This was linked to his recall of a previous incarnation as Yuö Bumme (literally, "intense turquoise light"), the aforementioned son of Danma, one of King Gesar's ministers. Since Yuö Bumme is said to be an emanation of Mañjuśrī and Gesar an emanation of Avalokiteśvara, this reinscribes his own close relationship to the contemporary Dalai Lama, as will be seen below. During a visit to the Potala Palace on his first trip to Lhasa, he identified several historically important rooms of which even the curators were unaware. His visions while visiting Samye Monastery during the same trip are related below.

A typical discovery of an unknown sacred site happened during his visit to a place known as Sacred Site Interior Monastery, which is said to be associated with the Buddha's Enlightened Speech.[58] Here he discovered and opened up a meditation cave of Vimalamitra and a secret Ḍākiṇī cave. At dawn on the seventeenth of the first lunar month in 1987, he sat for a while in silent meditation and then suddenly said, "Bring me some ink and paper!" He then related the following manifest concerning previously unrevealed sacred sites and had it transcribed (the first and fifth lines are written in esoteric Ḍākiṇī languages):

> *Pu-ta-ka-ru-hu-ma-li,*
> To the left direction of *Me lha skya ring,*
> One-third the way up a red heart,
> In the middle of a bright mirror-disc and amidst trees,
> *Ratna pustu mudri shre dpe,*
> A tiger-girl with white silk and intoxicated,
> Prize this time without letting it slip away.

In accordance with the mention of tiger-girls, Khenpo called together ten young girls (many of whom were born in a tiger year, according to the Tibetan calendar) and ten young boys and gave them the following instructions: "On this place's southern border, there is a cave about one-third the way up a heart-shaped rocky mountain. In front of it is a disc-shaped field, while trees surround the cave near its entrance. See if you can find it!" After sending the children to search for this meditation cave, Khenpo and his entourage went to a nearby guru meditation cave that was a sacred site of Avalokiteśvara. There Khenpo performed a ritual ablution, incense offering, and consecration of the site. He also took a chest from treasure concealment in the cave's depths, and at that time ambrosia spontaneously flowed from within the cave and the people outside clearly perceived melodious music and fragrant scents pervading the area. When the children who had been searching for the cave's location returned, he performed a ritual feast offering dedicated to Mañjuśrī.

The children related how they had found what they suspected to be the cave, and Khenpo sent several disciples to look for the sacred site's entrance with detailed instructions concerning the shapes of the mountain, cave, and surrounding field as drawn from the prophetic manifest. He predicted an additional cave would be found, a secret cave of the Ḍākiṇīs with imprints of their fingers, the syllables *Bam-ha-ri-ni-sa,* and their hand implements with offering-substances naturally engraved on its rock walls. Everything was clearly there just as Khenpo had described it. These discoveries were immediately inscribed within the web of prophecies that permeate the world of Tibetan Buddhism. The former cave was identified as a sacred site where Vimalamitra's emanation achieved contemplative realization; the latter was identified as the site where Vimalamitra taught spiritual doctrines and "turned the wheel" of feast offerings to a trillion Ḍākiṇīs such as Glorious Wisdom (Dpal-gyi blo-gros). It is said that some great figures had previously tried to find the former cave but were unable to do so. Khenpo located prophetic references to these two sites in a treasure prophecy:

> There is a meditation cave of Vimalamitra with his foot prints in stone . . .
> Esoterically it is the Glorious Copper Mountain in the Ngayab continent,[59]
> And in that glorious mountain there is an Assembly Hall of Ḍākiṇīs.

In addition, a Terton named Matiratna once revealed a treasure entitled *Prophecies Illuminating the Future, a Dialogue with the Ḍākiṇī Fierce Subduer of Demons,* which has a prophetic passage Khenpo interpreted as referring to his opening of these sacred caves to the outside world:[60]

> A power spot on the Tidro rock will be opened up, and by my, Urgyen Rinpoche's, magic powers, the door to a secret cave [an isolated sacred site of the Ḍākiṇīs] will be opened by an emanation of a small boy in eastern Tibet. Its internal door won't be opened except in the future, and the signs indicating that time are that border [i.e., foreign] troops will arrive in the hidden gorge and conquer, while religious activity will be no more present than a daytime star.

Khenpo thus identified this site as a previously unknown sister site to the famous cavern in Central Tibet within the Drigung district known as the Great Assembly of the Ḍākiṇīs Kere Yangdzong, a huge cave said to have been frequented during the dynastic period by the famous consort of Padmasambhava, Yeshe Tsogyel: both involve caverns functioning as "assembly centers for Ḍākiṇīs" and associated with the name Tidro.[61] Finally, Khenpo told his disciples how the caves' potent field of blessings meant that contemplation performed within them would be remarkably enhanced and result in direct visceral encounters with Vimalamitra and the Ḍākiṇīs respectively.

It is interesting to think of Khenpo's unusual commitment to celibacy in terms of Charlene E. Makley's argument for the importance of gendered practices in the reconstruction of Tibetan identity in contemporary China through the medium of sacred geography.[62] She argues that Tibetan women's adherence to traditional Tibetan gender distinctions with regard to the sacred space of Buddhist monasteries has played an important role in the subversive reconstruction of nationalistic models of Buddhist-derived authority that resists the "state-constructed map" of authority and identity. This is against the backdrop of emphasizing that for Tibetans "self" and "other" are played out to an unusual extent in terms of the opposition between sacred and profane, although my experience indicates that some type of distinction between domestic and public plays an equally important role, even if not as immediately visible. Clearly male-dominated institutional Buddhism is a key repository of Tibetan cultural identity,[63] in part because temple building is one of the few permissible public ways to express nationalistic pride and commitment with excess financial resources or donated labor. The complex cultural practices that then sustain these temples also play critical roles in shaping a distinctively Tibetan identity in resistance to the government's attempts to construct a suitably cleansed ethnic identity at home in the People's Republic of China. However, institutional Buddhism should not be overemphasized, given the importance of domestic residences,[64] the fact that lay religious practices are often only peripherally connected to such institutions, including pilgrimages where such institutions are often limited to mere markers,[65] the informal nonmonastic communities that inhabit Tibet's sacred geography, the evolving

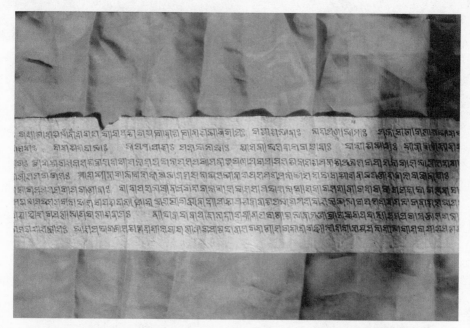

Figure 3.6. A famous yellow scroll (*shog ser*), the form in which a treasure text is often initially discovered. It is written in a special Ḍākinī script that only the Terton can decipher.

strata of nonmonastic Tibetan intellectuals, and in general the pervasiveness of lay religious contemplative rituals. My analysis suggests that while Khenpo's commitment to monasticism derives in large part from the key role of such institutions in the reconstruction of Tibetan identity and community, it is his blending of the role of monastic hierarch overseeing a huge community with that of a charismatic (and generally lay) leader in the "field" that has situated him at the center of these pervasive articulations of Tibetan resistance through the medium of the Tibetan landscape itself.

The most important aspect of these activities, however, relates to the Ter phenomenon, since no contemporary Terton is more renowned than Khenpo Jikphun. The reasons are clear: his treasures include a large corpus of philosophical treatises, poetry, contemplative manuals, and ritual cycles of undeniable eloquence, precision, and power; and his discoveries have been extensive, miraculous, and public events.[66] The background to his Terton status is his frequently reiterated claim to be the reincarnation of Nanam Dorje Dudjom, one of the twenty-five principal Tibetan disciples of Padmasambhava in the eighth century. Thus his Ter are supposed to be actual teachings that he received in this former life but only now is able to recall and retrieve. In fact, most of his corpus has been produced by spontaneous composition, whether understood as his personal work or a transmission from figures of the past—these days disciples use a handy recorder to tape such compositions as they emerge and later transcribe them. Along with these wisdom treasures, his Ter also include material earth treasures such as yellow scrolls concealed in odd-shaped rocks and various statues or ritual implements recovered from within rocks. To give a sense of the nature of these discoveries, I will briefly describe four such events (all of which transpired in the post–Cultural Revolution period), the final two also providing some sense of his ability to galvanize Chinese and refugee Tibetan interest as well.

Ter as a source of miracles and sacred power.   A famous example of public treasure occurred when Khenpo Jikphun was giving a Mañjuśrī empowerment on the tenth day of the first lunar month in 1981. In the morning while performing the preliminary recitations Khenpo kept looking up at the sky like a crazy yogi and, quite unlike his ordinary, ritually efficient conduct, he was not performing the ritual or the hand gestures properly, at times chanting the recitation very rapidly and at times very slowly. In the afternoon as the ritual feast offering was being performed, Khenpo Chöpe was acting as the attendant who handed Khenpo Jikphun the ritual items as required. Then as he presented the sacrificial cones (*gtor ma*) to Khenpo, Khenpo stood up instead of taking them and held a white offering scarf in his outstretched hands. A "chest" resembling a dark green bird egg then fell from the sky in front of his arms and landed on his desk (see Fig. 3.5). A number of people (several of whom I interviewed in 1991) witnessed it falling, and Lama Gakdor in particular mentioned first seeing it in the space in front of Khenpo's hands as it fell down. Khenpo then picked it up from the desk and allowed the thirty or so people there to pass it around, who found it a bit hot to the touch. This event details only one of his many reported miracles, ranging from receiving material treasures out of thin air to impressing his footprints in solid rock, and demonstrates the intense aura of power and sacrality with which his revelatory activities have imbued him. This conviction that his actions can step beyond the boundaries of corporeality and ordinary material limitations suggests to his followers that he may also be capable of a modern version of another impossible feat, namely leading them beyond the equally tangible confines of Chinese occupation, a presence now deeply rooted within the Tibetan soil and psyche.

Reawakening the geographic and mythic landscape of ancient Tibet.   While on a pilgrimage to the recently restored Samye Monastery in Central Tibet,[67] Khenpo went to the Blazing Turquoise Tiled Porch on the central temple's second floor, where he suddenly experienced a past-life memory of Padmasambhava expounding the Seminal Heart Great Perfection (*snying thig rdzogs chen*) teachings to a retinue of King Tri Songdetsen and his select subjects. Saying, "Though previously Padmasambhava taught the profound teachings in this very site, now in its present form I can't even recognize it!" Khenpo wept profusely and sang a song of lament. When I asked him about it in 1991, he told me that the reconstructed Samye

Figure 3.7. The reconstructed Samye Monastery in 1990. It was the first Buddhist monastery built in Tibet (at the end of the eighth century), an event that was made possible by Padmasambhava's taming of Tibetan spirits. Its complex of temples symbolically represents the traditional Buddhist cosmogram of the universe.

Monastery is unlike his past-life memories in many ways, particularly with regard to this porch. The porch is located on the second floor in the front part of the main temple as a wide balcony overhung by the roof above but without any external walls. Previously the roof below it had blue tiles, such that sun rays would reflect off its blue surface and suffuse the porch above with bluish light; at present that surface is instead covered with gold paint. His biography says that on seeing Samye in this condition, Khenpo suddenly recalled a wisdom treasure deriving from Padmasambhava's teachings to him in that very room, which his disciples immediately transcribed.

Then Khenpo went to the famous Chimphu retreat center located in the highlands near Samye Monastery. Along the way he had an intense contemplative experience of all ordinary impure appearances dissolving, followed by a vision of Padmasambhava emerging with countless Ḍākiṇīs from his pure land, the Glorious Copper Colored Mountain. Immediately after his vision he remained in meditative silence for a short time and then spontaneously sang many tantric songs. This was followed by a sudden vision of a demoness displaying unpleasant apparitions to indicate her displeasure at Khenpo's presence, such that he took the form of the fierce deity Lotus Heruka in response. Intimidating the demoness with this wrathful visualization, he confined her beneath the ground and ordered that she remain there for nine years. Finally arriving at Chimphu, Khenpo stayed at Keutshang Red Rock and became deeply absorbed in rituals of deity evocation. In the imperial period, Khenpo later said, Padmasambhava hid a treasure text at that spot in the center of two stone "chests" shaped like conch shells with clockwise spirals, the content of which summarized the tantric contemplative triad of deity visualization, subtle body practices, and the Great Perfection, for the sake of renewing degenerated teachings in subsequent times of strife. Padmasambhava had entrusted the stones to Yeshe Tsogyel, instructing her to hand deliver them in the distant future to an emanation of his disciple Nanam Dorje Dudjom, who would arrive at the gathering place of Ḍākiṇīs called Tidro and Chimphu. Since he recognized that the time had come for the treasure to be extracted, Khenpo Jikphun took one part of this treasure out from concealment during his stay at Red Rock. As for the other stone chest, subsequently Khenpo went to the upper part of the foot of the Drigung Tidro mountain north of Lhasa and then sent Khenpo Chöpe farther on with a white offering scarf, instructing him thus not to come back until he had found a rock exactly like the one recovered at Chimphu.

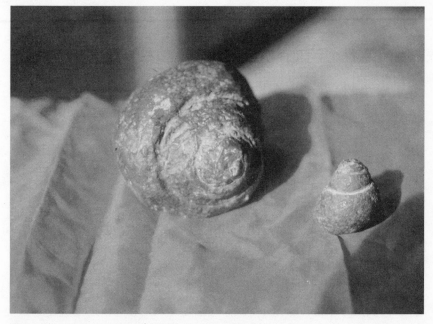

Figure 3.8. The two conch shell-shaped treasure chests mentioned in the account of Khenpo's revelations at Samye Chimphu. Items like the yellow scrolls are extracted from within such chests.

Khenpo Chöpe then obtained the stone from the hand of a woman staying in retreat in the Padmasambhava meditation cave at Tidro who is widely believed to be an emanation of Yeshe Tsogyel herself.[68] Though the time had not come to extract the treasure doctrines from these two stone chests, by virtue of there being an overriding necessity Khenpo revealed an empowerment ritual and evocation ritual for the goddess Kurukullā, as well as an empowerment ritual for the Fierce Guru, in the manner of a combined earth treasure/vision treasure deriving from these chests.

These incidents illustrate how Khenpo Jikphun's reanimation and extension of Tibetan mythology and its key icons is a dynamic process performed in close relationship to the Tibetan landscape, which is understood as a series of residences (*gnas*) inhabited by the Buddhist deities, ancestral spirits, local demonic entities, and the like, who have traditionally played a major role in the history of Tibetan culture.[69] Mythic history is thus retrieved through revitalization of the sacred landscape first created in ancient Tibet, a cooperative process with other Tibetans, both human and nonhuman, that involves encounters, exchanges, physical actions, and substances understood as productive of texts, or "treasures." These texts in turn give those encounters, actions, and substances significance, jointly creating a cultural density literally grounding Tibetans in Tibet once again. Thus Ter is one of the most striking crystallizations of the marked substance orientation of Tibetan pilgrimage and other practices relating to sacred geography.[70]

A common ground: Ter's extension of Tibetan culture into China.   In 1987 Khenpo went to the Wutai (Five Peak) Mountains in China, saying that from a very young age he had an intense desire to go there in person as it was the bodhisattva Mañjuśrī's main pure land here on Earth.[71] Classic Tibetan histories speak of Mañjuśrī gazing at Tibet from his home in the Wutai Mountains in the eighth century and deciding to emanate a form there as its next ruler. This was none other than the famous emperor Tri Songdetsen, such that the mountains are an integral part of Tibet's dynastic past and mythic present.[72] Khenpo became convinced the time had come during the late spring of 1986 when he was giving an empowerment of the *Magical Net of Mañjuśrī* tantric cycle to more than one thousand disciples,[73] after a large-scale *Wheel of Time* (Kālacakra) tantric initiation that he transmitted to more than six thousand people. During the blessings' descent, the phase of the ritual when the deity (the "gnostic being") is invited so that its inspiration descends and dissolves into the disciple's visualization of the deity (the "commitment being"), the empowerment deity descended in an inner visionary manifestation to Khenpo and gave him a prophecy: "Since there will be a great benefit to the teachings and living beings if you go to the Five Peak Mountains, you should go there." At that time an external sign of this vision was witnessed by everyone present: Khenpo was perceived to levitate three feet above the ground and hovered there for a short time. From that time on Khenpo encouraged all monasteries to perform thousands of ritual evocations of Mañjuśrī (involving recitation of his mantra with visualization of his form), and in the beginning of 1987 he set out for the Wutai Mountains, along with thousands of other Tibetans.[74] Along the way he visited such famous Buddhist sacred sites as the Imposing Elephant Mountain (Emeishan in Sichuan) and the huge Buddha statue at Leshan in Sichuan and finally arrived at Beijing. There Khenpo Jikphun consulted the Panchen Lama about the ongoing purification and reform of Buddhism he had undertaken and was reassured that he was on the right path. Making prayers for the sake of the teachings and living beings in front of the small stūpa located in a pagoda on the slopes of Beijing's Western Hills (Xishan), which is believed to contain one of the four cuspids of the Buddha, Khenpo Jikphun then departed for the Wutai Mountains.

Almost ten thousand individuals from areas in Amdo, along with members of various other regional and ethnic groups (Tibetan, Chinese, Mongolian, etc.), are said to have gathered there with Khenpo. He first taught them basic doctrines such as Tsongkhapa's *Three Principal Aspects of the Path* (*Lam gtso rnam gsum;* renunciation, the altruistic enlightened mind, and the authentic view), Tsongkhapa's *Summarized Meaning of the Path (Lam rim bsdus don),* and the Kadampa master Gyalse Thokme Zangpo's (1295–1369) *Thirty-seven Practices of a Bodhisattva (Lag len so bdun).* Then, before the Stūpa with a Nucleus of the Realized One's Relics he had all the Tibetans who had traveled there together create a virtuous foundation by reciting the *Prayer of Samantabhadra's Conduct (Bzang spyod smon lam)* thirty million times in total,[75] and Khenpo himself made potent prayers for all those spiritually related to him to be reborn in the Blissful pure land (Sukhāvatī), for the teaching to spread far and wide, and for all sentient beings to attain bliss. To bring benefit to the teachings in general, Khenpo had exquisite statues of Padmasambhava, Atiśa, and Tsongkhapa, among others, built with the appropriate ornaments and mantras inserted in them and also provided many such sacred objects for the other monasteries in the area. One day he traveled to a monastery on the far side of one of the key mountains, and immediately on arrival seven children are said to have magically appeared and received teachings from him, after which they suddenly disappeared into thin air. In a meditation cave called the cave of Sudhana (Shancai)[76] Khenpo kept a strict retreat for three weeks. While staying there, on the morning of the twenty-ninth of the fourth lunar month, he had a pure vision of Mañjuśrī's youthful body, accompanied by intense contemplative experiences.

Then Khenpo Jikphun went to a cave on the Eastern Terrace where the ocean can be seen which is identified with a spot mentioned in the *Avataṃsaka Sūtra* as Mañjuśrī's constant residence.[77] He did a two-week retreat there and later said that he experienced uninterrupted visions of radiant light day and night as well as other powerful contemplative experiences and visions. Then on the tenth day of the sixth lunar month when Khenpo was making a feast offering dedicated to Mañjuśrī while staying at the Clear and Cool Rock Monastery,[78] the sky became pervaded by strange patterns of rainbow light just as explained in the Clear and Cool Mountains guidebook reference to Mañjuśrī's emanations being present as multiform light rays. While Khenpo Jikphun had a vision of Mañjuśrī himself, these strange rainbow lights, including a very unusual rainbow-colored light sphere, were witnessed by everyone there. Subsequently, everyone present witnessed an extraordinary play of rainbow light from a cloud at sunset, and photographs were taken. During Khenpo's strict retreat in the Nārāyaṇa (Naloyanku) rock cave on the Eastern Terrace's slope,[79] his retreat house was encircled by a sphere of rainbow light, which again everyone witnessed. Khenpo Jikphun uncovered a miniature statue made of exquisite gold from this cave, which he later offered to the Dalai Lama, who was delighted by it. As Khenpo had on three occasions traveled to the Wutai Mountains in a dream body prior to actually going there in person, he often told his students he was able to identify all its sacred sites during this visit. One day while staying at the meditation cave of Sudhana, he said, "That area around the central mountain over there resembles a sacred site I came to in a dream.[80] If that's it, there's a damaged deity statue in that spot." He mentioned other related signs as well. Later his disciples found it was exactly as Khenpo had described. Khenpo also hid many statues and caskets as newly concealed treasures amid the Clear and Cool Mountains during his stay.

This extension of Khenpo Jikphun's Ter activity into parts of China in which Tibetan and Chinese Buddhism traditionally interacted creates a religious prospect of common ground, a shared physical and symbolic space of resistance to government ideologies and practices crossing, or at least intersecting, ethnic boundaries. In addition, his revelation and concealment of Ter at the Wutai Mountains invests the heart of the Chinese sacred landscape with a contemporary Tibetan presence, the precise inversion of the recent massive immigration of Chinese military and peasants into cultural Tibet. Unlike the Chinese caricature of Tibetans as uncouth and unkempt barbarians, it is a highly literate textualized presence that Khenpo represents, reveals, and leaves behind, a sophisticated maṇḍala with the capacity to organize time and space around it even within the dominating landscape of Chinese communism. In understanding the complicated Tibetan responses to "modernity," we must take into account not only the significant role of tourism in the revival of Tibetan sacred geography[81] and the role of Chinese and Western Buddhist appropriations of Tibetan culture for their own ends but also also the Tibetans as dynamic agents who construct as much as they are constructed, and who are thus both changing subjects and objects in a phenomenon of interaction that goes far beyond the pale confines of what is dismissively labeled "Orientalism." The Chinese fascination with Tibetan Buddhism is particularly important, and I have personally witnessed extremes of personal devotion and financial support by Han Chinese to both monastic and lay Tibetan religious figures within the People's Republic of China, often linked to the qi gong craze that continues to be an important force in Chinese resistance to the "state."[82] While I have more frequently witnessed Chinese dismissals of Tibetan culture as backward and barbaric, the pervasive importance of the qi gong movements in China again raises the possibility of a common ground where Chinese and Tibetan strategies of resistance, as well as oppressive otherness, and the construction (or deconstruction) of identity, encounter each other and overlap, even within an overall pattern of divergences.

Transcendent Ter in refugee Tibet.   Khenpo Jikphun in his previous incarnation as Lerab Lingpa had a particularly close spiritual and personal relationship to the thirteenth Dalai Lama, such that both Khenpo and the current Dalai Lama reportedly felt a strong desire to meet one other on the basis of this karmic connection. Khenpo expressed intense faith in the Dalai Lama. Thus he decided to travel to India to meet with the Dalai Lama and to visit the sacred Buddhist sites there. Penor Rinpoche, who in 1993 would become head of the Nyingma tradition, had invited him to come to his monastic seat in Bylakuppe, South India, on several occasions, but Khenpo postponed accepting that invitation because of pressing duties related to his activities in eastern Tibet as well as extenuating political circumstances.[83] However, toward the end of the first lunar month after the Tibetan New Year in 1990, Khenpo Jikphun finally made the trip accompanied by Khenpo Namdrol from Penor Rinpoche's monastery.[84] When visiting the famous Yangleshö Padmasambhava cave in Nepal just outside of the Kathmandu valley, he experienced past-life memories in which he recalled a teaching cycle entitled *The Single Dagger of the Tutelary Deity's Enlightened Spirit, the Dagger in a Small Neck Bag.*[85] The name is derived from a small bag that Padmasambhava wore around his neck which contained a ritual dagger embodying the essence of his tutelary deity. When Khenpo subsequently arrived in Dharamsala, he offered its empowerment to the Dalai Lama and subsequently during conversation, an auxiliary teaching of this cycle spontaneously emerged in Khenpo's mind, which the Dalai Lama wrote out on his behalf. In addition to exchanges of teachings and wide-ranging conversations on various topics, several attendants reported one encounter during which they discussed past-life memories of their previous relationship as the thirteenth Dalai Lama and Lerab Lingpa. Just prior to Khenpo's departure, the Dalai Lama finished a supplication prayer for the *Dagger* cycle that Khenpo had requested that he compose, and thus Khenpo received the verbal transmission for it from the Dalai Lama directly. Photographs of the two were subsequently widely circulated within eastern Tibet, although I did hear rumors of the local authorities' unhappiness with this.

Also during this visit Khenpo's niece Ani Muntsho was recognized by the Dalai Lama as the reincarnation of Migyur Palgyi Dronma, a Central Tibetan emanation of Yeshe Tsogyel, who was the daughter of the important Nyingma master Terdak Lingpa (1646–1714), also closely linked to the fifth Dalai Lama.[86] Khenpo was also invited to the Dalai Lama's Nechung College, where he gave the *Dagger* empowerment in their assembly hall. In the ritual phase at which the gnostic deity descends, the special protector of Nechung suddenly possessed the Nechung Oracle and in a highly unusual act gave prophecies and religious offerings to Khenpo; at the same time, the goddess Dorje Yudronma suddenly took possession

Figure 3.9. Khenpo Jikphun giving blessings to a group of laymen to whom he had just delivered a speech.

of her human oracle and gave prophecies. Khenpo himself experienced vivid past-life memories and wept as he recalled his former relationships and intimates.

This set of events points to the deployment of Ter within Tibetan refugee communities as a rare instance of a recent movement originating from within the People's Republic of China exerting powerful and positive effects on Tibetans still living outside its confines. His dramatic actions both within a major Tibetan monastery in India and within the sacred and political heart of refugee Tibet (Dharamsala) undercuts the paradoxical notion that traditional Tibetan culture only exists outside of Tibet and points to a possible forging of unity within the fractious Tibetan community through a potent brand of myth relocated within modernity, or at least some variant thereof.

DARKNESS AND RENEWAL: THE VALUE AND LIMITS OF CONTEMPORARY TER

I would like now to reconsider the themes of modernity, alienation, and renewal in a comparative manner that traverses the historical gap between the origins of the treasure cult in the eleventh and twelfth centuries and Khenpo's contemporary revival of Ter in the late twentieth century. I believe there is a strong subcurrent in the Tibetan imagination that associates the Chinese occupation, and above all the Cultural Revolution, with the dark period of Tibetan history following the collapse of the empire. In both cases Buddhism was persecuted, the ecclesiastical and economic structures collapsed, key religious and temporal monuments went into decay, formal education slowed to a standstill, and social chaos erupted. A key difference that is immediately evident is that between the self-engendered and self-governed collapse of central authority that occurred in the ninth century as the Tibetan empire disintegrated for internal reasons and the coerced and other-engendered devastation brought about by Chinese invasion and occupation. As Tibetans have begun to reemerge from this new dark period in the past two decades, there are thus unavoidable associations of this renewal of Tibetan identity with the "renaissance" of Tibetan culture beginning in the late tenth century. The points of similarity are as follows: (1) conflict with coercive temporal authorities and resistance through antinomian behavior are central; (2) a massive amount of new cultural information is flowing into Tibet from outside, much of it in literature written in alien languages (mostly Chinese and to a far lesser degree English, in contrast to the earlier predominance of Sanskrit and associated languages); (3) rebuilding monasteries and reestablishing religious lineages after an extended absence are foremost among many Tibetans' concerns; (4) there is controversy over purity in terms of religious infractions or corruptions; and (5) the institution of *tulkus*, or reincarnate lamas, has assumed renewed importance (an institution that first developed during the Tibetan renaissance). In terms of authority conflicts in early Tibet, hagiographies from eleventh- to thirteenth-century Tibet are pervaded by themes of social conflict as new religious and political institutions struggled to secure and consolidate power in the region.[87] Important themes include the strident criticisms of Nyingma traditions by the rulers of eleventh-century western Tibet,[88] suppression of populist religious movements,[89] and the hegemonic rule of the Sakya sect under the patronage of the Mongol Yüan Empire in the thirteenth century.[90] Accusations of antinomian behavior figuring centrally within many of these conflicts involved two distinct types: social transgressions cloaked in tantric rhetoric, ranging from a supposed subculture of unbridled sexuality and even ritual murder (such as reflected in the infamous "union and liberation" [*sbyor sgrol*] slogan) to powerful religious leaders' martial engagement in social conflicts,[91] and more institutional transgressions involving populist movements that seemed to dispense with clerical leadership,[92] criticism of monastic-based scholastic education, and general rhetorical opposition to ordinary institutionally defined Buddhist ethics and intellectual systems in favor of personal realization of the transcendent truth of the Buddha's teachings.[93] Finally, the institution of the reincarnate lama as a peculiar form of hereditary authority took shape between the eleventh and the fourteenth century as a strategy for institutionalizing spiritual legitimacy and charisma (among other things), and precisely this institution, along with its ideology of interconnected lines of reincarnations deeply intertwined with Tibetan history, has been at the forefront of religious change in eastern Tibet following the end of the Cultural Revolution.

There are of course crucial differences as well: as Chinese authorities maintain ultimate temporal control, Tibetans are in many ways not in control of their own future. Thus the new enemies—the Chinese and modernity—are common to most Tibetans and are colonial and extrinsic others, in contrast to the largely intra-Tibetan nature of conflicts during the eleventh and twelfth centuries.[94] In addition, the continuing vitality of refugee communities in South Asia results in a fissured self-identity, especially given the continued residence of key religious leaders, above all the current Dalai Lama, in these exiled and excised appendages of Tibet. The rhetoric often heard from Tibetan leaders in Dharamsala and their Western supporters echoes this state of affairs, often resulting in a strange inversion: the real Tibet is not in Tibet anymore, since the true, authentic culture of Tibetans is only maintained in uncorrupted form among refugee groups. Leaving aside the problematic nature of such rhetoric, it does capture a powerful sense of inadequacy, alienation, and abandonment that one often encounters in Tibetan areas of the People's Republic of China, particularly among the religious elite.

Thus it is essential that we ask how Tibetans have dealt with the literally dismembered body of Tibetans and Tibet, which was torn apart in a ritual sacrifice dedicated to the gods of modernism, communism, and Han imperialism. In particular, how have Tibetans turned to, and manipulated, the past in order to cope with the peculiarly dangerous manifestation of other cultures' enforced version of modernity that has so abruptly intruded into every dimension of their lives? In the present context, I have examined just one aspect of their response: the reliance on the Ter phenomenon among Nyingma traditions in a situation closely similar to that which first elicited its historical formation in the eleventh century. Prior to the opening of Tibet to the outside world in the early 1980s, the Ter movement appeared to have become quite limited in scope. In refugee communities only a few acknowledged Terton produced mainly wisdom treasures, and as far as I know, earth treasures were almost entirely absent, as one would expect, since the refugees carried with them Tibetan bodies but not the body of Tibet herself. It was unknown to what extent the Ter tradition was active in Tibet, if at all. However, my own experience in Tibet has revealed the existence of a vibrant, multipronged Ter movement that has emerged as one of the most powerful and vital strategies for the renewal of traditional Tibetan culture among Nyingma traditions in Tibet. Earth treasures—physical manuscripts in Ḍākiṇī language, special containers, statues, and ritual implements—are discovered in large quantities. I was told by one prominent lama, for example, that Tšopodorlo, a well-known Nyingma lama, had shown him a large chest full of such rediscoveries belonging to his recently deceased Bonpo spouse, Khandro Khachi Wangmo.[95] The phenomenon covers the full spectrum from the sublime to the absurd: at one point while I was living in Sichuan, a well-known Nyingma lama, of whom I had heard a number of incensed complaints from young women concerning his actions toward them, revealed to me several statues that he claimed to have revealed as "Ter" while in prison. An arguably more respectable Terton is the middle-aged, female

Terton Tare Lhamo from Golok, who reportedly is illiterate but has revealed a number of beautiful poetic Ter.

The contemporary Ter movement is thus similar in many respects to the initial development of Ter in the eleventh to the thirteenth century, right down to the material items taken out of the earth and the odd yellow manuscripts; both visionary retrievals also take place against the backdrop of more mundane recoveries of ancient manuscripts hidden or neglected during violent times. In addition, the movement seems to be functioning on the ground in similar ways in terms of establishing authentication and legitimacy in the face of oppressive temporal authorities.[96] The role of treasure revelations in revivifying the sacred landscape and pilgrimage sites is fundamental to the re-formation of Tibetan identity—not only is the uniquely Tibetan past again yielding its gifts, but the land itself is yielding concrete fruits intertwined with that past. The religious character of many of the shared "memories" that have historically played a key role in articulating collective identity for Tibetans entails that these actions perform a central role in the reconstruction and re-membering of this identity in a time of extreme pressures following a long period of violent darkness.[97] In many ways the rebuilding of sacred sites, along with the other ramifications of Ter, is a direct response to the loss of dimensionality in Tibet: during the Cultural Revolution, or more accurately the cultural devastation, everything in Tibet was flattened out culturally, just as physically the thousands of stūpas and monasteries were reduced to rubble littering the landscape. The Ter movement extends the roots of the present not only in the contemporary geographic landscape but also in the landscape of Tibet's remembered past. In this way, it is of unique value in imbuing the present with greater value and resonance for a very unsettled generation of Tibetans.

The potency of Ter as a Tibetan response to modernity is particularly clear in relation to Khenpo Jikphun's impact on some Chinese.[98] Not only are there Chinese monks and nuns resident in his Golok center and Chinese lay Buddhists periodically making the long pilgrimage there, I have heard reports of Khenpo literally being mobbed by Chinese Buddhists or simply the curious seeking his blessings or teachings during visits to Chengdu. I myself witnessed "transference of consciousness" (*'pho ba*) teachings he gave in Dartsedo which were attended by many Chinese. In Golok, I became friends with one Chinese monk from Beijing who had rejected his father, a famous qi gong master, to study with Khenpo Jikphun. Thus here finally is a Tibetan phenomenon that reverses the standard Han dismissal of "dirty, barbaric Tibetans" and raises the possibility of an acknowledged cultural superiority, at least in some respects. Khenpo's trip in the late 1980s to the Wutai Mountains was a major spectacle involving Tibetans and Chinese, numerous publicly reported miracles, revelation of Ter, and even the hiding of future Ter on Chinese territory. This same shifting of gravity by the Ter phenomenon has occurred with regard to perceptions of refugee Tibetan religious communities. Ter is much stronger in Tibet proper than in refugee Tibet, thus reversing the general feelings of inferiority aroused in Tibet with regard to the funding, autonomy, and scholastics of refugee centers. Thus Khenpo Jikphun's 1990 trip to India and Nepal stirred considerable interest among Tibetans parallel to the type of fanfare that has marked the return of prominent exiled lamas to Tibet since the early 1980s.

There is another aspect of Khenpo's biography that is standard for a Terton: controversy. The long-standing Tibetan concern for lineal purity, a matter that Ter addresses, has been a central issue in the post–Cultural Revolution era. Against the background of a larger cultural focus on continuity and lineage in Tibet,[99] Tibetan Buddhism has an exceedingly strong focus on religious lineage through an unbroken continuum of masters as the means of valid transmission of an intact tradition. In the eleventh and twelfth centuries, Nyingma groups were frequently attacked as being involved in corrupt lineages that may have possessed authentic texts but whose spiritual authority to use and understand those texts had corroded during the chaos of the dark period. The treasure mythos was the Nyingmas' most potent response to such criticism, as its "direct" transmission from Padmasambhava and other dynastic period saints not only provided an authentic lineage but also could even claim to be purer than ordinary lineages whose freshness and purity was inevitably eroded by the ravages of temporality and human nature.[100] The rupture of religious lineages of all types in modern Tibet—institutional, doctrinal, yogic—caused by the recent material devastation, massive deaths, and deep social ruptures has aggravated the traditional Tibetan concern with the fragility of continuity, especially in light of continued lack of control over their own sociopolitical future. This is also reflected in the frequent claims heard from refugee Tibetans that Buddhism in Tibet has become disrupted, such that pure religious traditions at populist and elite levels have only been maintained in refugee Tibet.

While Khenpo's revival of Ter has offered a potentially potent response to such concerns, controversy inevitably stems simply from the nature of a Terton: to hold that one is the reincarnation of a famous eighth-century figure with special direct access to new sources of scripture requires real self-assertion, as well as the ability to promote oneself so as to overcome resistance to such claims (the accreditation of Ter in many ways boils down to one's contacts).[101] Thus Khenpo Jikphun's Terton status has caused a considerable subcurrent of jealousy, particularly since it is linked to his leadership of movements to purify Buddhist lineages in eastern Tibet of breaches of *samaya* (tantric vows) that arose during the Cultural Revolution by his consistent opposition to the participation of violators in major tantric empowerments or high religious positions. This has also led to at least one minor Terton skirmish (see above); and it is connected to the tensions between lay tantric practitioners and monks (*dge slong*) that have resurfaced in the resurgence of Tibetan Buddhism. However, unlike earlier Ter movements, which were the frequent locus of attacks by reformists on ethical grounds given that its proponents tended to be nonmonastic, noncelibate, and often given to seemingly antinomian behavior,[102] and earlier Great Perfection movements, which were attacked on intellectual grounds given their antischolastic rhetoric and focus on contemplative experience, Khenpo has linked Ter and the Great Perfection to ethical reform, systematic study, and monastic institutions. This linkage to institutional and ethical conservatism has meant that the Ter cult, at least in his hands, finds itself in an unaccustomed position of supporting the criticism of ethical transgressions and corrupted lineages. However, I would argue that this renovated Ter includes a strong nationalist subcurrent in its romantic-historical focus on the Camelot of Tibet's Once and Future King,[103] its reanimating of uniquely Tibetan pure lands even as Chinese technology and colonization attempt to reshape that same geography, and the millenarian overtones of its miraculous revelations indicating the reemergence of the Buddha's potent authority and involvement with Tibet in the face of the onslaught of modernity. This unusual integration of personal charisma and authority, Buddhist rationalism and ethics, and a distinctively Tibetan cult of magic, miracles, and spontaneous manifestations of deities constitutes a revitalization movement that has managed to walk the thin line between morality and magic, charisma and institution, and, most important, Chinese authority and Tibetan tradition. The success of this integration can be seen, for example, when viewed in contrast to recent, overtly millenarian, populist movements in Tibet involving spirit possession, such as the aforementioned Heroes of Ling, that were quickly suppressed by alarmed Chinese authorities.[104]

A critical point of difference between ancient and contemporary Ter is the quite alien nature of the authoritarian other that current Ter combats and potentially assimilates. In the post-1978 era Tibetan horizons are dominated by a hegemonic foreign presence with a profoundly different ideological force, in contrast to the familiar, if at times antagonistic, otherness of imported Indian Buddhism and its Tibetan proponents from the eleventh century onward.[105] There is a new divide between secular scholarship and composition associated with Chinese literacy and translation activity conducted in the various Tibetan-oriented academic bureaus scattered across the landscape in modern Chinese cement-block architecture, on the one hand, and religious scholarship and praxis with its Tibetocentric concerns and agenda of institutional renewal and intellectual preservation, on the other.[106] This is altogether different from the situation of the early Tibetan renaissance, when the secular/religious divide was largely absent, translation was at the heart of the religious renewal, and Ter unabashedly and successfully raided the massive materials flowing into Tibet through the modernist translation projects. Unlike this earlier period, contemporary Ter takes place within a broader movement of institutional renewal and doctrinal preservation, not the dissemination or transformation of new religious teachings from abroad; in addition, with its power hierarchy stemming from Padmasambhava and his disciples, Ter continues ideologically to look back to the dynastic period with its ensuing darkness, but these periods are no longer its own immediate historical context. Finally, the antinomian behavior of Tibetans working the twilight zone between tantric rhetoric and social reality has receded in the face of preoccupation with both colonially induced transgression of traditional Buddhist norms during the Cultural Revolution and colonially defined transgressions of Tibetan Buddhist nationalists engaged in active protest against a totalitarian state's rule.[107]

This is probably one of the primary reasons that current Ter, despite being essentially the renewal of old stories and despite its positive value in re-membering the violently dismembered body of Tibet and Tibetans, does not yet seem to involve the digestion of new materials, or the performance of the alchemy of cultural transformation. On this point it does not appear to correspond in function to earlier Ter, which served to assimilate new Indic materials available in "modern" translation, in respect to its own modern others, namely Chinese or Western traditions. The abyss between a coercive modernity and Tibet's own Buddhist past has been so sudden and abrupt that it appears we may be nearing the outer perimeter of Padmasambhava's capacity to project forward from eighth-century Tibet, such that Tibet is entering an uncharted realm where the past is no longer an authoritative guide. Despite Khenpo Jikphun's tremendous openness and efforts to weave modern America into Ter's weblike reality during his as yet sole trip to the United States in 1993—thus proving Ter can span countries as well as centuries—one will look to no avail for any trace of Chinese, Western, or even Tibetan modernity within the traditional loose-leaf rectangular confines of the several volumes of his collected Great Perfection–based revelations.[108] In the last analysis, the modern other may simply be too foreign for the traditional Terton to digest in a Buddhist format, and at least for the moment, it appears to exceed even the capacity of the Great Perfection to create an alchemical buffer zone of rhetorical negation; only the future will tell if younger Terton may prove to be more adventurous in retrieving the enticing yet elusive intersection of Buddhism and modernity on their own terms. And then, at this imagined future moment, the long-suffering body of religious Tibet may complete its rise from the dead once again as a reconfigured gestalt with the capacity, will, and power to speak with its own distinctive yet transfigured voice in the modern arena.

FOUR

A Pilgrimage of Rebirth Reborn

The 1992 Celebration of the Drigung Powa Chenmo

Matthew T. Kapstein

In August 1992 the pilgrimage and festival of religious teaching known as the Drigung Powa Chenmo was revived after a hiatus of thirty-six years. Like certain other important Tibetan religious and cultural celebrations, it was traditionally held only once in every twelve-year calendrical cycle, in this case during the sixth lunar month of each monkey year,[1] and so had been last convened in 1956. Its performance in 1968 was prohibited by the relentless assault on virtually all aspects of traditional Tibetan life that marked the Cultural Revolution, then at its height; while in 1980 the partial relaxation of restrictions on religious observance in China, and above all on the cultural traditions of China's ethnic minorities,[2] had not yet advanced sufficiently to permit the reinception of an event of this scale. In this chapter, based on both textual research and firsthand observation of the Drigung Powa Chenmo during its revival, I survey its history and development, the pilgrimage as I witnessed it in 1992, and its implications for our understanding of the role of pilgrimage in Tibetan religious life and in the formation of Tibetan identity, in the past and at present.

Pilgrimage (*gnas-skor*) has long figured prominently among the characteristic religious activities in which Tibetans almost universally participate. Many, for instance, regard it to be particularly important to visit the religious shrines of Lhasa, where pilgrims can make the rounds of the numerous important temples and monasteries in the vicinity of Tibet's ancient capital. Before 1959 they could perhaps even have attended a public blessing given by the Dalai Lama, and today his absence is vigorously recalled by the many pilgrims who arrive in what is now a predominantly Chinese city. The pilgrims who flock to Lhasa bring offerings for the temples and monks and also frequently engage in trade so as to finance their journeys. Thus, in addition to its more purely religious significance, pilgrimage has generally played an important role in Tibetan commerce, both cultural and economic. In recent years the economic activity accompanying pilgrimage has to some extent resumed in Lhasa, though on a much smaller scale than in earlier generations and under greatly changed circumstances.[3]

The capital, however, was never the sole center of pilgrimage in Tibet. There was, in fact, a sort of national pilgrimage network, whose routes, extending throughout the length and breadth of geographic and cultural Tibet,[4] helped to maintain communications among even the most far-flung districts. The pilgrimage to the small valley of Terdrom[5] during the Drigung Powa Chenmo well exemplifies some pervasive themes relating to sacred places, emphasizing the symbolic significance of the landscape and of specific sacred objects to be found there, as well as legendary and historical associations with some of the great culture heroes of the Tibetan past. Configurations of stone, designs seen in the cliffs, and so forth, are described as the natural images and shrines of deities, or the tangible evidence of the great deeds of past masters. Uncanny occurrences, unusual features of climate and environment, are all also typically interpreted as being imbued with profound spiritual meaning.

Tibetan pilgrimage, then, as also pilgrimage in other cultural settings, involves much more than the mere physical journey to places deemed sacred.[6] Through religious teaching, ritual activity, and the attendant assimilation and replication of symbols, as well as through the formation of a rich network of social and economic relationships, pilgrimage has functioned in Tibet as an integral dimension of the construction of society and self, transforming the body, consciousness, and status of the pilgrim throughout the course of the journey. This certainly has been the case even if never brought to the level of deliberate reflection, though traditional Tibetan religious culture has in fact long been conscious of the transformative dimension of the pilgrimage experience, and so intentionally has sought to refine and thus to accentuate it.

THE LAND, THE LINEAGE, AND *PLANTING THE STALK*

The district of Drigung is located to the northeast of Lhasa. After reaching the town of Mendrogongkar, slightly less than one hundred kilometers from the capital, the main road swings toward the east, in the direction of the Kongpo district.[7] An unpaved track leads north, past the ancient temple of Katsel, and then, farther north, skirts a track leading to the almost equally old shrine at Uru Shei Lhakhang. These monuments, both severely damaged during the 1960s, recall the antiquity of Drigung and its connections with the Tibetan monarchy of the late first millennium. The first, associated with the very beginnings of Tibetan Buddhism in the seventh century, is said to be one of the temples founded by the Tibetan emperor Songtsen Gampo (617–49/50) to subjugate by geomantic means the great ogress who embodies the land of Tibet.[8] The second was the center of the estate granted to a famed monk who served as an imperial tutor at the beginning of the ninth century.[9] Desperately poor today, the rocky fields and poor pastures of Drigung provide little indication that this was once one of Tibet's great fiefdoms.[10]

Despite the presence of religious monuments dating back to the dynastic period, Drigung's emergence as a major center of Tibetan Buddhism began only in the late twelfth century. It was then that Kyopa Jikten Gönpo (1143–1217) established his monastery at Drigung-thil, dramatically situated in the upper reaches of the valley. Jikten Gönpo, who originally came from far eastern Tibet, had journeyed to the central region when he was in his twenties to study with Phakmotrupa (1110–70), one of the preeminent masters of the Kagyü school, an order renowned for its proficiency in advanced and esoteric techniques of Buddhist tantric yoga.[11] He quickly established himself as the master's favorite and lineage successor, but after Phakmotrupa's death he chose not to accept the responsibilities that that role would have entailed, and instead fled to the Drigung valley with some close companions. There he was offered a small monastic community by a yogin also affiliated with the Kagyü order and soon thereafter founded Drigung-thil. He became known for his compassion, learning, and strict adherence to the monastic code and was reputed to be an incarnation of the renowned Indian Buddhist philosopher Nāgārjuna. His charisma was such that it was said 180,000 monks once gathered for his teaching, and even if we allow for considerable exaggeration here, the conclusion is unavoidable that Jikten Gönpo was both a gifted and an exceedingly successful Buddhist teacher. It is highly probable that even during his lifetime hermitages adhering to his tradition were founded as far away as the Kailash region, in the kingdom of Guge in far western Tibet. His writings included highly respected expositions of Buddhist philosophy and meditational practice but came to be regarded in some circles as doctrinally controversial.[12]

The order Jikten Gönpo established, known as the Drigung Kagyü, after the location of its foremost seat, has remained one of the most successful of the Kagyü subsects, with affiliated monasteries in many parts of the Tibetan world: Ladakh (India), Limi (northwestern Nepal), and Nangchen (Qinghai Province) are among the main centers of its activity, besides Drigung itself.[13] These widely separated communities have continued to maintain their loyalty to the main seat of the order at Drigung, which has preserved an unbroken hierarchical lineage. The highest-ranking Drigung hierarch currently lives in India, where the order has established monasteries and educational centers in the Tibetan refugee community.[14] Like several of the other Tibetan religious orders in exile, it has extended its teaching activity beyond the traditional range of Tibetan Buddhism and now has some representatives in other parts of the world, including the United States.

According to tradition, it was in a monkey year during the sixth of Tibet's sexagenary cycles, perhaps in 1308,[15] that the ninth in the hierarchical lineage of Drigung Monastery, Dorje Gyelpo (1284–1350, head of the lineage from 1314 until his death), is said to have "reopened" the pilgrimage sites of Terdrom, which lies in close proximity to Drigung-thil.[16] Terdrom was famed for its mineral hot springs and for its many caves and other landmarks that had been hallowed by the eighth-century Indian tantric master Padmasambhava and his circle, above all his Tibetan consort Yeshe Tsogyel. In these places, it was said, the treasures—spiritual and material—that they had concealed for the benefit of the Tibetan people might be found. During the monkey month, the time when the birth of the master Padmasambhava is celebrated, Dorje Gyelpo ordered performances of the ritual dances associated with that teacher's favored deity, Vajrakīla (*Rdo-rje-phur-pa*).[17] In connection with this, he also began the custom of convening a regular public series of religious teachings, which were held every twelve years thereafter, though the location seems to have shifted from time to time, always remaining in the general vicinity of Drigung.[18]

Some two centuries later, the famous "treasure finder" (*gter-bton*) of Drigung, Rinchen Püntsok (1509–57), thoroughly reorganized these regular duodecennial observances that were followed in each monkey year. Rinchen Püntsok, a discoverer of the cached scriptural treasures, was a devoted adherent of the cult of Padmasambhava and as such promoted a syncretic form of tantric Buddhism.[19] This involved integrating elements of the traditional Kagyü teachings of Drigung Monastery together with the doctrines, rituals, and meditational practices of the Nyingma school, the ancient tradition of Tibetan Buddhism that was especially associated with Padmasambhava. Rinchen Püntsok also sometimes preferred to live as a contemplative hermit, outside the precincts of the large Drigung Monastery, and among his favored abodes was the upper part of the Terdrom valley, three hours trek beyond the hot springs, where, at an altitude of approximately 15,000 feet, he founded the hermitage of Drongur. Here he reconvened the cycles of public teaching, using these occasions to instruct those assembled in the treasure doctrines that he himself had recovered. Some of his discoveries had taken place in the high Kere Yangdzong Cave, the upper chamber of the large cavern known as the Great Assembly Hall (Tshogs-khang-chen-mo), situated in the peak looming above Drongur. The cave was reputed to have been Yeshe Tsogyel's favored place of meditation, and figures prominently in pilgrimage activity during the Drigung Powa Chenmo.[20]

The celebration appears to have been fixed in its modern form during the first half of the following century, when two famous Drigung hierarchs, the brothers Könchok Rinchen (1590–1654) and Rikdzin Chödrak (1595–1659), sought to renew and refine the combined Nyingma and Kagyü heritage of the Drigung succession.[21] They maintained Rinchen Püntsok's cycle of Nyingma instruction and are said to have augmented this by bestowing in addition such popular Kagyü rites as the empowerment of longevity according to the tradition of the yoginī Siddharajñī[22] and, as the culminating teaching to be conferred on the final full moon day, an especially treasured esoteric precept called *Planting the Stalk ('jag-zug-ma)*,[23] a means to achieve the safe passage of the consciousness principle from this life to the next at the moment of death. This final instruction of *powa*, literally "transference," henceforth would be the main attraction for the faithful, and so lent its name to this entire festival of pilgrimage and religious instruction. The event as a whole thus came to be known as the Drigung Powa Chenmo, "the great [conferral of the yoga of the] transference [of consciousness] at Drigung."

In general, the technique of powa, a special form of yogic exercise, is said to cause the consciousness of the dying individual to depart suddenly from the body through a forced opening at the crown of the skull and to travel immediately to a pure land, usually the Sukhāvatī realm of the Buddha Amitābha, in which enlightenment can then be swiftly attained. The technique is one that produces swift and unmistakable physical effects, as described here by a scholar of Tibetan Buddhism, H. V. Guenther:

> When a competent Guru imparts this instruction to his disciple, the region of the fontanel opening becomes highly sensitive to touch and remains so for some time. Moreover, when after the instruction he touches this region with Kusa-grass, symbolically representing the opening of the passage to the ultimate, the distinct sensation of being pierced from top to bottom is created. Needless to say, this practice is not without its dangers and under no circumstances can it be performed when there is any deformation in the bones of the skull or in the spinal cord.[24]

Indeed, powa has consistently been a topic of fascination for Western writers on Tibetan esotericism and yoga. Alexandra David-Neel has dramatically described the practice in her works, as has W. Y. Evans-Wentz.[25] More pertinent, perhaps, in our present context are the observations of an anthropologist, Martin Brauen-Dolma, commenting on the recent popularization of a version of the powa practice among Tibetan refugees living in Switzerland:

> Amitābha's paradise has become the focus of a salvation-practice for lay persons, with attainment actively being pursued.... To this extent, at least, its goal resembles that of a millenial movement. Secondary manifestations of this ritual are also reminiscent of characteristics of millenial movements: some participants in this rite— most are women—fall into trance-like states which are accompanied by rhythmic hyperventilation, moaning, whimpering, or loud sobbing, and less often by movements of the arms. For anyone accustomed to the quiet atmosphere of Buddhist meditation these seances are alien and extraordinary. The fact that this cult gains importance during the critical time of exile leads me to see yet another connection to the movements referred to by some authors as "crisis cults."[26]

However, the manifestations described here are by no means peculiarly characteristic of the community in exile. A recently published account in Tibetan of the traditional performance of the Drigung Powa Chenmo offers the following remarks on its performance during the seventeenth century: "The signs that accompanied the conferral of the transference included headache, the appearance of pus at the crown of the head, the opening of the fontanel, and, among some, momentary loss of consciousness."[27] Nevertheless, Brauen-Dolma's observations on the millennial dimensions of the ritual do contribute to our understanding of it, both in its past formation and in its present revival. For, as will become clear later in this chapter, the rituals of powa seem intimately connected with the construction of identities in an inherently unstable and so crisis-ridden world.

The particular version of the powa practice known as *Planting the Stalk* originated among the rediscovered treasures (*gter-ma*) that were traced back to the master Padmasambhava and his disciples. It had been discovered, probably during the fourteenth century, by an obscure figure named Nyinda Sangye, who is said to have recovered the texts from Black Maṇḍala Lake in southern Tibet. It was recorded that the esoteric methods he thus brought to light were so powerful that by means of them he was able to secure the liberation of all the spirits and animals inhabiting the lake itself. The association of the teaching's origins with the spiritual sublimation of the chthonic forces of Tibet is an important motif for the Drigung Powa Chenmo as well, though the precise location in which this connection is most apparent, interestingly, is removed from a lake to a mountain cave. Significant too is the report of some texts that Nyinda Sangye was the father of Karma Lingpa, the discoverer of the well-known "Tibetan Book of the Dead," for this association further strengthens the authority of the Drigung Powa teachings in connection with the rites of death.[28]

The title *Planting the Stalk* refers to a widespread test for the efficacy of the powa practice: after the adept has received the teaching and cultivated it in seclusion for several days, the opening of the fontanel grows sufficiently so that one is able to place a stalk of grass upright within it. In a famous passage David-Neel once reported witnessing this, and I can confirm that a similar degree of success in the technique has been observed also among contemporary Western Buddhist practitioners.[29]

This, then, was the teaching stressed by Könchok Rinchen and Rikdzin Chödrak. By making it, together with other valued elements of the Kagyü heritage, available to the assembled public, the hierarchy of Drigung was in effect inviting all to participate directly in the special charisma of the Drigung Kagyü line, an invitation that would no doubt enhance Drigung's standing among the Tibetan people at a time when several of the rival Kagyü lineages were in fact facing stiff opposition in Central Tibet.[30]

Until 1956 the Drigung Powa Chenmo continued to be held every twelve years, adhering to the general pattern of Nyingma and Kagyü teaching just described, combined with pilgrimage rounds through the sacred sites of Terdrom. In its traditional performance, however, the entire valley of Terdrom is supposed to have been in effect ritually sealed off from its surroundings, to become a self-contained realm for the duration of the pilgrimage. A description of this process was recently published in Tibetan and, as it has some importance for my analysis of the Drigung Powa Chenmo and much intrinsic interest, I offer a translation of it here:[31]

> The Monkey Year Powa Chenmo is convened at the place called "Drongur, the intersection of three valleys," situated in Zhotö Tidro (=Terdrom), during the period

from the seventh through the fifteenth of the sixth Mongolian month. Because the two Drigung lords of refuge—the Chetsang and Chungtsang—were the chief officiants for the religious performance, we state in brief the old custom whereby they rode [from Drigung to Drongur]. On an astrologically propitious day, having ridden from Dridzong to Tetrak-thang, they spent a day performing the propitiations of Achi, the chief protective deity of Drigung, at length. After exoteric and esoteric prognostications favoring the ride up from Dokashak the lamas, incarnates, and monks of the seat at Drigung-thil would guide the horseback journey by stages. Following casual ablutions and consecrations at the Dzenthang Kyopa Temple, the Lama of Drongur and the chief steward of Terdrom would welcome the party at Khatsel-gang with incense, whereupon the chief steward would offer the maṇḍala, the symbolic offering of the cosmos, together with an explanation of the sacred features of the site. Then, there would be further ablutions and consecrations at the Maṇi Temple. Following a monetary offering at Chötsel they proceeded to Tayak-thang. That afternoon, together with an offering of fragrant incense to the local deities (*bsang*) and other observances, they performed a circuit of the hot springs and proceeded to Drongur via Dinggyel. Then, with the nuns of Terdrom and the lamas of Drongur performing a procession known as the "yellow rosary," they entered the great stronghold of Drongur. Following the admonitions that issued from the residence, the monks and nuns of Drongur and Terdrom made the preparations for the great teachings of the Monkey Year by stages.

Besides that, the taxpayers and others belonging to the Drigung administration had to appear for an assessment of revenue and be forthcoming with their payments. Then, beginning on the sixth day of the sixth month, the monks of Gar College and those of the college at Drigung-thil, together with the eastern and western retreatants of the seat and those of Salt Cave, gradually had to assemble at Drongur. After riding up with the lamas who were officials of the two colleges, they then had to invite into their presence the representations of the Buddhas' Body, Speech, and Mind [in the form of the images, books and symbols that were installed at Drongur for the teachings]. On the seventh day, the colleges of Gar and Thil were asked separately to pitch their assembly tents—the assembly tent of Thil, "Blue Heaven," and that of Gar, "White Snow Peak," had been the presentations of the lord of refuges Peme Gyeltsen (the twenty-ninth head of the lineage of Drigung, b. 1770). These two colleges together would then request that the great tent of empowerment, the commission of the Ven. Thukje Nyima (the thirty-second head of the lineage), be pitched above the religious court of Drongur.

From Gar, four "servants of virtue" with four deputies from the larger taxpaying households, such as those of Khengchugyü, would have to shoulder the responsibility for the adherence to the religious laws according to Gar, along with the laws of the monastic and lay public in general. During the afternoon of the seventh day, at the valley closing the fortress of Drongur, all would have to listen to a proclamation of the ordinances of the religious law. Then by stages, following rounds in the habitations of the two colleges, and the most important campsites of the public, the path was closed, and it was arranged that neither mundane business nor affairs involving unclean sorts of things should arrive there. The entire legal power for the duration of the religious assembly was then held as the responsibility of the "servants of virtue" and the deputies.

Clearly, then, the lay and monastic populations of the Drigung valley were generally drawn into some degree of involvement with the pilgrimage, and this required a profound reconfiguring of ritual and economic and indeed even of spatial relationships. There have been, of course, many alterations resulting from the great changes that have taken place in Tibet since the festival's last fully traditional performance in 1956. Some of these will be discussed in greater detail below. Let us just note for the moment that the old revenue system has long been dismantled, so that the fiscal responsibility for the 1992 performance was in the hands of the Mendrogongkar district government together with Drigung Monastery, aided by a grant from the Tibet Autonomous Region's (TAR's) Council on Religious Affairs (*chos-tshogs*). Moreover, the ideal of a complete sealing-off of Drongur, so that it became for the duration of the festival a ritual and legal realm unto itself, could at best be recapitulated only symbolically, if, indeed, it had ever been fully effected in the past. Finally, given the greatly reduced monasticism of the region (as is the case throughout Tibet), the elaborate configuration of assembly tents described above was realized only in a much reduced form.

In the wake of the Tibetan revolt of 1959, followed by the onset of the Cultural Revolution in 1966, the observance of Drigung Powa Chenmo was forbidden, and Drigung-thil and other religious sites in the region, even some that were very remote and difficult of access, suffered almost complete demolition. Those monks and lamas who had not fled from Tibet in 1959 were mostly forced to disrobe and join rural work units in nearby communes or in their native districts. (The young Drigung Chetsang, for instance, prior to his 1975 escape from Tibet, was consigned to a work unit at Tsünmo-tse, between Mendrogongkar and Lhasa.) Some were subjected to much harsher treatment and as a result perished during the Cultural Revolution years. After the ouster of the Gang of Four in 1978 and the subsequent inception of Deng's reform program, which permitted a degree of liberalization to take place, Pachung Rinpoche (deceased during the late 1980s), one of the few learned monks associated with Drigung who had survived in Tibet, began initial restoration work at the monastery and attracted others affiliated with Drigung to join him in his efforts. At about this time, too, a charismatic woman, Tendzin Chödrön, appeared on the scene at Terdrom and came to be regarded as the Drigung Khandro. This title is traditionally conferred once in each generation on a female adept residing at Terdrom who is held to be the emanation of Padmasambhava's Tibetan consort Yeshe Tsogyel.[32] An extremely forceful personality, Tendzin Chödrön has played a pivotal role in the re-creation of the nun's community at Terdrom.

By the early 1990s the local government of Mendrogongkar, under whose jurisdiction the Drigung district falls, responded favorably to the requests of the monastery and the local public to convene the Drigung Powa once again, in August 1992, and they succeeded in securing the permission of the authorities of the TAR to do this. Remarkably, this happened despite the setbacks to liberalization policies in the wake of the Tibetan protests of the late 1980s and the martial law that followed, the pattern of deliberalization in Tibet having been compounded by the generally hard-line position on political and social protest that has come to characterize the Chinese Community Party (CCP) under Li Peng and Jiang Zemin.[33] This perhaps explains in part why the event was not well publicized in advance and the attendance of non-Tibetans not encouraged. Nevertheless, I had the good fortune to be among the handful of foreigners who made their way to the festival during its revival, to join the pilgrims who had gathered there in their treks to hallowed sites, and to attend the public teachings that were conferred in the course of the weeklong program.[34]

THE DRIGUNG POWA OBSERVED

In accordance with established tradition the teachings of the revived Drigung Powa Chenmo were conferred during the period from the eighth through the fifteenth lunar days of the sixth, or monkey, month of the monkey year. In 1992 this was the period from August 6 through 13. Normally, the occasion would be presided over by the two foremost hierarchs of Drigung, the Chetsang Rinpoche and the Chungtsang Rinpoche, the direct heirs to the incarnation lines of Könchok Rinchen and Rikdzin Chödrak. In 1992, however, both of these figures were living in India and were unable to return to Tibet for the celebrations, to the disappointment of many with whom I spoke. About a half dozen high-ranking lamas of the Drigung school, who remain in Tibet, were present to officiate at the Drigung Powa Chenmo. They included the Riwang Tendzin Rinpoche, Soktrül Rinpoche, Nuba Namka Gyeltsen Rinpoche, Nyedak Rinpoche, and Angön Rinpoche.

Some of the pilgrims I interviewed, expressing widespread Tibetan distrust of the Chinese government, reported that they regarded as prudent the decision by the Chetsang Rinpoche and Chungtsang Rinpoche to remain safely in exile, for some suspected that they would have courted kidnap by the authorities had they returned. Recent experience, however, suggests that such extreme fears are not in fact very well founded, though the possibility that they would have faced lesser difficulties cannot be ruled out.[35] Be that as it may, later that same year, in November, the teaching of the Drigung Powa was in fact granted by the two leaders of the sect to their adherents in exile in connection with the official opening of the Drigung Kagyü Center in Dehra Dun, India. Some Tibetans in India and Nepal later expressed to me the view that this was therefore the spiritually more authentic event, but in Tibet itself in August no one I interviewed was of the opinion that the authenticity of the revival was at all in question.[36]

Following tradition, the pilgrimage opened with the procession of the leading lamas and their attendants from Drigung Monastery to Terdrom, where ablutions were performed before proceeding to Drongur. By the sixth of the Tibetan month (August 4), many monks and nuns of Drigung, Terdrom, and adjacent convents had begun to assemble there and to make preparations for the teachings as well.

Figure 4.1. The campsite at Drongur. The pinnacle rising above is the Snake-headed Cliff *(brag sbrul-sgo-can),* the guardian of the gate at the Terdrom valley.

By this date, too, lay devotees and monastics from nearby districts started to arrive in large numbers, together with smaller numbers of pilgrims from distant locations, some of them connected through sectarian allegiance to Drigung, such as Nangchen in far eastern Tibet and parts of the Kailash region in the far west. The small area of relatively flat ground at Drongur soon became a little sea of tents, an overcrowded but jovial campground.

Beginning on the seventh (August 5), Drongur became symbolically sealed off from the world below by the proclamation of religious law, and during the remainder of the festivities monk policemen (*dge-skos* or *dge-gyog*, "servants of virtue," but popularly equated with the *rdab-rdob*)[37] would be conspicuously present as tangible evidence of this, though actual traffic between Drongur, Terdrom, and the Drigung valley continued unabated. Besides the authority of the religious law, contemporary Chinese civil law seemed but thinly represented: throughout the entire course of the revived pilgrimage there was no military presence, only a small company of local Tibetan policemen, not more than a dozen of whom were in uniform, though there were known to be some others present in plain clothes. It was clear that neither the monastic nor the civil authorities anticipated difficulties. My few encounters with the representatives of the Mendrogongkar government, however, left me with the distinct impression that they were not without some anxieties: the local government officials of the Mendrogongkar district, in whose precincts Drigung is situated, were clearly delighted with the reinception of the pilgrimage but very worried that it might become an occasion for nationalistic protest. When I first arrived at Drongur, I was made to feel very welcome by the pilgrims, but representatives of the local government were visibly unnerved by a foreign presence and told me in no uncertain terms that I could not be accommodated and would have to leave immediately. It was only after the monastic leaders provided them with some reassurance that the fear of possible foreign agitation was quietly dropped.[38]

The actual cycle of teaching began on the eighth (August 6), the commencement of the second half of the waxing phase of the moon and thus a date for regular religious observances. From this time, until the fifteenth, when all present assembled together for the instructions of the powa, the activities of most of those in attendance were only loosely connected with the formal rounds of teaching. These were delivered in a large tent set up in the field in front of the small Drongur Monastery, without the tents of the individual colleges described in the account translated above, thus simplifying to some extent the more elaborate arrangement of assembly tents that would have characterized the pilgrimage until 1956. Besides attending the teachings, many laypersons preferred to perform prostrations and circumambulations, or to pursue mundane but necessary occupations, such as trade.[39] Among those assembled, too, were religious specialists of various types, loosely or not at all affiliated with Drigung, who regarded the event as a special opportunity to pursue their own paths of practice. The presence of large numbers who were for the most part only peripherally connected with the

Figure 4.2. A "monk policeman" at the doorway of Drongur Monastery explains the monastery's rules of access to a lay pilgrim.

main teaching program, and engaged instead in activities otherwise regarded as suitable, lent a carnival atmosphere to the festivities, so that Drongur became increasingly like a Tibetan Buddhist Woodstock as the days progressed. The wide variety of costume, both the local dress of the laypersons who had arrived from remote districts and the many different styles of religious garb, further accentuated this impression.

The actual program of religious instruction, therefore, was followed throughout only by a minority of those present, above all by the ordained monks and nuns of Drigung and its affiliated monasteries and temples. Their routine began at daybreak each morning with the daily offering of fragrant juniper smoke (*bsang*) to the local deities, followed by a formal procession of the monks and nuns from the monastic quarters to the assembly in the main tent. The morning was then given over primarily to prayer services with offerings of tea and the dedication of the offerings that had been sponsored by the laity and others.[40] After a late morning break for the main meal of the day, the designated teaching was conferred to the religious and laypersons in attendance, with a different lama presiding each day. These daily programs were prominently posted on a wall of Drongur Monastery, permitting those present to select the particular teachings they wished to attend

Figure 4.3. Nyingmapa adepts from the nomadic region of Nakchukha gather before onlookers in the campground to perform the rite of *chö (gcod)*, Cutting, the visualized dismemberment of one's own body as an offering to all living beings.

Figure 4.4. The monks of Drigung assemble before Drongur Monastery at dawn to begin the procession to the morning's session of prayer and religious instruction. The monk seen in the portal holding a white offering scarf *(kha-btags)* is the Soktrül Rinpoche, who would confer the teaching of powa itself at the pilgrimage's culmination.

and to record accurately the titles of those in which they participated. The general schedule was given there as follows:[41]

Day 1. August 6. Nyedak Rinpoche confers the initiation of Buddha Śākyamuni and receives the formal request of those in attendance to bestow the powa-teaching.

Day 2. August 7. Riwang Tendzin Rinpoche confers the initiation of the six-syllable mantra of Avalokiteśvara (i.e., the well-known formula *Oṃ Maṇipadme Hūṃ!*) and receives a similar formal request. (This would be repeated on each successive day.)

Day 3. August 8 (= tenth day of the lunar calendar). Nangse Könchok Tendzin Rinpoche confers the initiation of the Vanquisher of the Lord of Death ('Chi-bdag-zil-gnon).

Day 4. August 9. Gambu Rinpoche confers the initiation of Padmasambhava in his peaceful aspect.

Day 5. August 10. Nuba Namka Gyeltsen Rinpoche confers the initiation of the goddess Parṇāśabarī (Ri-khrod lo-gyon-ma).

Day 6. August 11. Nyedak Rinpoche confers the initiation of Padmasambhava in his wrathful aspect.

Day 7. August 12. Riwang Tendzin Rinpoche confers the initiation of Amitāyus, the Buddha of Longevity, according to the tradition of Siddharajñī.
Day 8 (full moon). August 13. Soktrül Rinpoche confers an extended discourse
   on the merits of teaching the doctrine, and then bestows the actual instructions of the powa.

There is a general pattern of development to be discerned here, an initiatory
progression that would be clear at least to some of the monks and nuns, as well as
to religiously educated laypersons, who attended these teachings on a daily basis.
We may say that the progression of the teachings is one from universality within
the Buddhist tradition to specificity in relation to the particular tradition of Drigung and from teachings that govern the cultivation of positive attributes in this
life to those that focus on inevitable mortality and death. Thus the initiation of the
Buddha Śākyamuni represents the Buddhist tradition in the broadest terms, while
that of Avalokiteśvara more particularly addresses the outlook of the Mahāyāna.
Though this is still extremely broad, it must not be forgotten that the bodhisattva
of compassion is always regarded by Tibetans as the special patron of their land.[42]
The two initiations of Padmasambhava move beyond even this Tibetocentricity to
establish a special connection with the Drigung Kagyü lineage and the Drigung
Powa Chenmo, for both are derived from the "treasures" discovered by Rinchen
Püntsok in the peaks looming above Drongur, and were first taught by him publicly in the very place in which the pilgrims are now assembled. Further, there is
the contrast between the initiations of the Vanquisher of the Lord of Death and
of the goddess Parṇāśabarī, both teachings concerned with dispelling spiritual
and temporal obstacles overall, and the two culminating teachings, which focus directly on the specific obstacles to longevity and to the attainment of fortunate rebirth.
   The double progression just described is further reinforced by its correlation
with the waxing moon, splendidly visible above the valley's crags at night. Though
these and other similar relationships were articulated by members of the religious
elite who were present, clear consciousness of them was for the most part expressed only by such persons. For, as has been already noted, only a small per-
centage of those present actually participated in all these teachings, and were not
apparently expected to do so.
   In contrast, certainly the favored activity, for the lay pilgrims at least, as well as
for many of the nonmonastic religious,[43] was in fact pilgrimage. At daybreak every
morning, as the monks offered incense and the procession to the assembly began,
large numbers of persons set out to trek to the many sacred sites that are accessible from Drongur. The most famous and impressive of these expeditions is the ascent to the massive Kere Yangdzong Cave, the Great Assembly Hall in which
Rinchen Püntsok made his discoveries, the basis for the teachings bestowed on the
fourth and sixth days. The site is believed to be hallowed by the meditations of

Padmasambhava's consort, Yeshe Tsogyel, who, according to a tradition with which virtually all the pilgrims I met seemed familiar, dwelled in retreat here for seven years, practicing the widely revered Great Perfection (*rdzogs-chen*) system of meditation.

To ascend to the cave, one must first return to the Terdrom hot springs and from there turn to circumambulate the peaks that rise directly above Drongur, which are thought to house the guardians of the valley. The path spirals upward and the geographic configurations on all sides are described as embodying important aspects of the Tibetan esoteric Buddhist world. On the way I passed, for example, a site identified as the charnel ground (*dur-khrod*), a favored place for tantric practice, which is situated beneath a series of spires that are themselves regarded as the Ḍākiṇīs of the five Buddha families. When I stopped to rest there, I found a small congregation gathered to perform the rite of Cutting (*gcod*), a meditational and ritual practice that is renowned for its exquisite chants and whose practice is regarded as particularly well suited for cemeteries, whether metaphorical or real.[44]

The trail continued to ascend until, approaching the summit spires, I discovered myself to be now perched on the cliffs some 2,000 feet directly above Drongur. Turning to the highest peak, the pilgrim is greeted by the great, gaping mouth of the Great Assembly Hall. Inside, I first visited the small retreat cell of Yeshe Tsogyel, before beginning a harrowing climb up a makeshift series of wet and slippery ropes and ladders, for a tour of the summit of the peak from the inside. The configurations of the tunnels are all imbued with symbolic significance and are described as recapitulating the physiology of the subtle body, whose channels and energies are the foci of yogic methods including both the practices of powa and Cutting. In the cave the ordinary order of things is thus in a sense inverted, for now one finds oneself located within the body that, in meditation, one otherwise visualizes within the physical body. The pilgrims who complete the ascent to the cave, therefore, are granted, in virtue of their undertaking, an especially powerful performative initiation, introducing the esoteric lore that forms the background to the culminating teaching of the pilgrimage overall.

Following the tour of the cave, one makes a rapid descent via the steep slope of skree that falls from the side of the cliffs. This was perilous, and if it had any special symbolic significance, it was for the moment lost on this pilgrim, who was exclusively preoccupied with self-preservation. As it happened, it was at this point that I rejoined the teachings on the afternoon of the fourteenth (August 12), while the Riwang Rinpoche was bestowing the blessings of longevity to those in attendance.[45] I was by now in fact very grateful to be able to receive them. (Perhaps this was the point I had missed!)

The next day was the full moon. At daybreak all who were present began to gather around the teaching tent, trying to sit close, so that they would be certain to hear the powa instructions clearly. This would probably have been a real difficulty in former times, but in 1992 a primitive but adequate portable public address system was used. The teaching, in fact, did not begin until the early afternoon,

Figure 4.5. Pilgrims ascending to the cave of the Great Assembly Hall pause to practice the rite of Cutting at a sacred spot designated a "charnel ground" *(dur-khrod)*.

Figure 4.6. At the beginning of the perilous descent back to Drongur. The white specks seen below are the tents in the campground.

though all seemed content to stake their claims for choice places early. Following a general discourse on the benefits of propagating the doctrine, and of attending to it correctly, the actual teaching of the powa, which in 1992 was conferred by the Soktrül Rinpoche, lasted little more than a half hour. In my previous experience of large, public teachings among the Tibetans in India and Nepal, I have seldom seen a crowd that was not to some extent restless, even when such revered figures as the Dalai Lama and the late Gyalwa Karmapa have presided. On this occasion, however, the assembled crowd adopted contemplative attitudes and listened to the Soktrül Rinpoche's every word, completely still and silent. Some of the devotees wept softly as the Rinpoche explained the visualization of the subtle body, the gathering of consciousness in the heart-center at the time of death, and the means to swiftly project that concentration of energy to the pure land of Amitābha.

Though I would not suggest adopting Victor Turner's approach to the study of ritual as a general interpretive framework for the investigation of Buddhist and Tibetan rituals of all types,[46] this did seem to be a quintessentially Turnerian event. For in this public rehearsal of death persons from many different regions, representing diverse facets of the Tibetan world, had been brought together and introduced to that most characteristic of liminal states; and in participating then in a common set of meditations and exercises, something much like Turner's conception of communitas was surely engendered among them. Considering, in particu-

Figure 4.7. Early on the morning of the full moon, pilgrims gather around the tent from which the powa teachings will be given.

lar, Turner's insistence that religious pilgrimage generally does place pilgrims in a liminal passage and that the emergence of communitas is a characteristic feature of such pilgrimage experience, it would appear that the Drigung Powa Chenmo, by compounding pilgrimage with an imagined performance of death and rebirth, succeeds in accentuating these themes in a direct and striking manner. After concluding the transmission of the powa, final prayers of dedication were recited and then, in an instant, everyone was hurrying about in an effort to break camp in order to descend down the narrow path to Terdrom before nightfall, so that the trail became hazardously crowded. Within an hour, the entire camp site was virtually clear, and only the abundant garbage left by the pilgrims remained.[47] Following final ablutions at the springs, the pilgrims departed to return home, or to continue their pilgrimages elsewhere.

Before concluding this description of the revived Drigung Powa of 1992, I should add some brief observations of a political nature. The pilgrims themselves were well aware that political demonstrations would inevitably have had negative ramifications for the future development of such events and also seemed to feel the religious value of the pilgrimage was too great to compromise. However, those present were outspoken in the opinion that this was an especially *Tibetan*, that is, non-Chinese, happening, and small groups convened in the evening on several occasions to display furtively the flag of the government-in-exile and to hum the

Figure 4.8. As the powa is conferred, those in attendance adopt attitudes of concentration and devotion.

Figure 4.9. Following the teaching of the powa, the pilgrims break camp and begin to descend the narrow trail to Terdrom before they are caught by nightfall.

national anthem of free Tibet. Very few actually participated in these soirées, but virtually everyone I spoke to volunteered with pride that this was known to be taking place: "Last night we showed the flag!" they whispered. "Last night we showed the flag!"

TIBETAN PILGRIMAGE PAST AND PRESENT

It has often been remarked that Tibet, before its forced entry into the People's Republic of China, had only a very weak state structure, whose authority, such as it was, was supported by little coercive force.[48] Indeed, large parts of the Tibetan world were often outside of the Central Tibetan state altogether and were subservient to other states or to local princes or virtually stateless. Despite this, however, and despite the presence of strong tendencies, intensified by the exigencies of geography and poor systems of communication, to accentuate the particularisms of region, dialect, and sect, there were traditionally, and persist today, strong sentiments of affinity and cohesiveness running throughout the Tibetan cultural world. The relative coherence of Tibetan culture, considered in light of the powerful forces that seem to oppose any such unifying disposition, presents a general problem in the study of Tibetan civilization, requiring some attempt at explanation.

It seems plausible at once to seek such an explanation in part in the analysis of Tibetan religion. But here some caution is needed, for Tibetan religion, unlike, say, traditional Judaism or Islam, does not have even in theory a highly uniform body of religious-cum-legal obligations that apply to the entire community of the faithful.[49] The very great variations of Tibetan religious life, according to differences of status, education, and obligation, among monastics and laypersons and individuals of different sectarian and regional background suggest that Western models of religious commitment cannot be readily applied to Tibet. Indeed, in Tibetan scholastic philosophy there was even a bit of debate concerning just what was required in order for one to be considered a Buddhist at all, and the preferred answer was that the taking of refuge in the Three Jewels alone was definitive.[50] Obviously this is much too thin to account for the deep continuities running throughout the sphere of Tibetan civilization.

To indicate more precisely the nature of the problem, we may consider briefly some conclusions drawn by Sherry Ortner in her early work on Sherpa rituals. The issue we confront here is underscored in her supposition that Buddhism promotes individualism to a remarkable degree: "Sherpa Buddhism . . . retains the central Buddhist tendency to isolate and atomize the individual, and devalue social bonding and social reciprocity. Indeed it is hard to imagine how Buddhism could be Buddhism without retaining this bias. A Buddhism of social bonding and communal solidarity seems a contradiction in terms."[51]

Clearly, however (and as Ortner, too, seems to suggest), the coherence of Tibetan culture becomes unintelligible if understood solely in such terms. In *Sherpas Through Their Rituals,* Ortner sought to resolve this difficulty with allusions to the Tibetan state:

> In Tibet, where the Sherpas originated and where their religion took the form that it retains for the most part today, the religion was supported by the theocratic state. State support of religion, in turn, allowed the monastic community to cut itself off from society more completely, because it was not directly dependent on the laity for support. Thus although Tibetan Buddhism absorbed a great many elements of popular religious practice and belief, it did not get involved in popular social life as such.[52]

This perspective requires that we posit an almost ubiquitous and uniform "Tibetan state," capable of supporting a massive religious establishment while almost thoroughly concealing from laypersons their ultimate role in the maintenance of that establishment. Such a state must also be supposed to have been relatively stable over a very long period, if it was to have engendered the peculiar social arrangements that are demanded of it. However, this appears to be not adequate to explain the role of religion in the formation of Tibetan culture and identity, for, as a matter of fact, the ethnography and history of Tibet provide little evidence in support of this odd picture. Tibetan monks were routinely supported by their families, and the larger Tibetan monasteries depended in part on estates and other ap-

panages, requiring an ongoing involvement in "popular social life," for such purposes as recruitment and fund-raising and to fulfill the ritual functions they were
expected to perform on behalf of the laity. The religious life of Tibet, moreover,
was at no time limited to the great monastic centers and the activities directly
sanctioned by them. A whole range of small temples and shrines, local rites and
festivals, lay religious and itinerant preachers, to mention just a few of the alternatives, thrived with but tenuous ties to the "theocratic state," and that state, indeed, did not exercise authority in large parts of the Tibetan world.

With this in mind, it is clear that the symbolic dynamics of religious systems
within Tibetan culture should be considered in important respects as having primacy over state institutions in our investigations of the religious dimensions of Tibetan cultural and national identity.[53] In this connection pilgrimage may be examined as one of the paradigmatic phenomena contributing to, and perhaps even
to some extent engendering, the cultural unity of the Tibetans. Pilgrimage, among
other things, promoted trade in both goods and information. It brought persons
from far distant parts of the Tibetan world into direct contact with one another
and thus militated to some extent against divisive regionalistic tendencies. By ordering the cycles of pilgrimage according to calendrical cycles, by establishing the
locations visited and the routes traversed, and by promoting specific religious
teachings, historical narratives, and symbolic interpretations of the landscape and
the events taking place within it, the Tibetan religious world constructed for its inhabitants a common order of time, space, and knowledge.

But pilgrimage, even while engendering Tibetan communitas, also involved
various particularisms; for the pilgrimages themselves were specifically tied to particular times, places, and institutions. Thus, for instance, the Drigung Powa
Chenmo, though attracting Tibetans from all sorts of places and promoting cults,
like that of Padmasambhava, whose following extended throughout Tibet and involved adherents of all sects, was equally an event that enhanced the standing of
the Drigung Kagyü order in particular. And the Drigung Kagyü order, in its turn,
may be seen to embody precisely the problem confronted by Tibetan civilization
overall: how does one achieve some measure of unity, given great dispersion and
little coercive force? Besides the question, therefore, of enhancing Drigung's status
within the Tibetan world in general, there was a specific, perhaps more pressing
requirement that the Drigung Powa Chenmo may have to some extent addressed,
namely that of calling in the sect's own adherents and reinforcing, in this way, the
center of its authority in their eyes. There is perhaps a fractal logic at work here,
significant structural features of Tibetan culture and civilization being recapitulated at different levels, on different orders of scale.

This dialectical relationship between widespread, in some cases even universal,
Tibetan cultural symbols and the particularities of time, place, and person provides an appropriate point of departure for the interpretation of a particular
event, such as the Drigung Powa Chenmo. In this connection it seems worthwhile
especially to reflect on the apparent homologies obtaining among features of ge-

ography, ritual, and body and, in some instances, possibly history as well. Thus the ascent to the Kere Yangdzong Cave, the teaching cycle of the Drigung Powa, and the rehearsed passage of the principle of consciousness from the body at death are all, from a formal point of view, equivalent. For the homology of the cave and the subtle body, whence consciousness departs from the crown, is again recapitulated in the performance of the powa at the culminating moment of the entire sequence of teaching (much as it ought to be, too, at the culminating moment of life). Death is here thematized as a liminal passage, but at the same time as a culminating and, literally, peak experience. We may suspect as well that the historical displacement of the fundamental locus of the teaching of *Planting the Stalk* from a spirit-filled lake—in Tibetan mythology the very image of the underworld realm of corruption and death—to a mountain hermitage further exemplifies a similar principle. Thus, in the symbolic order exemplified in the Drigung Powa, body, ritual, landscape, and history come to be mutually embodying, and so cosignifying.

As described above, it may appear that the 1992 performance of the Drigung Powa was primarily a replication of similar performances in the past. Such claims made in other contexts regarding rituals revived after long periods of interruption have sometimes been greeted with skepticism, and I think some reservations about this must apply here as well. Bruce Lincoln has compellingly argued, for instance, with respect to the interpretation of the Ncwala ritual marking the supremacy of the Swazi king, that relatively "minor" changes had to be understood in the context of the changing colonial situation in which the Swazi have found themselves in this century. In the present connection Lincoln's remarks on our understanding of Swazi affirmations seem apt: "Of all grammatical forms, I know of none more subtle and problematic in their sociopolitical implications than pronouns of the first person plural that, when skillfully employed, permit speakers to construct groups in which they join with unnamed others and stand apart from others still: others who fall outside this 'we.' "[54] In the case of the 1992 Drigung Powa, it must be noted that the changes were not minor at all: the two lamas normally expected to officiate were in exile; the monastic population was considerably reduced; the Tibetan state and the Drigung estates had been dismantled and political and economic life now determined by the CCP—these and many other alterations escaped no one's attention.

If the general approaches to the interpretation of Tibetan pilgrimage sketched out here have some merit, then, we may expect to see the continuation, resumption, and revival of traditional pilgrimage operating in part as both an assertion of and an initiation into a distinctively Tibetan cultural and ethnic identity in the face of such changes. At the revived Drigung Powa Chenmo there was indeed some evidence that something of this sort was taking place, as was reflected both by the pointed remarks of some of those in attendance, their pride that the Tibetan flag had been displayed and the anthem hummed, if only for a moment, and the obvious concern on the part of the local organizers that the pilgrimage not become an overtly political event. As these observations suggest, the conditions prevailing in the Tibetan world are by no means what they once were, and we cannot expect that the practice of pilgrimage will simply recapitulate the past, without reflecting the great changes that continue to transform the Tibetan world throughout. Indeed, future researchers will have to ask how events like the revived Drigung Powa Chenmo are received and understood by, for instance, the growing numbers of unemployed Tibetan youth who cluster around the billiard tables and bars in the towns. The eventual answer to such questions will depend in part on the degree of success with which traditional cultural symbols are creatively redeployed given the harsh actualities surrounding the cultural life of contemporary Tibet.

To conclude in brief, the study of Tibetan pilgrimage contributes much to our understanding of the Tibetan past and certainly deserves more thorough consideration in this regard. The role of the pilgrimage in Tibet's present and future, however, must be assessed with some caution, taking care not to project the past too facilely onto a changing scene. It will be particularly important to follow Lincoln's counsel and weigh with special care each pilgrim's utterance of the pronoun "we."

FIVE

Ritual, Ethnicity, and Generational Identity

Lawrence Epstein and Peng Wenbin

Folk rituals involving village communities traditionally formed an integral part of Tibetan religious life. Although not focused on the preeminent Buddhist concerns of karma and rebirth, and often having nothing to do with monks and lamas, these communal rites were seen by participants as critical to the well-being of their villages and indirectly served to strengthen village solidarity and identity. They also, more broadly, fostered a pan-Tibetan identity by virtue of their focus on similar types of deities and spirits throughout the vast area inhabited by ethnic Tibetans. Many, like the one discussed here, were celebrated continuously until the onset of the Cultural Revolution in 1966 (or a few years earlier in some areas) when such activities were denounced and banned as backward remnants of the old feudal society.

The shift in Chinese government religious policy after 1978 gave Tibetan communities the possibility of reviving such rituals, although what constituted acceptable religion was not always obvious under the new Chinese rules of religious freedom. The state's religious policy was oriented toward dominant religions like Buddhism, with their literate traditions, educated specialists, and vast textual materials. Folk beliefs and practitioners claiming magical powers were often described as examples of false superstition rather than religion, although there was no unambiguous set of criteria against which to differentiate "religion" from "superstition." For example, were shamans who claim gods enter their bodies and speak through them or lamas who perform divination exponents of Buddhism or remnants of superstition? Despite such ambiguity, Tibetan communities have, by and large, opted to revive their major folk rituals, and this chapter examines one such ceremony as it is being conducted in a Tibetan area in Qinghai Province.

Villagers in the region of Repgong[1] claim to have celebrated a folk ritual known as *luröl* (*glu-rol*, literally, "music" or "musical festivity") for more than 1,100 years.[2] The festival, which takes place around the middle of the sixth Tibetan month, is performed throughout the vicinity of Repgong and the Gu (Dgu; Chinese, Longwu) River valley. Despite the considerable variation the rituals take in different villages, it is generally agreed that the luröl rite is of ancient provenance, originating in and commemorating old military or other legendary events, and it is aimed at pleasing local deities so as to obtain good crops, healthy animals, good luck, and fertility in general. The people of Repgong thus see the performance of luröl as vitally linked to the overall prosperity of themselves and their communities, and they generally consider the luröl festival to be their most distinctive and most important annual rite. While people may engage in a variety of other religious activities throughout the year, none but luröl compels attendance: a number of villages, in fact, have required each household to be represented by at least one member.[3]

Luröl is a part of what has been called Tibetan "folk religion," an area of Tibetan religious life that has been the focus of much discussion in Tibetan studies. Most recently, Geoffrey Samuel has argued that folk religion and folk practices are oriented to the contingencies of everyday life.[4] At the risk of oversimplification, we may say that folk religious beliefs and practices display a set of pragmatic concerns surrounding interactions with local gods and spirits (such as the mountain gods mentioned below) and communications with such deities through various modes of spirit mediumship and divination techniques. They also focus on personal or communal luck or fortune and avoiding supernatural malevolence.[5] Often such practices are carried on by lay practitioners such as shamans, oracles, or tantric practitioners (*sngags-pa*), or simply by people with no special religious training or status. The heavily "this-worldly" beliefs and practices of Tibetan folk religion stand in contrast to the "otherworldly" theological concerns expressed in Buddhism or Bon that are carried out by more formally trained practitioners such as monks. However, as Samuel and others have pointed out,[6] the Tibetan folk and more formal religious traditions have interpenetrated each other to the extent that it is difficult to disentangle them.[7] Monks, for example, often perform readings of religious texts for laymen, which, in the eyes of the latter, accomplish the same this-worldly ends as do, say, folk rituals of purification. They also confer some degree of otherworldly merit on them. Similarly, Buddhist or Bon rituals and texts are often employed in folk rituals.

The luröl festival, as will be seen, shares some of this interpretation but on the whole represents the more distinctively folk religion end of the continuum in that it is organized and carried out totally by laypersons to raise the luck, prosperity, and fertility of the community and its members and to avert any possible disasters stemming from the neglect of a powerful local deity. And despite the presence of a large and famous monastery, Ronggön, monks are not allowed to attend the luröl ritual, as they do many other folk rites.[8] There is, therefore, little concern with matters that typify normative Buddhist goals such as raising one's karmic merit, expiating sin, or worrying about one's rebirth.

We witnessed a performance of the luröl in 1991 when we visited Repgong to interview villagers about local religious sites as part of a research project on Tibetan pilgrimage. Neither we nor any of the people we were traveling with had heard more than vague descriptions of the luröl, which in any event was not the purpose of our trip. Our timing was fortuitous. We arrived the day before the actual ritual began, finding people in a frenzy of preparation, excitement, high spirits, and eager anticipation. Once the ritual began, we were immediately struck by the strong sense of communal effort and attention to carrying out in detail these ritual festivities that all and sundry proclaimed to us were the quintessence of their local traditions and local history.

Anthropological approaches to ritual have often drawn attention to the way in which rituals affirm a group's communal unity and solidarity by resolving and realigning the atomizing tendencies of everyday mundane life, with its burdensome problems and conflicts, into a sense of ideal form and timeless moral order. The luröl rituals are no exception. They adhere to a type long familiar to anthropologists from societies all over the world, where, as Catherine Bell has remarked, the past is invoked to (re)invent tradition "in order to afford a sense of legitimized continuity with the past and to experience tradition as fixed. In the fixity of ritual structure lies the prestige of tradition and in its prestige lies its power."[9] The same ritual setting also delineates group identity "which is based not only on generating a shared consciousness about an authoritative past but also on a set of distinctions, seen as rooted in the past, which differentiates the group from other groups."[10]

In the pages that follow we describe and discuss the aspects of the luröl rituals that refer to the idealized past that both we and our ritual actors recognize are played out in the ritual action itself, for example, the social relations of household and community, males and females, and senior and junior generations. Second, we hope also to describe the historical and social milieu that is both embedded in and emanates from the ritual process itself, precisely where the ambiguities of different modes of authority and ways of constructing them are generated. But as Bell has also noted,[11] ritual symbols and actions are often ambiguous enough to make them effective in generating new meanings. Thus, we suggest in this chapter that while the ritual structures and actions we observed emphatically contain the legacy of the past and perpetuate traditional customs as all our informants proclaimed they did, the ritual context or environment has both generated and acquired new meanings.

THE "ORIGINS" OF LURÖL

There are a number of stories throughout the Repgong area that account for the origins of the luröl.[12] Most of them refer to accounts of an old war and a peace settlement between troops of the Tibetan empire and China in the ninth century. A lay tantric specialist in Soru village explained the origins of luröl this way.

In the time of the Tibetan empire, Tibet and China were separate kingdoms that fought a border war, and because of the fierce fighting both sides suffered the loss of countless men, horses, supplies, and cattle. Both sides were weary. In 822, on the twenty-second day of the sixth Tibetan month, they negotiated a treaty and inscribed it on a stele at Targyekar in Gansu.[13] The Tibetan army leaders in Amdo sent copies of the treaty throughout the region. After that there was no fighting on the borders, and peace reigned in both Tibet and China. The leaders ordered that luröl be celebrated as a commemoration of this. The wise men who negotiated the peace are said to have first invited the gods, then the *lu* (Sanskrit, *nāga*), and then the people. The gods, lu, and people befriended each other; it is said to have been an effort for the good results of the peace. On the first day, the gods are celebrated and given offerings; on the second, the lu are celebrated; on the third, offerings are given to the people.

Two important subtexts emerge from the historical narrative of the luröl. First, the story situates the ritual and its practitioners in unique geographic space, which, once upon a time, two equal powers contested. It thus recalls and enhances ethnic pride in an irretrievable Tibetan epicohistorical past. Second, the ritual in fact celebrates neither conquest nor conclusive victory but the suffering and weariness of war and reconciliation with China. The story, however, elides present realities, in which one of the protagonists has come to dominate the other. The luröl ritual recapitulates afresh the battlefield scenarios, protracting a past that no longer really exists, bringing out the unsettling and unsettled aspect of Repgong's geographic space as a frontier. Whenever the story of the ritual's origins is invoked, people of Repgong experience a sense of pride, a sense of loss, and a sense of uniqueness that resist the absolute closure of history.

Michael Aris, in "The Tibetan Borderlands," his introduction to *Lamas, Princes, and Brigands,* has written that it is best to think of the Tibeto-Chinese frontier depicted in Joseph Rock's photographs "as a zone rather than a line, one in which all possible boundaries of geography, race, and culture cross and overlap to form a broad, north-south transitional area of great complexity."[14] Here the notion of the frontier can be regarded as a sense of cultural and historical flux and continuous negotiation of local identity. Viewed from the centers of power, places on the frontier, like Repgong, were relegated to the margins of history. Both China and Central Tibet have historically viewed populations like this as untamed and uncouth bumpkins, sometimes comical, sometimes dangerous. But as Aris correctly observes, where one might expect the local perspective of those who live on the frontier to be characterized by a "sense of marginality or alienation, so often one meets instead with a confident and ancient sense of centrality."[15] Bound up with a major historical moment, this ancient sense of centrality appears in an acute historical consciousness of the identity and contemporary situation of the peopling of Repgong, emerging as one of the defining features of the luröl ritual.[16]

THE PEOPLING OF REPGONG

Paralleling reference to the military history of the ritual, there are several stories about the peopling of the Repgong area. These established the way in which the area was to be domesticated, not only as a political space, but also as a moral one, in which a parade of ancient culture heroes, secular and religious, through a succession of endeavors, established direct lines of genealogical descent and spread Buddhist culture. These events form a backdrop to local perceptions of centrality in important historical episodes against which local identities and ritual practices may be negotiated.

The major written source is the excellent Ronggön history,[17] whose author uncovered a number of manuscript sources dealing with local family histories, and which contains several chapters concerning the secular history and sacred landscape of Repgong, the surrounding areas of the Gu River valley, and the eighteen Rong bo tribes that occupy the area. By and large, the information contained here is consistent with oral sources.

These sources state that the area was occupied by Tibetans as long ago as the imperial period from the seventh to the ninth century when Gar Dongdzen, a high minister of the Tibetan kingdom, left his son Gyandzenbum here and, according to his father's wishes, his lineage spread. During King Tri Songdetsen's time, Padmasambhava visited Repgong, as did his disciples.[18] Padmasambhava gave vows to hostile supernaturals in the area, including the mountain deities to whom the rituals we discuss are dedicated, and opened up eight holy sites (*grub thob gnas*) for eight saints, the disciples of Lhalung Bekidorje, in Repgong.[19] Additionally, there are a number of associations with famous Tibetan religious figures dating from the early thirteenth century. Several family lineages in the area are supposed to stem from these times.[20]

The most celebrated migrants from Tibet to the Gu River valley came in the late thirteenth century and are associated with the Sakya area in Central Tibet. Many local people attribute their roots to these immigrants. The lineage of the present "chief" (*nang so*), whose title is still extant, stems from a yogin-doctor, Laje Traknawa, who, it is claimed, was a member of the Sakya Rong lineage (although this cannot be substantiated in Sakya sources). He migrated at about the end of the thirteenth century at the behest of Drogön Pagba and married a sister of the chief (*dpon*) of Jamtsa, north of Repgong, becoming the chief's chaplain. His descendants include many famous regional rulers, lamas, and local lineages who are responsible for laying the foundations of Ronggön Monastery in the fourteenth century. The Repgong chiefs were the rulers of extensive lands and territories that extended a long way from this small valley, and they were honored with titles from the Chinese court throughout the Yuan, Ming, and Qing dynasties.

THE LURÖL RITUAL

The rituals consist of a series of dances, sacrifices, propitiation of local mountain deities, and rites that celebrate village solidarity and purity, long life and fertility. The rituals described here are from the villages of Saji and Soru.[21]

In Saji village, the ritual begins with a procession in which an image of the "supernatural" guardian (*gzhi bdag*) of the area, Anye Shachung, is brought to each house.[22] Some elder men tell us that Shachung is an eighth-station bodhisattva,[23] possessing the four different aspects or forms associated with the four ritual attitudes of pacification, enrichment, dominion, and wrath (*zhi, rgyas, dbang,* and *drag*). In accordance with the typical Tibetan story to account for such figures, Padmasambhava is said to have sent Shachung to Amdo to overcome the harm (*klu gdug*) that was being done by lu, or nāgas, to this then-untamed region. Nine centuries later, the famous seventeenth-century savant of Rong, founder of the Shar incarnation lineage, Shar drubchen Genden Gyatso, is reputed to have given lay (*dge bsnyen*) vows to him.

Anye Shachung, as befits his station, is depicted with a large retinue in his iconographic representation (*thang ka*) and by the statues in his temple. His attendants are as follows. His minister of the left is Lönbo Radzong, a godling or demon (*lha 'dre*) under vows (*dam-la btags-pa*) from Samye Monastery. He did not want to take part in building the monastery, so Padmasambhava exiled him. Shachung conquered Lönbo Radzong and granted him a small piece of land. His minister to the right is the apotheosized Chinese hero Erlang, invited to be part of the retinue some one hundred years ago, according to village sources. Shachung's wife is the female mountain god (*gnas bdag mo, gzhi bdag mo*) of Jagen, one of the eight holy sites mentioned above; his son is Bumpadöndrub. Sitting below them are Anye Magpön, said to be an apotheosized general exiled by the Ming or Qing court; the famous regional god of Amdo, Machenbomra, his wife, Gongmen lhari, and Anye Nyechen in Linxia, Gansu Province;[24] and their four bodyguards (*gnyan chen sde bzhi*).

It is useful to note here that both the lurol origin myth mentioned above and the iconography of at least some of the local mountain gods incorporate and obliquely refer to Chinese figures, a feature that seems to mark the fluidity of frontier regions and their historic vision of themselves. Such syncretic elements seem to have been a traditional part of the lurol ritual, marking an interpenetration of two cosmologies that give identity to the ritual and themselves. The interstitial nature of these elements provides a dynamic space for flexible maneuverings of (re)interpretation and (re)invention of local "little traditions." It can be claimed that a Tibetan center is incorporating a Chinese one, or a Chinese reading of such recognizable elements in the ritual makes it merely one among innumerable local variants of Han cultural influence, or a mark of the taming of the remote frontier.

The class of deities to which Anye Shachung belongs, the mountain and regional deities (*gzhi bdag, yul lha*), are usually regarded as having somewhat ambivalent "personalities" only partly subdued by Buddhism. Despite the insistence of some to see such figures in more abstract form, such as the village temple beadle who insisted on Shachung's status as a high Buddhist god, these deities also demand close attention to everyday behaviors that may be only partly related to

Buddhist morality. Unlike the forbearance that typifies the bodhisattva, they are often quick to take offense at human behavior that offends them and the geographic spaces over which they reign. These might include human acts that outrage their sense of morality and pollute their territories, such as incest or murder, hunting animals in their special preserves, and failing to do them proper homage in the form of various offerings and prayer. People and communities that fail to observe certain limits to their behavior and ignore ritual prescriptions may court disaster not only for themselves but also for their communities at large, such as accidents, famine, floods, and pestilence. Those that do, by contrast, are blessed with good luck and prosperity.

In the past, Shachung possessed the village shaman during the luröl ritual. Some elders tell us that if Shachung does not receive pious worship or a lama to guide him first, he will not possess his human attendants. Other people, however, seem to draw no such fine distinctions. Nor is it clear to everyone to which deities blood is offered (see below). Some who argue Shachung is a bodhisattva claim he never touches the blood and that it is offered only to the fierce supernatural attendants in his retinue. Others seem not to be bothered by such theological niceties and declare straightforwardly that their blood is for him.

Formerly at Saji, a male shaman (*lha pa*) went into trance and was possessed by the deity. He led a grand procession around the village, inviting the deity to each household, and finally performed divination in the mountain god's temple during the ritual to determine by throwing lots a number of issues such as whether the offerings were accepted and whether the signs were auspicious. This shaman was confirmed each year by a lama through divination. However, Saji's principal shaman died in 1965, and he has not been replaced. In the year we observed the rite, there was no shaman from this village. Instead, a teenaged boy acted as a substitute shaman (*lha pa tshab*). Complete with various shamanic accoutrements and a false pigtail, he led the procession and performed the ceremony of offerings. This boy was chosen by the senior men of the village on the basis of his ability to dance and was not in trance.

This situation, however, is not found in other nearby villages where trancing shamans have continued to perform their traditional roles for the luröl.[25] It is not certain why a "real" shaman was also not selected in Saji. It may be simply that no one has recently become possessed by the deity, but we suspect that Saji's close physical (and social) proximity to Tongren town and the fact that many Saji villagers hold official positions in the local government or work in the town are relevant. A leading local (Tibetan) cadre whom we interviewed about this admitted, somewhat reluctantly, that the presence of a trancing shaman was slightly "touchy," in that such ritual specialists still lay under a small, ever-decreasing, shadow of ambiguity of what is and is not acceptable according to state religious policy.[26]

It should be emphasized, however, that this does not stop the genuine shamanic trance from occurring at Saji. First, during the course of the ritual, senior men

Figure 5.1. Substitute shaman offering ritual items before the sedan of Anye Shachung.

become "symbolic" shamans anyway (see below). Second, a shaman or sometimes several of them, from other villages where shamans operate without embarrassment, show up and go into trance, perform offerings, make interpretations of the gods' signs, and so on.

When asked why no one tried to stop the real shamans from going into trance, the leading cadre referred to above explained that those shamans were not from Saji village and that while their presence was perhaps ambiguous according to state religious policy, it was sanctioned under the guidelines for ethnic policy that allow minority nationalities to practice their cultural traditions.[27] Such "contradictory" situations are not at all uncommon. The ambiguity over the presence of shamans, in fact, illustrates well the complex interaction among local religious values, state religious policy, and the attitudes and interpretations of local-level officials that has typified the religious revival of popular religion in Tibetan regions. In this case of Saji, the local inhabitants have been able to adapt traditional practices so as to renew a ritual in a manner that satisfied the concerns of local officials with national law while maintaining the rite's cultural authenticity and integrity.

In Saji, the ritual began early on the sixteenth day of the sixth Tibetan month (6/16). A statue of Shachung was borne throughout the village in a sedan chair veiled and decorated with cloth so that the deity would not be polluted by the gaze of the onlookers. The procession visited each and every house, where standard offerings of bread, yogurt, flowers, butter lamps, grain, fruit, liquor, money, and ceremonial scarves (*katak*) were made. The homes had been ritually purified to receive Shachung, and people wore their best clothes as a mark of respect. An old man told us that people feel the real presence of Shachung and pay much attention to this event, asking Shachung to bless their lines, property, and future happiness. When Shachung returned to his temple, Anye Nang,[28] above the village, the courtyard had already been filled with the purifying smoke of evergreen bough incense (*bsangs*) that had been stockpiled there in preparation for his divine return. Shachung was so filled with power from the day's offerings that the men bearing his sedan chair lurched around the temple courtyard for almost an hour before the god could be coaxed back into his temple. This, we were told, was an auspicious sign of Shachung's pleasure. His renewed power forecast his good blessings in the coming year.

On the seventeenth day, males alone congregated at the temple and then proceeded to the *labdze*[29] located halfway up the hill above the village whose site commemorates Saji's military victory over a neighboring village about one hundred years ago. Men and youth proceeded to the labdze in generational age order, although nowadays, some of the oldsters complained, things were not properly done and people often proceeded by order of status or wealth. Generally, the labdze ritual consists of erecting anew ritual implements—spears and arrows representing village leaders and bushy decorated twigs representing village households and their inmates—and performing purificatory (*rlung rta*) ceremonies, calculated to raise supernaturally the real luck of the village. It is this form of luck which, if

Figure 5.2. Young men performing a military dance.

it is sufficiently "high," averts disease and demonic attacks (*bar chad*).[30] While there are various explanations for this ritual, in keeping with the military aspects of the overall ritual, some said that the arrows and spears inserted in the labdze are weapons, admired by the war gods (*dgra lha*).

The dances at the temple began the next day and were generally referred to as offerings to gods (*mchod*) or sportive/recreational/entertainment offerings (*rtsed mchod*).[31] In the morning, the following events occurred.

1) Young men performed the Pehwa dance[32] and honored (*bkur sti*) the four directions;
2) Young men performed a military dance offering (*gar stabs mchod*);
3) Young girls performed a dance offering (*gar gyi mchod*);
4) Senior men performed a drum dance to delight the immortal gods (*'chi med dga' ba'i lha rtsed 'jo*);
5) Two young men performed a stilt dance, a respectful offering of a staff (*ber kha*), and beat the god's drum to offer entertainment to the emperor (or the lineage of important lamas of the past [*gong ma*]);[33]
6) Senior men performed the offering of a staff for long life for those from ages one to one hundred;
7) Young men performed a luck-granting song (*kha gyang gi rtsed 'jo*);
8) Senior men beat drums to please the god;

9) Young men and girls performed a dance, likened to a rainbow twist (*'ja mtshon 'khyil ris 'dra*), offered to the Tibetan patron bodhisattva Tujechempo (Sanskrit, Mahākāruṇika).[34]

These dances were repeated in the afternoon with the addition of the following:

1) Elder men performed a weapon offering (*mtshon 'bul*), during which time they gashed their heads as a blood offering (*khrag mchod; dmar mchod*);
2) Elder men made sportive/joking offerings (*rtsed mo'i ku re'i mchod*) to create good luck for crops and domestic harmony;[35]
3) Senior men offered flower garlands and songs (*glu*) to please gods and men;
4) Senior men performed a sportive offering to delight Anye Magpön and Radzong, the attendants of Anye Shachung.

All households with young men and women were required to send at least one performer to dance. The types of line dances performed by males alone were considered military in nature (*dmag rtsed*). The latter are performed by younger men only and their military aspect is emphasized by the bearing of the dancers who assemble and break ranks in military fashion. The dances performed by young women are considered dances to entertain the lu (*klu rtsed*). Maidens (or at least unmarried girls of no more than twenty) performed a languorous dance consisting of slow steps and dips, highly organized in lines, said to have its origins in imitating

Figure 5.3. Elder men preparing to cut their heads.

Figure 5.4. Elder man making a blood offering.

Figure 5.5. Young women performing a nāga dance.

Figure 5.6. Young man dancing with skewers in his mouth.

the graceful movements of the lu. Married or parturient women never dance or participate in any way other than as onlookers.

In contrast to the straight-line, highly organized, and dictated dance formations of the youth, elder men perform free-form dances to entertain the gods (*lha rtsed*) before the sedan chair containing the god and throughout the temple courtyard, singly or in pairs or threes as the inspiration takes them. Their dances imitate the somewhat out-of-control motions of the entranced shaman, and they bear the relevant shamanic paraphernalia, such as a frame drum, a knife, or other implements.

When the youth are not dancing, the shaman also dances freely throughout the temple plaza, making offerings of various kinds, such as libations of liquor or yogurt, which are said to "feed" the respective "hot" and "cool" deities who attend the ritual. Additionally, late in the afternoon of the last day, the shaman or an experienced senior man uses a knife to open a wound on the heads of senior men, who let the blood stream dramatically over their faces or their backs, as an offering to the gods. Sometimes young men, approximately eighteen to thirty-five years old, allow the shaman or senior men to skewer their cheeks (*sha mchod* "flesh offering"; also *kha dmar* "red mouth"). There are various claims regarding the latter custom. Senior men, at least in Soru village, tended to tell us that skewering is compulsory for all young men of the age group, while senior men perform their offering as the inspiration takes them.[36] Others, principally younger men, claimed that there are no fixed numbers of requirements and that people do these things as they are so inspired.[37] The general reason given is that the skewering is a prophylactic against diseases that enter through the mouth. A great deal of local prestige is accorded to young men who do this.

SOME RITUAL SYMBOLS

Anthropological theory often views ritual as an occasion that displays life's contradictions and then resolves them, setting mythic or ideological clocks back to primordial beginnings. Certainly for the elder men this would seem to be the case in the way they explained to us the significance of the luröl. Elder men invariably referred to two aspects of ritual meaning. First, they explained it in terms of their historical and military origins. They were clearly interested in their "glorious past" and their identity as descendants of a tradition that stemmed from such heroes as Padmasambhava, the Tibetan imperial dynasty, the Sakya hierarchs, and countless others who seem to weave in and out of explanatory consciousness as one inquires after the meaning of these things. Second, they also explicitly recognize the local meanings of intravillage and intervillage solidarity (whether this is a matter of having the same mountain deities or having been under the same brigade in more recent times) and the blessings of the gods on matters of local fertility, be it in the guise of good crops, healthy animals, general prosperity, or the fertility of their women, especially the unmarried girls.[38]

While historical and military aspects of the ritual seem to dominate people's consciousness, other themes emerge from ritual actions which are perhaps not so overtly recognized. Among these are a set of oppositions that would appear to have to do with gender and generational relations. While people told us quite plainly that the luröl guarantees fertility, such explanations did not reach much beyond saying that if the gods are pleased with what they receive in offerings, obedience, and entertainment they will confer good things in return. On the other hand, we think that certain ritual actions can be read to lend us insights into the mechanisms involved in this exchange.

This aspect is far more apparent in other places. In Langja and Meba, places several kilometers to the north of Saji which we were unable to visit, the luröl, we are told by members of the local Cultural Bureau with whom we discussed the area's rituals, is designed specifically for fertility, which, for many reasons, they say, was low (especially before "liberation") and so depended on ritual enhancement. The village shamans dress up as yak bulls and imitate the action of bulls on women. It was considered a token of luck for a woman to be jumped on. Nowadays, our informant (an official of the local Cultural Bureau) reminds us, a man cannot jump freely on a woman because of the state's policy of limiting family size. But infertile women may invite a yak-man to jump on them.

There is also a ritual in which the shaman imitates the motions of coitus using oversized genitalia made of wood and other materials. Hence, our informant said, people are also embarrassed about Langja village's practices, which cause people from other areas to think Tongren folks are vulgar. Our informant in the Cultural Bureau was in fact so embarrassed at having revealed some of the region's dirty secrets that, after we had left the offices, he literally chased us down the street to tell us he had "changed his mind" about what he had said. In discussions with our colleagues later on, they, too, to our surprise, denied that these rituals had anything at all to do with sex but instead constituted an unfathomable religious "mystery." Even after we told them that such goings-on were common in agricultural societies, which, after all, have a perfectly comprehensible mundane concern with fertility, and that in Europe and other places such periods of ritual license, during which people practiced ritual intercourse freely in the fields, were not uncommon, they still would have none of it. Their concern was with the primitive unseemliness of it all, which might besmirch the ethnic image of Tibetans.

However, it is also apparent to the perfervid imagination of the anthropologist that more than mere sex is buried in the ritual symbols at Saji. First, to choose only a limited topic, what do the highly dramatic blood offerings signify? We are told time and again that married women are not allowed to participate in either the labdze ritual or the dances because they menstruate. If they did participate, they would pollute the gods and disaster would befall the village. Women's blood defeats ritual purpose—fertility. Blood may index their potential fertility, but its monthly appearance means they are not pregnant. Girls' blood does not count; they are infertile because they are unmarried. Where then do they get their fertility from? Clearly, the gods. But then, where does the god get his potency? Just as clearly, from the heads of senior men, the ones who cut themselves during the dances. It is not blood per se that offends Shachung, it is women's blood; men's blood is necessary to sustain his energy.

One revealing ritual moment, however, stands out beyond all others: the girls' last dance. The moment it was concluded, a number of senior men came forward, bearing gifts. They changed the girls' ceremonial scarves from the white ones worn during the dance to red ones made from the silk worn by Anye Shachung—from the cold, "premenstrual," sterile maiden state to the state of hot, fertile womanhood. They then placed a large loaf of special bread (called *kha rte'u*) and some money in the folds of each dancer's robe. We were told that originally the bread was given by the shaman to Anye Shachung and then to the people as a form of communion or blessing. But now it is given only to Saji girls under twenty. Bread, a lucky food, the men say, should be carried around for success. However, as the girls leave the dance field, the front of their robes bulging with bread, their symbolic pregnancy readily reveals itself to any onlooker.

Thus, through the lüröl, the preceding year's problems are purged, village solidarity is affirmed, and fertility and fortune are reestablished in their proper order through the ritual offering of blood by and under the authority of elder men. For the elder men, the rituals portray and affirm, first, their sense of village solidarity (even in the face of increasing rationalization and privatization of village economic strategies) and their traditional generational authority without which the good things of this life are impossible. Second, it ties them to a glorious Tibetan cultural, religious, and historical tradition, centering them in their Tibetanness. Throughout the rituals references to Tibetan deities, ritual objects, texts, heroes, kings, armies, landscapes, and conquests, both sacred and secular, are conspicuously paraded. The revival of the luröl ritual in Repgong, therefore, plays a major role in valorizing Tibetan ethnicity and erects an emotionally vibrant bulwark against the powerful forces that threaten to drag Tibetans along the road to assimilation.

At the same time, however, some younger participants expressed ambivalent feelings about the ritual, interpreting its meaning in a manner somewhat different from that of their elders. This generational difference reflects in large part the somewhat divergent manner in which the generations are adapting to the new conditions to which the local people are adjusting.

THE YOUNG MEN AND GENERATIONAL IDENTITY

At Soru, a group of young men recognized a member of our party, a well-known and highly respected teacher. They took him aside and complained that they did not want to have skewers inserted in their cheeks. They offered two reasons: it is potentially unhealthy, they said, and pointed out that someone a few years ago had ended up in the hospital with an infection;[39] worse, they thought it was primitive and therefore embarrassing. Nevertheless, they said that they still felt constrained to participate because they are Tibetans of Repgong, and because their elders make them do it and the village will criticize them if they do not. Despite their embarrassment, when the older men cut their heads first, they said that it would be shameful if they did not fulfill their part of the ritual. However, they wanted to know what the teacher thought about all this and, playing on their status as educated people, what he thought they could do to get out of or modify the situation to make it less offensive to them.

As mentioned above, for elders the rituals seem always to have celebrated several things: military history, village solidarity, and the order of the generational authority of elder men over the very bodies of their young men and women. However, the young are now very different from the elders when they were youths. They have received a modern education, and this includes the Chinese version of the modern view of history, of linear cultural evolutionary development in the Morganian mode from slave societies through feudal ones to socialist scientific ones.[40] Thus their objection. Being skewered through the cheeks or the upper back might reveal an unseemly and suspect backwardness lurking in the breast of modernity. For the young, increasingly educated in historical and developmental theories of the modern Chinese state, the issues inherent in the ritual are more complex and ambivalent than for their elders. Many of these young people are cadres and teachers, who in part see their futures developing within the wider context of the nation, and who are well traveled and have seen more of the world than their elders. Thus they are less happy to indulge in the "primitive" and the "superstitious," and would like to see the ritual modified to fit the new social realities as they see them.[41] Through its uniquely local elements and processes, the ritual ensconces participants in an identity that is in opposition to the discourses of the state that promote more elevated views of minorities in terms of their cultural achievements, such as high religion and literary sophistication. Thus some younger participants find that on the one hand the ritual connects them with a primordial place that instills a powerful and satisfying sense of valued ethnic identity while on the other it devalues their worth and identity in the larger sociopolitical arena of modern China. And, of course, if ritual meaning is consciously read at all, it is also a mark of local social subordination to their less educated, but socially and politically powerful, elders. In any case, for the present at least, the traditional organization of the ritual is dominant and the young men of Repgong submit to this prideful indignity, but pressure for change is already active.

THE STATE AND THE LURÖL RITUAL

During the early years of the People's Republic of China, state policy toward nationalities strongly articulated the right of Tibetans to follow their cultural and religious traditions. The political rationalization for this was that nationalities were backward and needed many years of development before they would be ready and able to discard such beliefs and practices in favor of socialism. During the Cultural Revolution, that view was replaced with an assimilationist policy that emphasized the paramountcy of class struggle; class identity would subsume and eliminate ethnic identity. Rituals like the luröl, therefore, were totally prohibited.

In the post-1978 era, the state made a major about-face and reinstated the earlier policy in which ethnic culture and religion were again valid activities. The state, in fact, has made a major effort to present itself to the world as a model multiethnic state in which nationalities like Tibetans can maintain their language, culture, and religion. Ann S. Anagnost has recently commented on this: "From 1986 on, religious belief became recognized as an ethical basis for everyday life that was as effective as (if not more effective than) socialist ethics in producing good civic behavior."[42]

However, the state's conception of religious freedom relegated a residue of folk religious and ritual practices to a somewhat dubious and suspect category of "superstition." In general, clearly "superstitious" practices are ones in which religious "fakes" under the guise of performing various ritual services bilk their clients for personal gain. Such activities are likely to be vigorously prosecuted. However, some rites and rituals in the popular religious arena are not financially exploitative, so fall into an ambivalent status in that they are not valued manifestations of high religion but also not clearly illegal instances of exploitative superstition. They fall into a gray area between religion and superstition and are generally seen by the state as primitive and backward. The state does not favor these because in one sense they are "an unequivocal 'sign' of China's backwardness" in the transnational setting.[43] On the other hand, Beijing's powerful commitment to a multiethnic state in which minority nationalities have the right to practice their ethnic culture makes it difficult to prohibit such nonfinancially exploitive religious activities. Consequently, in the post-1978 period, China's laws on religious freedom treated much of this type of popular religion inconsistently, sometimes ignoring it, sometimes discouraging its practice, and sometimes prohibiting all or part of it. Often, as in the Repgong area, this was done on a local basis, different villages in a single area having different policies and even the same village having different policies in different years (as officials and attitudes shifted). Thus, despite the state's negative view of much of popular religion, rituals like the luröl have been widely revived and perpetuated.

These tensions have been complicated in recent years by the explosion of market economics, in particular, the economics of tourism. The rush toward a market economy in China has created incentives to package and market ethnic culture for profit in China's ever-growing tourist industry. There has been, for example, a rush in many areas of China to create "ethnic villages" where members of different minorities dance and sing in costume for paying tourists. And the presence of ethnic religion and culture are key selling points for creating tourist sites. Stereotypically, in these "ethnic villages" ethnic culture is condensed to its performative value, the enactment of "timeless" cultural performances, displaying cultural diversity and the richness of cultural traditions contained within a benevolent and unified state.[44]

Repgong, with its famous monastery and its unique schools of religious art and embroidery, is not immune to economic forces. It is, for example, an "open area" for foreign visitors which already hosts a substantial, if not yet booming, tourist trade that is actively promoted by both state and local interests. Although we do not have statistical evidence, we are under the impression that a not insubstantial portion of the area's income flows from tourism, and discussions with local leaders have led us to believe they are counting heavily on the development of the tourist trade to sustain and finance the area's development. This would seem to add a new and powerful motive for preserving and perhaps even "museumizing" the more colorful parts of the luröl ritual—the dances, the bloodletting, the skewerings, and so on.[45] Economic gain is a potentially powerful new player.

CONCLUSION

The ritual of the luröl reveals the complex and ambiguous place of Qinghai Tibetans in the modern Chinese state. The luröl's revival clearly was an autonomous, genuine expression by a people who had just experienced more than a decade of state-sponsored policies of assimilation. It proclaimed to all who witnessed and participated in it that those who practice this are Tibetans and that they choose to preserve their religion and traditions, regardless of how Han and others perceive and evaluate it. It asserted local ethnic identity and enlivened the memory of local history and the grandeur of Tibetan civilization and past political power. It was, therefore, unabashedly antihegemonic. As such, it illustrates vividly a basic contradiction of contemporary Chinese political philosophy. In its desire to promote its vision of a nation in which different ethnic groups (nationalities) are happily subsumed under the authority of the state, the state feels compelled to allow localized discourses to emerge which reclaim in part a heterodox vision of history in which separateness and Tibetanness are highlighted and valorized.[46]

For the moment, therefore, the luröl ritual for the people of Repgong is a vital and important religious act that links them to their place, their gods, and their Tibetanness. And no matter how colorful the attraction, or how important a financial factor it may become in Repgong's modernized future, it has not yet, nor is it likely soon to become, a pure commodity. The luröl ritual clearly retains powerful local cultural significance. Its meanings will continue to be negotiated among the ritual actors, but as modernity continues to make its inroads on the people of Repgong, its very performance may condemn its participants to a form of second-class citizenship in which they must choose between their ethnic or their national identities. Or worse, it may be transformed into a meaningless theatrical performance. But at present, Repgong's luröl ritual reflects the breadth of the revival of Tibetan religion in China.

SIX

Concluding Reflections

Matthew T. Kapstein

I

To speak of "religious revival and cultural identity" in contemporary Tibet may convey to many readers images of protest demonstrations, cries for freedom, and reported violations of human rights. The close relationship between resurgent Buddhism in Tibet and the Tibetan independence movement began to receive intensive international attention in the wake of the series of riots that erupted in Lhasa during the autumn of 1987. Videotaped images of monks being beaten senseless by police and continuing reports of the arrest, detention, and sometimes torture of monks and nuns who have demonstrated on behalf of Tibetan freedom and the leadership of the Dalai Lama have been among the most prominent representations of religion in contemporary Tibet, indeed for many the only representations they are likely to have encountered in print or broadcast journalism. To the extent that scholars and writers have turned their attention to this subject matter, understandably they have also focused on the protest movement in and around Lhasa. For besides being the most dramatic expressions of religious and political activity in Tibet, the events in Lhasa have been the most accessible to outside scrutiny.[1] Despite this, as the events and circumstances discussed in this book make clear, the post–Cultural Revolution religious revival has involved considerably more complexity and variation than such a picture alone suggests. Accordingly, too, the relationship between religion and nationalist aspirations proves to be less straightforward than it had seemed.

The studies presented here are notable for the breadth of coverage they do provide, but Tibet is vast, events have been varied, and our case studies accordingly cannot pretend to be comprehensive. Our researches were conducted in three of the five Chinese provincial units with substantial Tibetan populations (chapters 2 and 4 in the Tibet Autonomous Region, chapter 3 in Sichuan, and chapter 5 in

Qinghai). Religious activities among both monastics and laypersons are discussed, as are questions relating to sustained institution building (chapters 2 and 3) and more short-lived celebratory events (chapters 4 and 5). We have examined circumstances in proximity to major urban settlements (chapter 2) and in smaller towns (chapter 5), nomadic districts (chapter 3), and mountainous wilderness (chapter 4). Three of the major sects of Tibetan Buddhism are topics here (chapter 2 on Geluk, chapter 3 on Nyingma, and chapter 4 on Kagyü), as is what R. A. Stein has termed the "nameless religion" (in chapter 5).[2] In short, though the quantity of the data discussed is necessarily limited, when considered in relation to the extent of the geographic area and the diversity of the population of Tibet, their variety helps to ensure that the sample is nevertheless broadly representative. Later in this chapter some important issues and topics that are not discussed in these pages will be surveyed in brief, above all to indicate directions for future consideration.

II

Following Eric Hobsbawm and others, we must stress that *national identity*, the identification of oneself as belonging to a particular national group, and *nationalism*, the conviction that the national group ought to be politically embodied in a unique nation-state, are to be carefully distinguished.[3] While the former may supply some of the background conditions for the occurrence of the latter, it in no way necessitates or entails that occurrence. That this is so as a general principle is well exemplified in the case of Tibet.

It is seldom precisely clear what constitutes national identity; all of the usual suspects—ethnicity, history, religion, language, and so on—have important exceptions, as Hobsbawm has shown. National identity, it would seem, is plastic and malleable, not a matter of rigid determination but rather of a broad set of loosely shared characteristics, practices, and beliefs. Like religions, national groups are probably only capable of being defined polythetically, if they are to be defined at all.[4] By virtually any of the criteria that have been widely discussed, however, the assertion of a Tibetan national identity remains unusually powerful: besides the Tibetan folkloric notion that Tibetans are those who speak the Tibetan language and eat tsampa (parched barley flour) as their staple food, one can point to the geographic coherence of the Tibetan world (including its traditional lines of trade and its sacred geography), the sense of a shared history among the Tibetan people, and their use of a common literary language (including the implications of this for the formation of an educated elite sharing, at least in part, a common literature), as well as to aspects of geneology, myth, and folklore, in addition to Tibetan religion per se. And Tibetan religion, it must be stressed, reinforces the Tibetan sense of identity in part by engendering a shared culture in many areas of life that in postindustrial, secularized societies are no longer often treated as religious. In short, the Tibetans, quite apart from the special issues raised by the emergence of modern nationalism among them, have ancient and abiding reasons for identifying themselves as a distinct nation, despite the differences of regional, tribal, or sectarian identity that may otherwise divide them. This much is generally acknowledged; indeed, the identification of the Tibetans as a distinct national group is fundamental to Chinese nationalities policy, which regards the Tibetans as one of the leading nationalities of China.[5]

China, like the former Soviet Union, has never formally considered itself to be a nation-state, representing the political aspirations of a single nationality.[6] The communist ideal early on privileged not national identity but class identity, and both the Soviet Union and China were conceived by their theoreticians to be multinational states in which the supposed aspirations of workers and peasants for a revolutionary and egalitarian socialist community would be realized.[7] In the Soviet Union, however, the actual dominance of the Russian nationality was sufficiently resented by the not inconsiderable numbers of non-Russians so that, given the economic failure of Soviet communism, the conditions for a breakup of the union along nationalist lines were immediately realized. But China, so far, has developed somewhat differently, in part no doubt because the nationality that in fact dominates, the Han Chinese, accounts for almost 95 percent of the total population of China. Potentially, at least, intra-Han conflict would present a much graver challenge to the unity of China than attempted secession by disgruntled minority nationalities.[8]

The comparison between China and the former Soviet Union is instructive in other respects. Several of the former Soviet republics had well-developed *nationalist* movements of their own even prior to the revolution of 1918, or to their incorporation in the Soviet Union.[9] That is to say, modern nationalism, not just national identity, already had a relatively long history in some areas prior to the special conditions obtaining during the last years of the Soviet empire. While a similar story might be told of some non-Han groups in China—some might adduce the ill-fated East Turkestan Republic as an example—it can be argued that this was not true of Tibet: despite the existence of an independent Tibetan state and the distinct identity of Tibetan culture and civilization, and although the bare beginnings of a modern Tibetan nationalist movement may be detected in some pre-1951 political developments,[10] Tibetan nationalism has emerged primarily as a reaction to the incorporation of Tibet into the PRC in 1951. Because the Chinese have been determined to squelch this tendency whenever it has forcefully emerged, there has never been an extensive, organized Tibetan nationalist movement, except to the extent that one has emerged within the Tibetan refugee communities in South Asia, Europe, and North America.

The religious revival in Tibet following the Cultural Revolution has therefore been a matter of great delicacy: to the extent that it appears to foster Tibetan national identity, within the context of Tibetan inclusion in the multinational Chinese state, it remains (in principle at least) ideologically unobjectionable, and on this basis local governments have been able to protect and in some cases even support revival movements (see especially chapters 3 and 4). At the same time, when religious revival has provided the background for the emergence of genuinely nationalistic expression, the Chinese state has brought its instruments of control, and, if it deems necessary, repression, to bear.[11] Drepung Monastery, studied in chapter 2, is a poignant example of a religious institution struggling to survive in the volatile atmosphere that is thus created.

III

Religion, then, is by no means uniquely definitive of Tibetan identity; and even where religion plays a significant role in its formation or articulation, it does not entail the nationalistic expression of that identity. Nevertheless, it is also true that religious practices and symbols have been particularly prominent in the context of nationalist protest[12] and that some of the most striking nationalist manifestations have come from the ranks of the religious. Religion, therefore, at the very least seems to provide a field in which the issue of identity is intensified and brought into full consciousness.[13] Based on the cases studied in this volume, three themes seem particularly pertinent for the roles they play in national identity formation, namely, religious conceptions of Tibetan history, geography, and education. In these areas, religious views strongly promote conceptions of Tibetan difference and uniqueness while also elaborating a distinctive set of values and ideals.[14]

History frequently plays an important role in religious nationalisms: the notion that a particular religion is tied to the historical development and destiny of a nation may prove to be powerfully compelling both emotionally and intellectually. Tibetanists have discussed to some extent the manner in which traditional Tibetan historiography engenders a view of the Tibetan world in which its historical station is intimately intertwined with Buddhism.[15] It is not surprising, therefore, that historical themes and associations should be strongly emphasized in connection with three of the movements or events studied here. Khenpo Jikphun (chapter 3), for instance, explicitly relates his mission to recollections of the old Tibetan empire, and in the celebrations examined in chapters 4 and 5 historical memory is also a prominent theme. In these cases, it is clear that religious revival has entailed, and in turn been reinforced by, forceful reaffirmations of the Tibetan past. There is also a certain irony about this, for in the expansion of Tibetan-language publishing activity and the development of Tibetan-medium educational curricula in post–Cultural Revolution China, the study of Tibetan history has been encouraged as a more or less secular aspect of traditional Tibetan learning.[16]

History, of course, is also tied to Tibet's special place in the world, both figuratively and literally. As Melvyn Goldstein suggests in the introduction, the historical reality of Tibet's role in its relationship with the Mongol, Ming, and Manchu emperors of China as a special repository and source of Buddhist learning and spiritual virtuosity plays no small part in Tibetans' self-image and pride that they are the representatives of a great and indeed exemplary civilization. Moreover, as the other chapters in this volume also stress, the Tibetans' sense of their place in the world is also intimately connected to specific places in the geographic body of Tibet. Tibetan identity is embodied in the Tibetan land and reinforced by the knowledge of that land's special features and powers. Pilgrimages like the Drigung Powa Chenmo, the rites of local deities such as those propitiated at Repgong, and the geomantic insights of respected teachers like Khenpo Jikphun are among the primary vehicles through which Tibetans continue to assert their privileged relationship to Tibetan soil.[17]

The third theme mentioned above was the role of education, and here, too, the Tibetan religious revival shares a significant feature with religious nationalist movements in other parts of the world.[18] For traditional systems of education are above all concerned with the inculcation and embodiment of particular human ideals, whose form and value are particularly accentuated within a given cultural system. The person formed within such a system, therefore, though exemplifying some virtues that may be claimed to be universal, always embodies a unique and distinctive way of life. Well-formed traditional systems of religious education aim to produce exemplary exponents of such ways, and in this respect at least Shi'ite mullahs, Tibetan lamas, Orthodox Jewish rabbis, and Roman Catholic priests all may be said to exemplify similar cultural phenomena.

The role sometimes played by an educated, literate elite in the crystallization of national sensibilities has been widely discussed.[19] The intelligentsia, of course, need not be, and often are not, defined by elite religious formation (for example, the early Zionist movement had its strength among Jewish secularists and progressives, not among the religious traditionalists). Indeed, where the religious intelligentsia have felt a primary loyalty to supranational, or non-national, religious institutions, they have sometimes militated against nationalisms.[20] However, where the national destiny is regarded as peculiarly tied to a specific religion, the religious elite also may become focal points of national feeling. Something of this sort has occurred in the renewed valuing of higher religious education in Tibet, as is evident in connection with the revival of Drepung Monastery, near Lhasa, and the training of young khenpos under Khenpo Jikphun in Golok. Significantly, when national feeling spills over into genuine nationalism, as noted in chapter 2, it is often among some of the most talented of the younger monk scholars. At the same time, it has by no means been axiomatic that such a shift to active nationalism must occur. Chapter 3 offers the example of a dynamic center for the training of a new Tibetan religious elite that, in marked contrast to Drepung and other monasteries that have been highly politicized, has fostered national identity and pride apparently without the by-product of manifest political activism.[21]

It is clear that for many Tibetans at the present time, the construction of identity must be negotiated between competing and often hostile alternatives, and, because the public culture of China does not permit the free expression of alternatives that are regarded as challenging the officially sanctioned structures of power, individuals are often compelled to adopt what has been termed, in similar contexts elsewhere, a "dimorphism of values," by adhering publicly to the official culture while masking their true sentiments.[22] With reference to a centrally located monastic center, for instance, Goldstein observes,

> Every Drepung monk believes in the sanctity of the Dalai Lama and wants him to return to Tibet, and virtually all support his efforts to secure Tibetan independence. Nevertheless, some monks believe the efforts are not only unrealistic but also harmful to the monastery and the revival of religion. The DMC, for example, has tried to persuade the monks that Drepung's interests are best served by focusing their efforts on religious study and eschewing political activism. Some senior monks have similarly tried to persuade their young wards to reject political activism because of the personal and monastic dangers. However, by and large, such efforts were not successful. (P. 42)

And Epstein and Peng, in treating popular religion among the laity of a district on the periphery of the Tibetan world, speak of a "ritual [that] ensconces participants in an identity that is in opposition to the discourses of the state" (p. 136). The movement from a generalized national feeling to positive nationalism may be one way of resolving the internal tension and conflict that such dilemmas inevitably involve, and clearly that tension will occur in an unusually high degree precisely among the aspiring religious elite who are exposed at once to the full force of opposing currents, as they are in monasteries like Drepung where the efforts of the CCP to exert some level of ideological control have been most pronounced.

There are, of course, many variables at work here, and we do not expect to find a formula that will satisfy every case. One further factor that must be borne in mind, paradoxical though it may at first seem to some, is that Tibetan identity is still perhaps not the identity commitment felt as most important in the daily lives of many Tibetans.

IV

In studying the Tibetan refugee community in India during the late 1970s, sociologist Margaret Nowak found that the Tibetan government-in-exile was faced with the task of actively forging a clear Tibetan identity that would override the regional and sectarian identities that kept the Tibetans divided among themselves.[23] Though there are, as we have seen, strong bases for the assertion of a Tibetan identity, it is an identity that has been emphasized above all when it is challenged, or when dealing with non-Tibetans; for among Tibetans themselves there are very often other affiliations that first come into play. As chapter 2 points out in the case of Drepung, a monk's first loyalty was usually to his residence house, then to his college. His monastery and sect were somewhere in the background, and the Tibetan people or the Tibetan state not often (if ever) considerations at all. Tibetan identity, in short, came into the foreground above all when it was felt to be under attack.[24]

The foregrounding of Tibetan identity in recent decades, however, has by no means annulled the membership of Tibetans in particular communities within the Tibetan world. And it is surely the case that for many Tibetans, in their day-to-day affairs, these are still the affiliations that count. As several of the chapters here (especially 4 and 5) show, traditional and revived religious activities often serve primarily to reinforce these particular affiliations, though within the framework of a more generalized and abstract Tibetan identity.

As we see most dramatically in Epstein and Peng's study of intergenerational conflict in Repgong, traditional local identities have also begun to be felt as problematic by younger Tibetans. One response, of course, that is sometimes encouraged by contemporary authorities in the TAR and neighboring regions is to adapt oneself to the dominant culture of contemporary China. But at the same time, this may engender precisely the disquieting "dimorphism of values" to which we have referred above, and so issue in a renewed insistence on a distinctively Tibetan identity. It is not surprising, therefore, that, besides those who have entered monastic life in the region of Lhasa, many outspoken young Tibetan nationalists have emerged from the ranks of those who have pursued modern secular educations in the cities of China. Their stories, which are crucial for a fuller consideration of contemporary Tibetan national identity and nationalism, have yet to be considered in detail.[25] As the present studies show, an alternative response to the sense of conflict is the reaffirmation of traditional Tibetan religious identities, and it is of course this tendency that has in part fueled the religious revival.

We should note, too, that it would not be correct to argue that local identities simply militate against or undermine the formation of a broader Tibetan identity. That they do not is in part because such particular identities are of significance primarily in the larger context that the Tibetan world provides. Our study of the Drigung Powa offers a case in point: "though attracting Tibetans from all sorts of places, and promoting cults . . . whose following extended throughout Tibet and involved adherents of all sects, [this] was equally an event that enhanced the standing of the Drigung Kagyü order in particular." In sum, though local, tribal, and sectarian identities often play a divisive role in the Tibetan world, they presuppose, and so in some respects also maintain, the very fabric of that world.

V

While the Tibetan government-in-exile and the People's Republic of China have emphasized diametrically opposing visions of religion in contemporary Tibet, most of the religious Tibetans we have encountered here seem to be attempting to steer a delicate course between them. As Chinese citizens, they have sought take advantage of the post–Cultural Revolution liberalization to revive and preserve their cherished traditions, and generally they do this within the bounds of the present system. At the same time, as persons who are determined to see a distinctively Tibetan culture and identity survive and flourish, they have strong feelings of affinity with their compatriots in exile and cannot easily relinquish their sense of loyalty to the Dalai Lama. The experiences of the Cultural Revolution and the extreme marginalization of Tibetans in contemporary China, to an increasing extent even in traditionally Tibetan regions owing to the substantial influx of Han workers and entrepreneurs, have produced enduring sentiments of alienation and mistrust, so that a wholehearted affirmation of their position in China is difficult even for the many who accept that they must work within the system at this time. The Tibetans are, as it were, suspended between Dharamsala and Beijing.

But the political polarity is by no means the only source of tension in religious Tibet. To varying degrees in different settings, as suggested above, generational, regional, sectarian, and educational difference all inform the emerging scene. Many of the relevant forces were present in the Tibetan world long ago but have taken on new meaning, and in some cases new urgency, under the special circumstances that exist today. Not surprisingly, symbols of Tibetan unity and focal points of common allegiance have also gained a new emphasis, and most prominent among these have been the figures of the two leading Tibetan Buddhist hierarchs, the Dalai Lama and the Panchen Lama. Though we have obviously not been able to deal fully with events that have only been unfolding as this volume was being produced, some that concern these two leaders are of great significance in the present context and cannot be passed over in silence. These include the 1995 dispute over the succession of the Panchen Lama and the 1996 campaign to restrict the display and distribution of images of the Dalai Lama, the violent reactions this provoked, and the ensuing crackdown, above all at Ganden Monastery. Though detailed consideration of these events must await future study, a few words may be said to relate them to our present concerns.[26]

Nowak, in her study of the refugee community, found that the promotion of personal loyalty to the Dalai Lama played a key role in the government-in-exile's efforts to strengthen the sense of a unified Tibetan identity.[27] The Dalai Lama has become the best-known symbol of Tibetan aspirations, in the world at large and also for Tibetans themselves. One result in post–Cultural Revolution Tibet has been the formation of a renewed cult of the Dalai Lama, most often manifest in the distribution and display of photographs of him. This was directly attacked by the CCP in April 1996 with a campaign to remove such images from view, particularly from public and otherwise high-prestige venues, such as schools and the homes and offices of Tibetan officials. In protest, a riot is reported to have broken out at Ganden Monastery, which resulted in some deaths, many arrests, and new restrictions placed on the monastery.

In some respects, the extraordinarily high value placed on images of the Dalai Lama in Tibet in recent years represents a genuine symbolic innovation, supported tangentially by the more general religious revival, but in some respects distinct from it. It represents a particularly striking instance of "the power of symbols against the symbols of power," to borrow the expression of Jan Kubik, writing on Polish resistance to Soviet domination.[28] There is an interesting sense in which the

Dalai Lama, in virtue of his absence from Tibet and visibility on the world stage, has acquired for many an aura of supranational authority, though this may not be true of Tibetan Buddhism institutionally.[29] Though the Gelukpa sect, with which the Dalai Lama is affiliated, does have the strongest sense of a corporate identity among the Tibetan Buddhist schools, the sectarian and regional divisions we have mentioned earlier continue to be factors limiting religious mobilization in Tibet.[30] The remarkable successes of lamas like Khenpo Jikphun and of events like the Drigung Powa therefore appear to have occurred not as the result of an overriding ecclesiastical strategy but through a sort of free agency.

This appearance, however, may be misleading in some respects, and it would be wrong to conclude that religious activity among Tibetans in China has been uncoordinated except for the symbolic unity provided by the image of the Dalai Lama. Among relevant topics not directly studied in this volume, but alluded to at various points throughout, is the complex network of county and provincial offices of publication, cultural relics, and religious affairs, among others, whose relations with government at several levels, with the lamas and monasteries, and with one another have facilitated and lent some measure of coherence to reviving Buddhist activity. Moreover, throughout the initial phases of the revival during the 1980s, a guiding hand behind much of this network was that of the late Panchen Lama.

As the foremost arbiter, during the period following the Cultural Revolution, between the Chinese government and Tibetan religious and cultural life throughout China, the Panchen Lama was uniquely influential in matters relating to the restoration and construction of temples, the creation of monastic schools, the publication of religious literature, and other similar activities. In the decade before his death in 1989, he succeeded, for example, in arranging for the return of looted cultural treasures from Beijing to Drepung, in encouraging and gaining authorization for the reestablishment of some impressively large monastic centers, such as the massive Nyingmapa Monastery at Mewa in far northern Sichuan, and in creating an academy for the education of incarnate lamas at the Yonghegong, the old center of Tibetan Buddhism in Beijing.[31] Regardless of the misgivings some Tibetans harbored about him, owing in part to his long-standing public stance in favor of reconciliation with China, there was very widespread support for his efforts here, and it was widely believed that he was doing the best one could under the circumstances. Thus, besides the Dalai Lama, the Panchen Lama served as a second unifying point for Tibetan Buddhists, and it is in part owing to this that the controversy that erupted in 1995 over his reincarnation became so virulent as it did almost immediately.

This dispute received worldwide attention when on 14 May 1995 the Dalai Lama and the Tibetan government-in-exile preempted the announcement of the discovery of the young incarnate in Tibet. The Chinese reaction was fast and furious: the acting abbot of Tashi Lhunpo, Chadrel Rinpoche, was placed under house arrest in Chengdu, Sichuan, and Gendun Choekyi Nyima, the young boy who had been recognized as the Panchen Lama by the Dalai Lama, was detained with his family. (It was eventually announced that they were being held in "protective custody" in Beijing.) Shortly thereafter, his recognition was rejected by the Chinese government, and a lottery was held on 29 November 1995 to choose a new Panchen Lama from among several officially approved candidates. In the end, one of these was enthroned as the Panchen, and Gendun Choeki Nyima apparently remains in Beijing.

Obviously, control of the office of the Panchen Lama has been regarded as crucial by both sides, and this reflects both the symbolic and the practical power with which that office has come to be invested. It is also the case, however, that the dispute, far from being uniquely the product of very recent Tibetan and Chinese relations, recapitulates an ongoing series of disputes between Tibet and China throughout the past two centuries over the appointments of Dalai Lamas and Panchen Lamas and that the most recent such dispute before this one indeed involved the recognition of the previous Panchen Lama.[32] It is striking that here, as in much else, China and Tibet seem to be locked in patterns of conflict that emerged and became established long ago, in this instance under China's Manchu rulers of the eighteenth and nineteenth centuries.

With these matters in mind, then, it seems that neither the disputed recognition of the new Panchen Lama nor the campaign against the display of photographs of the Dalai Lama should be regarded as fundamental changes in Chinese policy toward Tibetan Buddhism, though as seen in the epilogue to chapter 2, they have resulted in significant alterations of specific policies. Nevertheless, this reflects a consistent pattern since the late 1980s, with roots established even before, of dealing stringently with manifestations of Tibetan nationalism, particularly when these involve overt expressions of support for the Tibetan government-in-exile in Dharamsala. Many of the types of revived religious activity discussed in these pages may be only marginally affected by such events, though it will surely seem that they form an ominous background for current religious revival activity in general. At the same time, the Chinese attitude toward the Dalai Lama has increasingly hardened in recent years, and whereas it was once possible to separate his political and religious roles, and in this way to justify the public display of his likeness, the developing tendency has been to regard any show of allegiance to him as fundamentally political in nature. Moreover, for the time being at least, there is no Tibetan religious figure in China capable of acting on behalf of Tibetan Buddhists with the authority of the former Panchen Lama. In the absence of the latter, and with the former under sharp attack, feelings of loss and desperation may be expected to surface in some quarters with renewed force.

VI

Despite the struggles and hardships of recent decades, Tibetan national identity remains a potent cultural force in the Tibetan regions of China, and its vitality is powerfully supported by the ongoing revival of traditional Tibetan religious activity. The factors that have encouraged the emergence of genuine nationalism, however, have not grown out of the traditional religion per se; rather, antipathy to Chinese domination as it has developed so far combined with the positive ideal of Tibetan autonomy and freedom, embodied for many in the figure of the Dalai Lama, are probably the key factors here. But the national religion, by offering innumerable reminders of harm done to Tibet under Chinese rule and by accentuating distinctively Tibetan beliefs and values, does underscore both. This places China in something of a quandary: by suppressing Tibetan Buddhism, Tibetan resentment and hence the longing for freedom are increased; but by adopting a liberal policy, the very cultural system that most encourages the Tibetans to identify themselves apart from China continues to flourish. The dilemma this creates will perhaps be resolved if Tibetan self-understanding is radically transformed, or if the political evolution of China eliminates the fear of repression and provides real and enduring assurances of local autonomy. At the time of this writing (November 1996), however, such outcomes seem far removed.

APPENDIX

SPELLINGS OF TIBETAN NAMES AND TERMS

Throughout the volume, for the convenience of most readers, the authors have used simplified spellings of Tibetan proper names and terms employed in the main body of the text, to indicate their approximate pronunciation. Some terms introduced in notes, or parenthetically, however, are given according to their correct Tibetan orthography. The following list provides those conversant with Tibetan with the exact spellings for those words given only in simplified form in the text.

Aba	*Rnga-ba*
Achi	*A-phyi*
Amdo	*A-mdo*
Angön Rinpoche	*A-mgon Rin-po-che*
Ani Muntsho	*A ni mu mtsho*
Anye Magpön	*(A-myes) Dmag-dpon*
Anye Nang	*A-myes nang*
Anye Nyenchen	*A-myes Gnyan-chen*
Anye Shachung	*A-myes Bya-khyung*
Black Maṇḍala Lake	*Mtsho Maṇḍal-nag-po*
Bargor	*Bar-'khor*
Batang	*'Ba'-thang*
Bon(po)	*Bon(-po)*
Bumpadöndrub	*'Bum-pa don-grub*
Chamdo	*Chab-mdo*
Che College	*Byes Grwa-tshang*
Chetsang Rinpoche	*Che-tshang Rin-po-che*
Chimphu	*Mchims-phu*

chöra	*chos-rwa*
chösi nyindre	*chos-srid gnyis-'brel*
Chötsel	*Chos-'tshal*
Chungtsang Rinpoche	*Chung-tshang Rin-po-che*
Danma	*'Dan-ma*
Dartsedo	*Dar-rtse-mdo*
Dawu	*rta-'u*
Deyang	*Bde-dbyangs*
Dinggyel	*Sding-rgyal*
Dodrub Kunzang Zhenphen	*Rdo-grub kun-bzang gzhan-phan*
Dokashak	*Rdo-kha-shag*
Dorje Gyelpo	*Rdo-rje-rgyal-po*
Dorje Yudronma	*Rdo-rje g.yu-sgron-ma*
Drepung	*'Bras-spungs*
Dridzong	*'Bri-rdzong*
Drigung Kagyü	*'Bri-gung Bka'-brgyud*
Drigung Khandro	*'Bri-gung Mkha'-'gro*
Drigung Powa Chenmo	*'Bri-gung 'pho-ba chen-mo*
Drigung-thil	*'Bri-gung-mthil*
Drogön Pagba	*'Gro-mgon 'Phags-pa*
Drongur	*'Brong-ngur*
Dzenthang Kyopa Temple	*Rdzan-thang Skyob-pa'i lha-khang*
Gambu Rinpoche	*Sgam-bu Rin-po-che*
Ganden	*Dga'-ldan*
Gar College	*Sgar grwa-tshang*
Gar Dongdzen	*Mgar Stong-btsan*
gegö	*dge-skos*
Gelugpa	*Dge-lugs-pa*
Gendun Choekyi Nyima	*Dge-'dun chos-kyi nyi-ma*
Gen Lamrim	*Rgan Lam-rim*
gensogang	*rgas-gso-khang*
Gesar of Ling	*Gling Ge-sar*
geshe	*dge-bshes*
Geshe Sherap Gyatso	*Dge-bshes Shes-rab-rgya-mtsho*
Golok (Serta)	*'Go-log (gser-rta)*
Gomang	*Sgo-mang*
Gongmen lhari	*Gong-sman lha-ri*
Gonjo	*Go-'jo*
gönye	*sku-gnyer*
Gu (river, valley)	*Dgu (chu)*
Gyalo Thundrup	*Rgya-lo Don-grub*
Gyalse Thokme Zangpo	*Rgyal-sras thogs-med bzang-po*
Gyalwa Karmapa	*Rgyal-ba Karma-pa*
Gyandzenbum	*Rgyal-mtshan-'bum*
Gyelrong	*Rgyal-rong*
Jamtsa	*Gcam-tsha*
Jamyang Chöje	*'Jam-dbyangs chos-rje*

Jayan Günjö	*'jang-dgun-chos*
Jonang	*Jo-nang*
Kadampa	*Bka'-gdams-pa*
Kagyü	*Bka'-brgyud*
Karma Lingpa	*Karma Gling-pa*
Katsel	*Ka-tshal*
kegya gegen	*khas-khyag dge-rgan*
Kelzang Namgyel	*Bskal-bzang rnam-rgyal*
Kere Yangdzong	*Ke-re-yang-rdzong*
Keutshang	*ke'u-tshang*
Kham	*Khams*
khamtsen	*khang-mtshan*
Khandro Khachi Wangmo	*Mkha'-'gro Mkha'-spyod-dbang-mo*
Khatsel-gang	*Kha-'tshal-sgang*
Khengchugyü	*Kheng-chu-rgyud*
Khenpo Chöpe	*Mkhan-po Chos-pad*
Khenpo Jikphun	*Mkhan-po 'Jigs-med phun-tshogs*
Khenpo Namdrol	*Mkhan-po rnam-grol*
Könchok Rinchen	*Dkon-mchog-rin-chen*
Kongpo kamtsen	*Kong-po khang-mtshan*
Kusum Lingpa	*Sku-gsum-gling-pa*
Kyopa Jikten Gönpo	*Skyob-pa 'Jig-rten-mgon-po*
labdze	*la-rtse*
Labrang	*Bla-brang*
Ladakh	*La-dwags*
Laje Traknawa	*Lha-rje Brag-sna-ba*
Langdarma	*Glang dar-ma*
Langja	*Gling-rgya*
Larung	*Bla-rung*
Lhalung Bekidorje	*Lha-lung Dpal-kyi rdo-rje*
Limi	*Gli-mi*
Litang	*Li-thang*
Lodrö	*Blo-gros*
Lönbo Radzong	*Blon-po Ra-rdzong*
Longchenpa	*Klong-chen-pa*
Loseling	*Blo-gsal-gling*
lu	*klu*
Lukhang	*Klu-khang*
luröl	*glu-rol, klu-rol*
Machenbomra	*Rma-chen spom-ra*
Maṇi Temple	*Ma-ṇi lha-khang*
Meba	*Smad-pa*
Mendrogongkar	*Mal-gro-gung-dkar*
Mewa	*Rme-ba*
Migyur Palgyi Dronma	*Mi-'gyur dpal-gyi sgron-ma*
Minyak	*Mi-nyag*
Mipham Rinpoche	*Mi-pham Rin-po-che*

Nanam Dorje Dudjom	*Sna-nam Rdo-rje bdud-'joms*
Nangchen	*Nang-chen*
Nangse Könchok Tendzin Rinpoche	*Gnang-gsal Dkon-mchog-bstan-'dzin Rin-po-che*
Nechung	*Gnas-chung*
Ngagba	*Sngags-pa*
Ngayab	*Rnga-g.yab*
Nuba Namka Gyeltsen Rinpoche	*Nub-pa Nam-mkha'-rgyal-mtshan Rin-po-che*
Nyarong	*Nyag-rong*
Nyedak Rinpoche	*Gnya'-ldag Rin-po-che*
nyerba	*gnyer-pa*
Nyinda Sangye	*Nyi-zla-sangs-rgyas*
Nyingma	*Rnying-ma*
Pachung Rinpoche	*Dpa'-chung Rin-po-che*
Panchen Lama	*Paṇ-chen Bla-ma*
pechawa	*dpe-cha-ba*
Pehwa dance	*pe-hwa'i gar*
Peme Gyeltsen	*Padma'i Rgyal-mtshan*
Penor Rinpoche	*Pad-nor rin-po-che*
Phakmotrupa (Dorje Gyelpo)	*Phag-mo-gru-pa (Rdo-rje-rgyal-po)*
powa	*'pho-ba*
Ratna Lingpa	*Ratna gling-pa*
Repgong	*Re-skong, Reb-skong, Reb-gong*
Rikdzin Chödrak	*Rig-'dzin chŏs-grags*
rikshung	*rig-gzhung*
Rinchen Püntsok	*Rin-chen-phun-tshogs*
Riwang Tendzin Rinpoche	*Ri-dbang Bstan-'dzin Rin-po-che*
Ronggön	*Rong-dgon*
Saji	*Sa-dkyil*
Sakya	*Sa-skya*
Salt Cave	*Tshwa-phug*
Samye	*Bsam-yas*
Sera	*Se-ra*
Shachung	*Bya-khyung*
Shar drubchen Genden Gyatso	*Shar grub-chen Skal-ldan rgya-mtsho*
Shigatse	*Gzhis-ka-rtse*
Soktrül Rinpoche	*Srog-sprul Rin-po-che*
Songtsen Gampo	*Srong-btsan sgam-po*
Soru	*Sog-ru*
sungjö	*gsung-chos*
Tare Lhamo	*Tā-re Lha-mo*
Targyekar	*Dar-rgyal-mkhar*
Tashi Lhunpo	*.Bkra-shis-lhun-po*
Tayak-thang	*Rta-g.yag-thang*
tendrel	*rten-'brel*

Tendzin Chödrön	*Bstan-'dzin-chos-sgron*
Tengyeling	*Bstan-rgyas-gling*
Ter	*gter*
Terdak Lingpa	*Gter-bdag gling-pa*
Terdrom	*Gter-sgrom*
Terton	*gter-ston*
Terton Lerab Lingpa	*Gter-ston Las-rab gling-pa*
Tetrak-thang	*Lte-khrag-thang*
Thrakthung Dudjom Dorje	*Khrag-'thung Bdud-'joms-rdo-rje*
Thukje Nyima	*Thugs-rje nyi-ma*
torma	*gtor-ma*
tragyü	*grwa-dkyus*
tramang	*grwa-dmangs*
tratsang	*grwa-tshang*
Trijang Rimpoche	*Khri-byang Rin-po-che*
Tri Songdetsen	*Khri Srong-lde-btsan*
Trugpa tsheshi	*drug-pa tshe-bzhi*
tsamba	*rtsam-pa*
Tshongon	*Mtsho-sngon*
Tsongkhapa	*Tsong-kha-pa*
Tsünmo-tse	*Btsun-mo-rtse*
Tujechempo	*Thugs-rje-chen-po*
tulku	*sprul-sku*
umdze	*dbu-mdzad*
Urgyen Rinpoche	*U-rgyan Rin-po-che*
Uru Shei Lhakhang	*Dbu-ru zhwa'i lha-khang*
Yangleshö	*Yang-le-shod*
Yeshe Tsogyel	*Ye-shes-mtsho-rgyal*
Yuö Bumme	*G.yu-'od 'bum-me*
Zhotö Tidro	*Zho-stod ti-sgro*
zi	*gzi*

NOTES

CHAPTER 1

1. Welch 1972: 4.
2. Ibid., 2.
3. McInnis 1972: 13.
4. This was the program of the first meeting of the Chinese Political Consultative Congress. It served as a temporary constitution until the official constitution was promulgated a few years later.
5. McInnis 1972: 21.
6. Ibid., 38.
7. Welch 1972: 7.
8. McInnis 1972: 23−24.
9. New China News Agency (NCNA), 18 April 1982, cited in McInnis 1989: 7.
10. And, of course, now as refugees in South Asia and the West.
11. Richardson 1984: 1−2.
12. For a longer discussion of the boundary issue, see Goldstein 1994.
13. Many monasteries in ethnographic Tibet expected their young monks to go to one of the great monastic centers (like Drepung; see chap. 2) for at least a few years after finishing their introductory studies.
14. In modern times these monk officials neither lived in monasteries nor participated in monastic life, although they were clearly still monks in the sense that they maintained monks' vows, especially the vow of celibacy.
15. In Tibetan: *Bstan-pa chos-sbyin-gyi mnga'-bdag.*
16. Harrell 1995: 3−36.
17. They were known as *mkhan-mgron-lo-gsum.*
18. Goldstein 1989: 542.
19. For a detailed discussion of this agreement, see Goldstein 1989.

20. Goldstein 1989: 766.

21. For discussions of the nature of Tibetan peasantry, see Goldstein 1971a, 1971b, 1986.

22. The constitution of the CBA specified its goals as "to unite all the country's Buddhists so that they will participate, under the leadership of the People's Government, in movements for the welfare of the motherland and the defense of world peace; to help the People's Government fully carry out its policy of freedom of religious belief; to link up Buddhists from different parts of the country; and to exemplify the best traditions of Buddhism" (Welch 1972: 19-20).

23. International Campaign for Tibet 1990: 20.

24. The activities in Sichuan were later criticized by the central government for their failure to first create proper ground-level conditions for reform.

25. *Ta-kung Pao*, Tientsin, 24 July 1955, cited in Union Research 1968: 38.

26. McInnis 1972: 221.

27. There were a few exceptions to this such as Tashilhunpo, the monastery of the pro-Chinese Panchen Lama.

28. The Panchen Lama, in fact, was shocked by what was transpiring, particularly the decimation of monastic religion, and sent a highly critical (70,000-character) report to the central government in 1964.

29. At the heart of this was the campaign to "Destroy the Four Olds"—old ideas, old culture, old customs, and old habits.

30. Many of the more valuable ones were also taken to inner China where a good number of them ended up being sold abroad or melted down to recover their gilding.

31. A detailed narrative of the Tibetan Red Guard movement is found in Goldstein, Seibenschuh, and Tsering 1997.

32. Epstein 1983: 431.

33. In October 1982, for example, the Office of Tibet in New York City submitted a 14-page document entitled "Chinese Human Rights Abuses in Tibet: 1959-1982."

34. One Tibetan scholar has written that the exiles raised these points at the 1982 meeting, but that appears to be incorrect (Dawa Norbu 1991).

35. The new strategy was finalized, it appears, after a series of high-level meetings between key Tibetan and Western supporters in New York, Washington, D.C., and London in 1986-87. The history of these developments has not yet been well documented and details are still sparse.

CHAPTER 2

This paper is based on fieldwork conducted in Drepung Monastery in the Tibet Autonomous Region between 1989 and 1995. Prior to the official project's beginning, informal visits were made over several years. The research project focused both on reconstructing Drepung's socioeconomic organization in the traditional society and on the monastery's revival after 1978. It was conducted as part of a general research agreement between Case Western Reserve University's Center for Research on Tibet and the Lhasa-based Tibet Academy of Social Sciences. It involved extensive interviews with Drepung monks and officials. The project was sponsored by grants from the Committee on Scholarly Communication with China and the National Endowment for the Humanities.

1. Some Tibetan Buddhist subsects such as the Nyingma allow monks to marry in the sense that they permit them to take the *dge-bsnyen* or *sngags-sdom* vows that do not prohibit marriage.

2. *Beijing Review*, 26 August 1985 and 26 October–1 November 1987, 23–26; International Campaign for Tibet 1996: 25; LAWASIA 1991: 12. It should be noted that there are no available records to document such numbers precisely, so these figures are really estimates. Moreover, these figures would be higher if monks and monasteries in what is now Sichuan, Gansu, and Qinghai were included.

3. Tambiah 1976: 266–67.

4. Goldstein 1964.

5. Goldstein 1989, 1990a; Shakabpa 1967: 241; Richardson 1984: 169–73.

6. The term "old society" is used in China to convey the era before the implementation of socialist reforms. The term "new society" refers to postreform society. These terms are used here with no pejorative meaning.

7. Three other named "colleges" no longer had monks, i.e., they were defunct but continued to have abbots.

8. This does not imply that there was no change for we have already seen that three of Drepung's colleges had become defunct.

9. There were several levels of geshe, the gap between the highest and lowest being almost as much as that between scholar monks and common monks.

10. Some monks from other Tibetan Buddhist sects and from Bon monasteries also occasionally enrolled in these great monasteries.

11. Epstein 1983: 421.

12. Telegram from the Central Committee of the CCP, 19 May 1952. Emphasis added.

13. Many ethnic Tibetan areas outside of political Tibet, e.g., in Sichuan, Qinghai, Gansu, and Yunnan provinces, had experienced these changes a few years earlier.

14. A distinction was made between monasteries involved and not involved in the uprising. Those not involved, such as the Panchen Lama's Tashilhunpo Monastery, received compensation payments for the confiscation of their land. Tashilhunpo, e.g., received about 9 million yuan (Epstein 1983: 417).

15. Epstein 1983: 421.

16. The DMC is defined as follows: "Every monastery has its own democratic administrative committee (or group) composed of a director, one or several deputy directors and several committee members. The committee, elected by all the monks in the monastery on the basis of full consultation, is responsible for overseeing the monastery's Buddhist activities, its repair and upkeep, selecting administrative personnel and any work that goes on. The Committee receives guidance and support from relevant government departments in charge of religious affairs, and keeps them informed of any problems in implementing state policies" (Jing Wei 1989: 61).

17. Dorje, interview. Pseudonyms are used throughout the chapter for interviewees who are still alive because of the political sensitivity of this topic.

18. Sonam, interview.

19. Epstein 1983: 422.

20. Ibid.

21. Ibid., 430; Tsultrim 1979.

22. Most of these first arrivals were former monks who had just been released from labor camps. In accordance with Chinese law, such released prisoners were allowed to return to their original place of residence if they wanted, which these monks specified was Drepung.

23. Pema, interview.

24. Wangjung, interview.

25. New China News Agency, (NCNA), 18 April 1982, cited in McInnis 1989: 7. Although many critics of the PRC reject the validity of prohibiting a political voice for religious institutions, it should be noted that when religious freedom is examined cross-nationally, many nations that profess adherence to religious freedom actually maintain some restrictions. Germany's restrictions and persecution of the Church of Scientology are a prominent example of this in the West. The United States also has restricted religious freedom. It bans the use of poisonous snakes in the services of fundamentalist Christians in West Virginia as well as polygamy among Mormons. It also has, at various times, banned the use of peyote in Native American religions, forced Christian Scientists to use hospitals, and compelled the Amish to send their children to school. This is not offered as a justification of China's mix of restrictions; it is offered rather as a caveat that claims of religious freedom often include restrictions that the country involved deems eminently reasonable.

26. Goldstein 1990b: 141; Goldstein 1995: 26–27; Wang Yao 1994: 285–89.

27. Summary of World Broadcasts, 30 May 1980.

28. Because the staple food of monks was tsamba mixed with tea, the provision of tea at prayer chanting sessions allowed monks to bring their tsamba to the prayer assembly and eat a meal, thereby avoiding the costly expense of buying fuel to make their own tea.

29. The Lhasa Municipality's Religious Affairs Bureau (*chos-don-jus*) is the political entity that is administratively immediately above Drepung.

30. Sonam Tashi, interview.

31. The three days set aside each month for assemblies were the eighth, fifteenth, and thirtieth (of the Tibetan lunar calendar). The success of the assemblies prompted an addition of two more sessions on the tenth and twenty-fifth.

32. Some contemporary writers on religion in Tibet such as Schwartz (1994b: 63) have confused the presence in Drepung of both official and unofficial monks with the presence of monks with and without *them tho* (permanent residence). Every citizen in China has an official place of residence (normally his or her place of birth) that tied individuals to their home areas until the reforms of the 1980s. At this time, individuals became free to travel and work in other areas. However, legally changing one's them tho was and is very difficult, so most individuals who migrate to work continue to have their permanent residence as their home village. Consequently, with regard to Drepung, a boy monk moving from a village to the monastery remains an official resident of his village unless the government agrees to change his residency to Drepung when he is accepted as an official member of the community. The government initially did this but since the mid-1980s has generally refused. Thus many of the younger (newer) official monks do not have Drepung as their permanent residency and are not eligible for some of the small subsidies residents receive from the state as well as retirement benefits later in life. The presence or absence of them tho, therefore, is an important issue for the monks because it differentiates two types of official monks, not official versus unofficial monks. Further complicating the issue of who belongs to Drepung are a number of individuals who are not monks but have their permanent residence as Drepung. These individuals are the former monks who married in the 1960s and 1970s and remained in the monastery. They (with their families whose residency is also Drepung) now

live in an area located below Drepung where they farm land owned by the monastery. However, despite their permanent residence being Drepung, they are not part of the monastic community and do not receive a share of any distributions such as alms.

33. Interestingly, in doing this the monastery ignored the government rule prohibiting recruitment of monks under the age of 18. Tibetan monks and laymen believe, as indicated above, that recruiting monks as children/youths is critical to producing good monks. So ingrained is this attitude in Tibetan society that the Religious Affairs Bureau of Lhasa and the TAR agreed to turn a blind eye to the age of these new enrollees. Drepung today is replete with young monks in the under-18 age bracket.

34. Gendün Nyima, interview.

35. Gendün Nyima, interview.

36. Although one of the persistent complaints aired in the exile community and among their Western supporters has been that full-time study is not possible in monasteries like Drepung, my fieldwork did not find supporting evidence for this assertion. As will be shown below, hundreds of Drepung monks are engaged in full-time study (and funded to do so) and do not work at the monastery's various enterprises.

37. In 1993, the exchange rate was 5.6 yuan to the U.S. dollar.

38. Tibet Statistical Bureau 1993: 129.

39. During the Cultural Revolution, Drepung monks planted roughly 10,000 apple trees just below the monastery. This huge orchard now holds about 8,500 apple trees that are maintained by monks who also sell the apples at the monastery and in Lhasa. Economic data derive from interviews with monastic officials and monastery accounting records.

40. Drepung also owns about 80 mu of farmland (1 mu = 0.06 hectare) below the monastery which it leases to a group of about 30 households of its married former monks at token rates.

41. Almost all of this came from the fees paid by foreign visitors.

42. Drepung had several other substantial sources of income that were not used to support the monks. The first of these was the monastery's million-yuan fund, which it keeps in a bank account drawing interest. It was obtained in 1982 when the state agreed to pay Drepung 800,000 yuan in compensation for the losses it experienced during the 1959–76 era. Payment of this was completed in 1988, and with interest, has now grown to 1 million yuan. It is used only occasionally for repairs and renovation, so is not relevant to the monk's salary issue. A second source of income comes from the small donations that the thousands of pilgrims leave in each of the monastery's shrine rooms they visit. Estimates put this at 250,000 yuan for 1993. This money is used only for monastic renovations and repairs.

43. Net income is the gross income mentioned above minus expenses and a 3% contingency amount that is set aside.

44. For the first six months of 1993 this value was 0.75 yuan; for the second six-month period of 1993, 0.9 yuan.

45. They were actually paid 4.5 yuan a day for the first six months and 5 yuan a day for the second six months.

46. Another group of monks who did not earn work points but were partially supported by the monastery were the shrine room caretakers. They, like the elderly monks, received a salary from the government that was far too low (50 yuan per month), so the monastery paid them a supplementary wage out of its income. It should also be noted that the members of the DMC also did not receive work points; their salary (roughly 140–150 yuan per month) came from the government.

47. This is an abbreviation of *chos-lugs-kyi rig-pa'i gzhungs-lugs.*

48. Drepung's DMC has to ask the RAB for permission to hold a teaching for a specified number of days. When asked why they only hold two of these a year, a leader of the DMC explained, "It would be hard for us to organize more than two a year. First, Gen Lamrim is old, and second, the government is worried about these teachings interfering with the work of farmers and nomads and the work of the monastery. Consequently, the best times of the year to hold these are in spring [before planting] and in fall [after harvests and shearing]. We haven't had any [political] disturbances at these teachings so the RAB gives permission easily" (Tashi, interview).

49. Gen Lamrim also received a substantial amount of alms in the form of foodstuffs, which, like the cash, he distributed to the other Drepung monks. In 1992 this yielded for *each* monk approximately 12 bricks of tea, 15 jin (16.5 lb) of butter and 15 jin (16.5 lb) of rice and flour.

50. In 1993 they received 636 yuan annually in government welfare and monastery supplementary funds, plus 973 yuan in alms distributions.

51. Tibet Statistical Bureau 1993: 48.

52. It was not unusual, moreover, for a single guardian monk to have two or three young wards.

53. A recent book on Tibet levels the serious charge that the Chinese government is obstructing the traditional relationship between the people/community and the monastery by prohibiting donations from laymen to monks, for example: "Particular emphasis is placed on curtailing voluntary contributions to religious institutions" (Schwartz 1994b: 68). Although many government officials believe the money laymen donate to monks is a waste of valuable economic resources and should be curtailed, and although they often express this in speeches, actual government policy, as indicated above, is not doing that. Any Tibetan can go to the office of the rikshung on the day of a collective prayer session and give the rikshung officials money (alms) for the monks which is then distributed that same day. I have done that on a number of occasions myself. Moreover, large patrons are permitted to help the rikshung officials physically distribute the money to the seated monks at the prayer sessions and the gegö official reads the names of patrons before the full monk assembly as traditionally occurred in the old society.

54. Goldstein 1990a, 1995; Dawa Norbu 1991.

55. A version of this became an amendment to the State Department Authorization Bill that was signed by President Ronald Reagan in December 1987.

56. Goldstein 1995.

57. After arriving in India in 1959-60, Tibet's refugee monks gradually rebuilt their monasteries there and began their own revival of monastic traditions. Drepung's monks have reestablished themselves in two refugee settlements in South India. In the mid-1980s a number of monks from Tibet were able to visit relatives in India and once there, their sister monastery. At the same time, Tibetan monks and lamas from India visited their home areas in Tibet. Thus the hope that this would become regularized was not far-fetched at that time.

58. The DMC in 1995 consisted of 15 committee members, 14 of whom were Drepung monks and 1 of whom was a former Drepung monk who has remained associated with the monastery since 1959. Of these members, one is considered the chairman, the Senior Trurin (*kru'u-rin*) and four are Junior Trurin. The other ten function as ordinary members (*uyon; u-yon*). An election of sorts to fill these posts took place in 1985, but subsequent ap-

pointments were made by the existing DMC members with the approval of the government. Although DMC leaders after 1959 were all former monks with strong leftist views, today's leaders are very different. Three of the five trurin are former "class enemies" (*trerim; gral-rim*) who themselves were persecuted after 1959, and one is a new monk who entered in 1982. Moreover, all are monks with vows. The fifth leader is the former monk who was appointed initially in 1959. He is the only leader left from the category "poor monk."

59. Schwartz 1994b.

60. Young monks were shown the letters of the Tibetan alphabet on cards and that way learned to identify, pronounce, and ultimately read.

61. Tashi, interview.

62. Sera Monastery in Lhasa has also created a school for its unofficial monks.

63. In the old society, monks from all over the Tibetan Buddhist world, including China, Mongolia, and India, were accepted in Drepung. In the current era, government law stipulates that only permanent residents of the Tibet Autonomous Region may become official Drepung monks. However, the ancient tradition of monks from smaller monasteries in Qinghai and elsewhere coming to Lhasa's monastic centers for advanced theological study has reemerged, and the monastery and government have worked out a compromise wherein these monks are permitted to stay in Drepung and study in the dharma grove program, although they are not official Drepung monks and do not receive salary. They also cannot attend the prayer chanting assemblies or receive alms designated for Drepung monks. Drepung, however, assists them by allowing them to live there rent-free.

64. Scholar monks from the main monastic seats in Central Tibet traditionally went to Jayan (*jangs*), a monastery located about 40 kilometers southwest of Lhasa, for a month in December to engage in theological debate. This was important because it was the only opportunity scholar monks in the old society got to test their skills against monks outside of their college. Sera Monastery first sent its scholar monks there for several weeks in 1993 on its own, and Drepung's scholar monks joined them in 1994. In 1995 government permission was sought and received to make this event official.

65. This section was written in 1997 and appended to the manuscript after it was accepted for publication. It is based on interviews in Drepung and Lhasa and materials and assessments provided by the Tibet Information Network in London.

66. In Tibetan, *rgyal-gces ring-lugs kyi slob-gso*.

67. There has been a somewhat parallel campaign against the leaders of the underground Catholic church, i.e., those Catholics who have refused to join the official Catholic organization set up by the government (the Catholic Patriotic Association).

68. In Tibetan, *las-don ru-khag*.

69. Although this campaign had ended in Drepung by the end of 1996, it was just beginning in many smaller monasteries in 1997.

70. Tibet Information Network, document dated 15 July 1996 and issued by the work team and the Sera Democratic Management Committee; Tib doc. Ref. 21 (VG).

71. More, it is said, were ready to leave the monastery but changed their minds when older monks persuasively argued that the monastery needed them for its future and that in a short time the work team would be gone and their "agreeing" would be meaningless.

72. Anonymous interviews.

73. Interestingly, a tacit decision was made also not to enforce the prohibition of Dalai Lama photographs in the realm of the monks' private quarters, and six months after the campaign I encountered his photographs on altars in the monks' apartments.

74. If, on the other hand, one focuses on the total number of both official and unofficial monks present at the start of the campaign, Drepung's size has decreased by about 20 percent.

75. Another concession to the monks concerned the rights of these monks from outside the TAR. In the past these monks could not attend prayer sessions or receive alms. Now this restriction was moderated and they are permitted to attend prayer sessions if a donor specifically requests this, and can receive 10 percent of the alms given the official monks.

76. It is not clear, however, whether the government will be able to prevent the reemergence of a class of "waiting" monks. Six months after the work team left the monastery, a number of the underage monks who had been sent home had returned to live with their guardian monks. They generally claimed they were unable to enroll in local schools so wanted exemptions to live in Drepung. The new Management Committee says it will send them home again, but it may well be easier for them to make more exceptions.

77. It is headed by a Senior Trurin (president) and seven Junior Trurin, three of whom are lay officials (of Tibetan ethnicity). A new house was built in the monastery this year to accommodate these lay cadres. Two of the nine other members (*uyön*) of the administrative committee are also lay cadres.

78. In Sera Monastery the political reorganization was somewhat different: the new Management Committee consists only of monks, but this is balanced by a second administrative committee consisting entirely of lay officials.

79. A second, subordinate, committee called the Religious Affairs committee (*chos-don u-yon lhan-khang*) was also established to oversee strictly religious issues. It consists of the abbot, the prayer leader (umdze), the disciplinary office (gegö), the kitchen head (chabri), and two stewards (nyerba).

80. Another important change concerned the settlement of a long-standing dispute between Drepung and a group of ex-monk families living below the monastery on farmland Drepung owns. Since the official residence status (them-tho) of these ex-monks was Drepung, the monastery could not take back control of this land, and legally Drepung consisted of monks and nonmonks. The work team rectified this situation by dividing the land equally between the ex-monk families and the monastery. At the same time, it arranged for the residence status of the ex-monks to be shifted to a village at the foot of Drepung, thus finally separating these laymen administratively from the monastery. This change has allowed Drepung to increase its income since it has leased its share—26.4 mu of farmland— to Chinese vegetable farmers for three years at a fee of 400¥/mu this year (with a 50¥ increase in rent each of the following years). This represents a 400 percent increase in the monastery's yield from this land.

81. Other changes sparked by the campaign included starting a modern medicine clinic for the monks by arranging for two monks to obtain training at one of Lhasa's hospitals for one year and by helping the monastery to obtain a grant of 20,000¥ to purchase modern medicines. The monastery is also in the process of building a solar-powered bathhouse for the monks. The government also gave the monastery a set of movie projection equipment and a new policy was established wherein a movie will be shown each Sunday for the monks.

82. The recent decision of the U.S. secretary of state to appoint a special officer for Tibet, for example, was interpreted by many Tibetans in Lhasa as important evidence that the United States is genuinely interested in supporting the Dalai Lama and pressuring

China to change its policies toward Tibet. By making opposition to China seem less futile, this could well encourage some Drepung monks to continue political dissidence.

CHAPTER 3

I would like to express my deep gratitude to the Committee on Scholarly Communication with China for their funding and support of my research in eastern Tibet from 1990 to 1992, without which much of my present research would have been either impossible or considerably impoverished. I would also like to thank my two host institutions in the PRC—the Sichuan Research Institute of Nationalities and the Tibetan Academy of Social Sciences—as well as all the individuals who aided me so generously during my stay. Finally, I am indebted to the editors of this volume, Melvyn Goldstein and Matthew Kapstein, for their extensive and insightful comments on various drafts of the present chapter.

1. A very prominent Tibetan mythic history of the dynastic period presents the Tibetan landscape as a vast supine demoness, who is pinned down and controlled through a network of Buddhist temples. See Gyatso 1987.

2. The historical founder of Buddhism, Śākyamuni, was from an early period in India discussed in terms of two Bodies: his physical presence, or form bodies (*gzugs sku, rūpakāya*), and the corpus of his teachings, or teaching bodies (*chos sku, dharmakāya*). In this chapter, I play off this ancient Buddhist emphasis on the Buddha's many bodies.

3. Although there was systematic government looting of Tibetan art earlier, these days it is often Tibetans themselves who are involved.

4. The movements involved in such excavations all maintained deeply Buddhist traditions but were divided among those who maintained standard Buddhist historical discourses (known as the Nyingma [*rnying ma*]) and those who maintained idiosyncratically Tibetocentric traditions (known as the Bonpo) that subsumed orthodox Buddhist history into a quite different account of origins and lineages.

5. See Thondup 1986 for an excellent survey of the treasure tradition in Tibet; Gyatso 1996 provides a succinct overview of the textual side of these treasures. In the standard presentation discussed by Thondup, the dynastic period concealment of these treasures was understood to have taken place via placing these texts within the Tibetan earth as well as within the transmigrating subtle bodies of Tibetans of the time. By "subtle bodies" I refer to the widespread late Indian Buddhist tantric notion that there is a more fundamental subtle body of energy currents within the ordinary physical body. By "physically" I refer to concealment that seems to have been a straightforward burial of items; "mystically" refers to the paranormal concealment of texts within solid rock, consciousness, and so on.

6. See Kunsang 1993 for a translation of an important early biography of Padmasambhava.

7. The ecumenical, or "non-partisan," movement originated in eastern Tibet in part as a reaction to the dominance of the Geluk (*dge lugs*) regime nominally headed by the Dalai Lama line of incarnations in Central Tibet. Intellectual and social in nature, it involved all the major traditions of Tibetan religion with the significant general exception of the Geluk. Particularly interesting for the present context is the fact that the Great Perfection (*rdzogs chen*) tantric tradition in many ways formed the religious heart of the movement. The Great

Perfection tradition is renowned for its strong deconstructive rhetoric undercutting analytical thought and its equally consistent positive celebration of the primordial enlightened nature of all life. It presents itself rhetorically as the "peak" of all Buddhist teachings which embraces all of them as partial truths. See Samuel 1993: 533–43 for a brief overview of the ecumenical movement and the Great Perfection's role.

8. At least one contemporary Bon scholar has explicitly identified the twentieth-century concealment of texts as a major "Treasure concealment" (Gyatso 1996: 152). Also, in an interview with the Dalai Lama printed in the 6 March 1996 edition of the *New York Times* international edition, he refers to the past forty years as "our own dark period."

9. See Hanna 1994 for an interesting eyewitness report of a contemporary revelation in Tibet by a famous female Bonpo Terton whom I refer to below.

10. The individual in question is Dondrub Gyel (*Don grub rgyal*), whose story was repeated to me on more than one occasion by lay Tibetan scholars in Sichuan. All made a point of directly linking his death to the current domination of Tibetan cultural areas by Han Chinese (particularly the population transfer and dominance of Chinese language in education), which they claimed was made explicit in the suicide note. I have no access to the note and thus cannot verify its contents, although the rumors attest to their own social reality. See Stoddard 1994 for an interesting account of his life and death. She mentions (p. 826) the famous note or "testament" (*bka' chems*) but appears also to have not had direct access to its contents; she adds an unhappy love life and criticism of Tibetan traditional attitudes (p. 827) to his list of woes (in the more generalized rumors I heard, there was an exclusive focus on political problems stemming from Chinese control). See Don grub rgyal 1994 for a collection of his writings, including a biographical essay by Padma 'bum.

11. While certainly it is true that traditionally at some large monasteries serious academic study was limited to a fairly select portion of the resident population, religious education in Tibet includes ritual competence, contemplative instruction and practice, and general grounding in the principles of the Buddhist worldview, in addition to rigorous scholarship. Although the Western misconception that monasteries were exclusively havens of dedicated contemplation and scholarship needs to be rectified, we must not ignore that contemplative practice and intellectual education were deeply grounded in many parts of Tibet. During research in Tibet, I observed widespread interest in and practice of both dimensions, such that the lack of competent teachers and institutions was viscerally experienced and repeatedly commented on. While one may argue that recent plights have generated renewed interest that was not present prior to 1950, I think the pre-1950 hagiographic literature clearly attests to both the mundane concerns of many monks and a more limited yet still widespread serious involvement in Buddhist study and practice.

12. I have in mind here such eminent figures as Dudjom Rinpoche, Dingo Khyentse Rinpoche, Urgyen Tulku, and Penor Rinpoche.

13. Most of the ensuing biographical details are drawn from a biography of Khenpo Jikphun written by Tshul khrims blo gros, Bsod dar rgyas, and Bstan 'dzin rgya mtsho. The work, entitled *Snyigs dus bstan pa'i gsal byed gcig pu chos rje dam pa yid bzhin nor bu 'jigs med phun tshogs 'byung gnas dpal bzang po'i rnam thar bsdus pa dad pa'i gsos sman*, was published locally in the late 1980s in modern book format. I have translated the work in its entirety at the authors' request and may publish it in some limited fashion in the near future. I would like to thank Slob bzang tshe ring and Bstan 'dzin rgya mtsho for their extensive help in translating the biography, as well as Khenpo Jikphun himself for helpful elaborations.

14. The word *bardo* literally means "intermediate state" and is used in the famous *Tibetan Book of the Dead* to refer to the state of ordinarily chaotic visions said to confront someone between death and rebirth. See Freemantle 1987.

15. See below for an account of how King Gesar is woven into his Ter activities.

16. See Kapstein 1992: 86, 88 for his suggestion that Arthurian legends are an apt analogue for understanding the elaborate mythic romance that developed in Tibet around the seventh-century Tibetan emperor Songtsen Gampo (*Srong btsan sgam po;* d. 649 c.e.).

17. Zi (*gzi*) stones are polished beads of varying sizes with highly distinctive black and white stripes and circles known as "eyes" (*mig*). Genuine ones discovered from the ground can be exceedingly expensive as they are highly prized as ornaments and potent talismans. Dorje and Kapstein (1991: 38) identify them as "agate." See Nebesky-Wojkowitz 1956: 505–7 for a detailed discussion, including various legends of their origins.

18. This well known seven-line prayer runs as follow:

> Hūṃ!
> On the pistil-stem of a lotus
> In the northwest border land of Oḍḍiyāna,
> Is the one renowned as Lotus Born (Padma-sambhava)
> Who has attained the supreme amazing spiritual attainment
> And is surrounded by a retinue of many Ḍākiṇis—
> I pray that you come to grant blessings
> To me who practices in your wake!
> Guru Padma Siddhi Hūṃ!

19. Ḍākiṇī refers to female tantric spirits who are, broadly speaking, understood to be of two types: impure ones termed "flesh-eating" (*sha za*) and pure ones termed "gnostic" (*ye shes*). The latter are particularly important as visionary agents in the Ter cult.

20. Dreyfus 1994: 210–12.

21. Ibid.; Schwartz 1994a: 227–29.

22. See Dreyfus 1994 on the importance of certain shared paradigmatic memories that have historically shaped a sense of imagined community among all Tibetans which was not confined to political boundaries. I agree with Dreyfus (p. 216) that there is a certain continuity with this "protonationalism" and modern Tibetan nationalism. I would argue further that it is precisely such a continuity that accounts in part for the dynamic success of Khenpo Jikphun's peculiarly Tibetan revival of the Ter cult.

23. See Thondup 1986: 68.

24. Literally, "Blood Drinker Vajra Demon Destroyer" (*Khrag thung bdud 'jom rdo rje*), he was also known by the name *Lcags khung sge'u gter.* He is said to have been reborn as Dudjom Rinpoche, a famous Nyingma lama active in Europe and America until his death in 1987.

25. This is the traditional fourfold classification of an enlightened figure's activities: pacifying, enriching, magnetizing, and subjugating (*zhi rgyas dbang drag*).

26. Another prophecy indicated that Khenpo could preside over the academy for thirteen years without obstacles; thus when he decided in 1993 to continue for another six years, it was necessary to perform a complex series of rituals.

27. During my stay there were no special sites for doing retreats apart from personal residences. Most monks bring their food—meat, butter, roasted barley flour, and so forth—in large quantities from home; others (the Chinese in particular) must purchase such from the other monks at varying prices. There are also periodic trips by vegetable

sellers in pickup trucks, mainly peddling Chinese cabbage and onions; in 1991 a small private general store had just opened at the monastery, and in 1996 I heard from a friend at the institute who was traveling through India that material conditions had improved quite a bit since my visit. A few residents have a younger monk as servant, often a relative, a childhood friend, or someone for whom they are providing housing; most live by themselves, but a few live with relatives. Each residential unit pays a set price for electricity, which is piped in from a water-powered generator created specifically for the school with expenses borne by the Serta county government. Fuel for cooking and heat mostly comes from yak dung, partially brought from home and partially purchased at the monastery. In general the academy and nunnery are thus financially self-sufficient and do not rely on government grants, which enables them to preserve their independence and integrity. All their financial resources derive from private donations, from which Khenpo Jikphun pays monks a sustenance allowance of variable amount (food, clothes, money) per month if they specifically ask for help, or if he comes to know of their difficult financial position. Some benefactors also make general contributions that are divided equally among all the monks and nuns.

28. The labor was done by the monks and nuns, supplemented by donated labor by parents as well as a small number of paid Chinese laborers. The stones and other materials were largely donated, though a small amount had to be paid for the trucks bringing timber in. Much of the donated labor in this instance came from the city of Serpa (*Gser pa*) 100 miles to the east (famous for its stonework). Some were relatives of monks while others just wanted to contribute to the monastery; altogether about 300 people worked off and on for two months.

29. This was reported to me in the summer of 1996 by one of his disciples traveling outside Tibet, though I have been unable to confirm this at the time of writing.

30. While masked dances are only done on special occasions, they are popular events that only monasteries are allowed to perform under contemporary political guidelines. Thus it was repeatedly mentioned to me by residents as being one of the few things they could not do as the institute was not considered a monastery, the point being that this was not considered a particularly significant loss.

31. The entire Tibetan Autonomous Region is locally referred to as "Lhasa," even areas formerly considered part of Kham, or eastern Tibet.

32. See below for a discussion of the veracity of such a number.

33. The main practices of the Great Perfection involve a technique-free contemplation of self-awareness called "breakthrough" (*khregs chod*) and contemplation of a spontaneous flow of light imagery called "direct transcendence" (*thod rgal*).

34. The two translators are Södargye (*Bsod dar rgyas*) and Tshultrim Lodrö (*Tshul khrims blo gros*).

35. Of course the realities of such relationships are difficult to judge, but certainly in the gossip circuits there is an intense interest in the supposed quarrels and sexual infidelities that seem to be linked to so many Tertons' relationships to their sexual partners.

36. See Thondup 1986: 82–84 for a discussion of the importance of consorts in the recovery of Ter.

37. While it is said Khenpo had revealed Ter from childhood, the karmic momentum fueling these revelations was disrupted when he refused to take the aforementioned woman as his destined consort. Thus he was subsequently unable to reveal "earth treasures" until much later during a trip to the Lhangdrak power-mountain in Nyarong. Most of his trea-

sures are understood to have been concealed by Guru Padmasambhava some twelve hundred years ago in dynastic Tibet, who transmitted his wisdom to certain advanced disciples in latent forms designed to become manifest in their future rebirths when most needed. Having arranged that wisdom in the symbolic form of written texts, he concealed them in special "adamantine" rocks, sacred lakes, inviolable containers, and so forth, sealing them with special prayers. The destined revealer was endowed with a special karmic momentum enabling him or her to reveal those texts and objects at the appropriate time when their contents could function to renew and revitalize the teachings. In general it is said that without the visionary relying on actual sexual yoga with his destined consort to intensify and enhance his energy, it is difficult to extract these treasures, which accounts for Khenpo's prolonged dry spell after refusing his destined consort. When he subsequently began to uncover treasures once again, his lack of a consort resulted in his excavated statues of Padmasambhava lacking their traditional hand-held tridents, which are symbolically understood as signifying the consort.

38. Longchenpa (1308–63) and Mipham (1846–1912) are arguably the two most prominent postdynastic figures in contemporary Nyingma circles.

39. See Schwartz 1994a: esp. pp. 730–34.

40. Schwartz 1994b: 22, 226; also Schwartz 1994a.

41. The five corruptions relate to life span, emotional distortions, sentient beings, time, and outlook.

42. The three jewels are the traditional objects of refuge for Buddhists: the teacher (*Buddha*), the teachings (*dharma*), and the community (*saṃgha*).

43. This is verse 125 of the sixth chapter of Śāntideva's famous *A Guide of the Bodhisattva's Way of Life*. I have used Batchelor's 1979 translation.

44. Although, as discussed above, Khenpo Jikphun has decided against casting his community as a formal monastery, in terms of behavioral guidelines, curriculum, and residents it is for all intents and purposes a deeply monastic institution.

45. The character of Ngakpa lineages in eastern Tibet and their relationships to celibate religious institutions have been barely researched. For interesting comments on the subject in western Tibet, see Aziz 1978: 51–56.

46. Married "monks" (*grwa-pa*) have been discussed at length by Aziz 1978: 76–94 in western Tibet under the rubric *Ser khyim*, but the extent and nature of such a phenomenon in eastern Tibet is not clear to me. Certainly I have met such individuals who informed me that their clerical dress and married status was a custom in their locale, but I have also heard criticisms of such behavior which attributes it to more recent origins, such as the disruptions of the Cultural Revolution conjoined with attempts by unemployed youths to eke out a living based on performing rituals and/or begging under a clerical guise. The extent of traditional versus recent origins is thus at present unclear.

47. Schwartz 1994a: 730; Schwartz 1994b: 22. Also it should be noted that others (Samuel 1993 in particular) have argued that there is a much more ancient pattern of relative "rationalization" and "clericalization" of religion operative in Central Tibet that involved a greater stress on hierarchically governed ethical systems; Samuel argues this was in large part due to the centralization of the Lhasa-based polity with its religious stress on large monastic institutions. Based on my own experience in various parts of contemporary Central Tibet, it is clear that this highlighting of ethical and political dimensions only extends so far and in no way has elided the so-called magical element, or the individual and collective importance of tantric practices among lay and monastic populations.

48. Davidson 1994 made an excellent analysis of the initial emergence of this renaissance.

49. See Samuel 1993: 217-22, 454, 571-72.

50. See Davidson 1990 for a discussion of Indian Buddhist models and Gyatso 1993 for a discussion of the use of Ter in Tibet for legitimation.

51. This notion of dual concealment within individuals' bodies and within the actual earth, rocks, and water of Tibet itself is discussed below.

52. I argue this at length in Germano 1994 and forthcoming; also see Kapstein 1992; Gyatso 1993; Davidson 1994 for related comments. Kapstein 1989 directly addresses the various Tibetan reactions to Ter, including polemical literature.

53. As noted in Gyatso 1996: 152, there was a historical transition from simple digging up of concealed objects to a complex "dependent upon visionary inspirations, the memory of past lives, and especially the compulsion exerted by the prophecy." However, it should be stressed that there continued to be a distinction made between physical recoveries and simple psychic recollections, though both were equally bound up in this complex of reincarnation and vision.

54. Gyatso 1996: 154 stresses the "Tibetan ground or Tibetan mind," but Gyatso 1986: 16 says the treasure site can be called "the adamantine body," a term for the subtle body. Given the importance tantric Buddhism places on the body, its paradigm of the body being the locus of Buddha-nature and gnosis, the visceral nature of Tertons' discoveries, and my own use of the trope of the body here, I have used "body" instead of "mind" in this context.

55. Davidson 1994 and Gyatso 1993 both have excellent discussions of the functions of Ter, to which I am indebted.

56. See Germano 1994 for a more detailed presentation of this argument.

57. This is a technical term in the treasure cult that most commonly refers to smoothly polished medium-sized stones from which the treasure is then extracted. See the photos included herein for examples; also see Thondup 1986: 84 for a brief overview of their significance.

58. *Gnas nang;* also referred to as *Bsam gtan chos 'khor gling.* The former name derives from the monastery's foundation on a site said to be a special locus sacred to all three of the main bodhisattvas: Mañjuśrī, Avalokiteśvara, and Vajrapāṇi.

59. This is a reference to the pure land of Padmasambhava himself.

60. Matiratna is given as a sixteenth-century Terton in Thondup 1986: 194.

61. See Matthew Kapstein's chapter in the present volume for an extended treatment of the more famous Tidro, which reveals interesting interpenetrations between our two accounts. The particulars of Khenpo's prophetic exegesis are that "the emanation of a small boy" referred to himself while "the hidden gorge" indicated the site was surrounded with forest.

62. See Makley 1994. Though the relevance of gendered practices here requires further thought that lies outside the parameters of my present inquiry, I would emphasize Khenpo's key role in the revival of Buddhist nunneries in eastern Tibet in addition to his role with male celibate institutions.

63. See Makley 1994: 79.

64. For example, the role of tightly knit traditional neighborhoods in the Lhasa demonstrations comes to mind, as well as the seemingly systematic Chinese efforts to break up these neighborhoods as central secular cauldrons of Tibetan identity and mutual alliance networks. The strong Tibetan sense of "home" (*nang*) as an inner sanctum (*sbug*), with

boundaries controlled by the family, has played a major role in preserving distinctively Tibetan spaces from the increasingly Chinese-reshaped public spaces: there is a tangible sensation one feels on being invited across the threshold of a Tibetan home into its private interiors (*sbug*), so unlike most contemporary American residences. In addition, linked domestic spaces in kinship networks provides a series of such Tibetan enclaves that provide a haven of Tibetanness that crisscrosses the wider contested public spaces they are situated within, and which I believe is a very visceral experience for contemporary Tibetans. This is the significance of not only the government breakup of traditional neighborhoods but also the recent explosion of private residence construction by Tibetans in Lhasa.

65. See Huber 1994b for an excellent analysis of how a Buddhist-centric analysis of Tibetan pilgrimage practices can distort our understanding of their lived reality on the ground.

66. His renown also derives from factors discussed previously: his personal charisma has been reinforced by intellectual brilliance and ecumenical learning; his religious center is one of the largest in Tibet, despite its not being founded on a preexisting institution; he has emphasized strict monastic discipline despite the traditional association of the Terton with noncelibate lifestyles; and he has created rigorous academic programs that rival those in the major refugee monasteries.

67. Samye Monastery is one of the most famous religious sites in Tibet, since it was the first Buddhist monastery constructed in Tibet at the height of the Tibetan empire. It holds particularly important associations for the Nyingma tradition, since it is said Padmasambhava played a key role in taming the demonic forces that initially prevented the monastery's construction.

68. This woman is none other than the Tendzin Chödrön discussed in Matthew Kapstein's chapter as a pivotal figure in the revival of the community of nuns at Drigung.

69. See Huber 1994b for a discussion of the significance of sacred places in Tibet being termed "residences" (*gnas*).

70. See Huber 1994b: 36–45.

71. The following account has been saved from a number of inaccuracies, as well as enhanced with detail, because Raoul Birnbaum graciously shared with me his wealth of knowledge concerning the famous Wutai Mountains. Any remaining errors no doubt are due to my own inadequate recording of his suggested revisions and additions. When Buddhists refer to the Wutai Mountains, they have in mind a central area 150 miles in extent that includes five famous flat-topped peaks, or terraces, that are spoken of as directional (east, north, south, west, and central) but in fact form a crescent-shaped circle (I have translated it as "five peaks" in accordance with the Tibetan [*ri bo rtse lnga*]). Thus the area enclosed by these terraces, as well as the terraces themselves, are considered to be the special residence of Mañjuśrī on Earth, though the boundaries are somewhat loosely defined.

Mañjuśrī is the bodhisattva of wisdom and hence closely associated with scholarship, writing, and monasteries. A statue of him constantly accompanies Khenpo, while his main contemplative cycle is centered around the visualized figure of Mañjuśrī. In addition, Khenpo's strong ecumenical orientation has manifested in his consistently teaching from the corpuses of three masters widely considered to be the three main incarnations of Mañjuśrī in Tibet as well as his experiencing of visions of each: Longchenpa (*Klong chen pa*, 1308–63, one of the most important Nyingma figures), the Sakya Paṇḍita (*Sa skya paṇḍita*, 1182–1251, a key early figure in the Sakya sect), and Tsongkhapa (*Tsong-kha-pa*, 1357–1419, the founder of the Geluk tradition). The cult of Mañjuśrī has thus been an important factor in transcending monastic sectarian boundaries, though not as significant in wider contexts as the cult of Avalokiteśvara (on which, see Kapstein 1992). However, it is noteworthy that in the present context, Mañjuśrī serves in part to bridge the distance between Tibetan and Chinese cultures. In fact, a controversial photograph (in the 1980s?) of an apparition of Mañjuśrī taken by a Chinese man at Wutaishan proved to be exceedingly popular among Chinese Buddhists to the point that it supposedly became the target of government suppression.

72. One of the earliest examples is found in a twelfth-century history, Nyang Nyi-ma-'od-zer 1988: 272.

73. *'Jam dpal sgyu 'phrul drwa ba.* This is another title for the famous *Mañjuśrīnāmasaṃgīti.* See Davidson 1981 for a translation.

74. The number "thousands" here and the number "ten thousands" given below are difficult to evaluate. While I was assured they were accurate, traditional Tibetan hagiographies tend to use stylized enumeration and Raoul Birnbaum has informed me that it would be difficult to conceive of ten thousand individuals receiving teachings at the site in question (see below). At the same time, ten thousand was also a number given to me as attending significant empowerments at Khenpo's residence in Golok, and photographs of the event seemed to indicate at least several thousand monks in attendance. Thus I have chosen to use the numbers provided, with the above caveats.

75. The Stūpa with a Nucleus of the Realized One's Relics is a large and famous structure located in a monastery named Yuantongsi. It was built in the Ming period and is believed to contain the genuine relics of Śākyamuni Buddha, which have a complicated history of burial, reappearance, and reburial. Aside from the obvious connections to the Ter cult, the stūpa's importance for Khenpo also appears to relate to its functioning as an important site for Chinese monastic ordinations.

76. Sudhana is the hero of the *Gaṇḍavyūhasūtra*, the culminating episode of the *Avataṃsaka Sūtra.* See Cleary 1993: 1135–1518, for a translation. There is an upper Shancai cave controlled by Tibetans and a lower Shancai cave controlled by Chinese; presumably Khenpo stayed at the former.

77. The Eastern Terrace is one of the five directional peaks, all of which are supposed to be sites where it is particularly easy to make contact with Mañjuśrī. The reference to the "ocean," which is far beyond visual range from Wutaishan, refers euphemistically to the "sea" of clouds visible from the peak.

78. Qingliangshan (lit., Clear and Cool Mountains) is one of the older names for the Wutai range, especially the central area conventionally thought of as Wutaishan, and is the name given in the famous *Avataṃsaka Sūtra* as the home of Mañjuśrī. One of the oldest Buddhist monastic sites at Wutaishan is Gu Qingliangsi (Ancient Clear and Cool Monastery), which currently is abandoned. Nearby, however, the relatively new Qingliangsi (Clear and Cool Monastery) consists of structures built around the Qingliangshi (the Clear and Cool Rock). The latter is a famous rock with a large flat upper surface on which Mañjuśrī is said to have once preached to a vast number of beings, who were all able to fit on its surface (conventionally, it would appear no more than about nine people could simultaneously stand on it). The Tibetan reference here combines the two names as Clear and Cool Rock Monastery (*Dwangs bsil rdo yi gling*).

79. This name occurs in the *Avataṃsaka Sūtra*'s account of dwelling places of bodhisattvas (according to a conversation with Raoul Birnbaum). It is said that long ago the Nārāyaṇa

Buddha practiced here before proceeding westward. In line with the general Chinese notion of caves as sacred places linking to hidden places, there is a well-known story of a monk disappearing in this cave, indicating it to be a link to hidden worlds. Thus again we see a natural connection to the Ter activity that Khenpo performs at the site.

80. From this site the Central Terrace can be seen directly.

81. See Makley 1994: 81ff.

82. See Ots 1994; Alton 1997. Qi gong is a traditional Chinese Taoist and Buddhist set of practices that involves manipulating subtle currents of energy called "qi" that exist within the body and external environment. As such, they are closely connected to martial arts, traditional medicine, and paranormal bodily feats. Contemporary qi gong involves both quiet sitting forms using contemplation to move the qi around within the body and more active forms using "automatic movements" of wild, spontaneous bodily movements. Alton provides an excellent explanation of the latter's contemplative and healing functions, as well as firsthand accounts; Ots's recent study focuses on the sociopolitical conflicts that have surrounded its immense popularity and government strictures. In the past decade, not only have numerous small qi gong communities formed in China, but there have also been enthusiastic rallies of thousands of Chinese centered around charismatic qi gong masters. Basing himself on the government's advocation of quiet sitting qi gong and condemnation of the wildly cathartic "spontaneous movements" form of qi gong, Ots argues that the former supports social and mental control over the lived body (*leib*), in line with a general principle that bodily experiences are silenced by highly structured social domains. In contrast, the latter practices rupture the culturally inscribed and constructed body with their invocation of highly personalized and spontaneous events originating in the body itself.

Chinese at times refer to Tibetan lamas as "qi gong" masters, or even valorize them as spiritually "higher" than Chinese qi gong masters with their merely physical feats of strength and energy manipulation. One middle-aged Tibetan acquaintance who had been recognized as a reincarnate lama (*sprul sku*) as a child, but later had married and become an editor, acquired an influential following in Beijing based on what were reputed to be his "qi gong" abilities. These Chinese disciples later entirely funded the construction of his lavish large monastic-style residence back in Lhasa and were quick to perform other services on his behalf, such as picking up his relatives in stretch limousines from the Beijing airport. One of the Chinese monks resident in 1991 at Khenpo Jikphun's institute was in fact the son of a famous qi gong master in Beijing. Although qi gong secrets are often transmitted in a hereditary fashion, which was his father's desire, he had for the time being spurned his legacy to instead study Tibetan Buddhism. In discussions with him, he frequently cited the mundane concerns of Chinese qi gong masters with money, popularity, and bodily feats, contrasting that to what he perceived as the more transcendent concerns and realizations of the major Tibetan Buddhist lamas. Finally I know a young Tibetan lama who recently spent several years in Shanghai, where he acquired numerous Chinese disciples. Their contributions subsequently enabled him to do such things as make lavish religious offerings back in Lhasa and construct a large old person's home (*rgan gso khang*) in eastern Tibet.

83. The political circumstances apparently related to the difficulty of securing government permission to travel abroad as well as the need for his personal attention during key stages in his academy's development.

84. Khenpo's original home monastery (*Gnub zur*) was actually a branch of the Nyingma Palyul (*dPal yul*) lineage, currently headed by Penor Rinpoche who also is the current overall head of the Nyingma sect (base monastery in Bylakuppe, Karnataka State, India). Penor

Rinpoche had met him on an earlier trip to Tibet, and Khenpo Namdrol had developed a close relationship to Khenpo Jikphun.

85. *Phur pa mgul khug ma'i thugs dam thugs kyi phur gcig.*

86. Dudjom Rinpoche 1991: 833; Dorje and Kapstein 1991: 81.

87. See Dudjom Rinpoche 1991 and Roerich 1976 for a wide selection of hagiographies from this period.

88. Karmay 1979, 1980.

89. Martin 1996.

90. Petech 1990; Jackson 1994.

91. See Karmay 1979, 1980; Ruegg 1984. It is not clear how much social reality the at times lurid polemical attacks reflect, at least in terms of the nature of the actions imputed to the "transgressors."

92. See Martin 1996 for a very valuable analysis of the limited written traces of such movements.

93. See Germano 1994: 228–34.

94. I am sensitive to the problem of the essentialist reification of both the "Chinese" and the "state" in polarized opposition to "Tibetans," and would agree that the actual situation is "complicated patterns of convergences and divergences of interests and projects among the different groups encountering each other" (Makley 1994: 73). Anyone who has lived for an extended time in the People's Republic of China knows how much more complex the "otherness" of the Chinese and the state is for Tibetans there than for Tibetans raised in refugee camps in South Asia. In addition, there are numerous internal and charged differences among Tibetans within the PRC concerning the value of traditional monasticism, the relation between social classes, the extreme variations in regional identity and practices, and so forth. However, lived realities are always a web of contradictions, such that many Tibetans live with both a clear sense of daily complexities and blurred boundaries and a strong sense of hegemonic otherness that is predominantly experienced as the Chinese and the state. In this way, Chinese workers at the lowest level are seen as extensions of the state's control over Tibetan culture, which makes their presence possible, while coercive Tibetan political, military, or religious officials are generally seen as mere puppets of the profoundly Chinese state, Tibetan externally but Chinese at their core. A "Tibetan" who is ethnically half-Chinese, whose sister may be married to a full Han Chinese, and who has numerous Chinese friends may have no compunction at all in articulating such otherness with strong emotional valences. These representations are as strong in Tibetans working for the government as they are for those outside it, and form a reality of their own that simply cannot be dismissed because of its contradictions with the lived complexities of life for ethnic "nationalities" within the PRC. My point in the current context is that these "others" are shot through with a far stronger sense of alienness and difference than was ever the case during the Tibetan renaissance period.

95. See Hanna 1994 for a firsthand encounter with one of her revelations.

96. The religious norm in the eleventh to fourteenth century, which tended to be supported by political authorities, was to deemphasize ongoing revelation in Tibet in preference for considering a valid Indian manuscript and lineage as the necessary criteria of validity, and to embrace the scholastic norms and conventional Buddhist values of monastic institutions as primary. Thus the open canon of the treasure cult, its preference for continuing old dynastic period translations, and its predilection for the deconstructive rhetoric of

the Great Perfection's emphasis on "sudden" experiences of indwelling enlightenment all rendered it the object of polemical attacks.

While the constraints of my contemporary focus prevent a full elaboration, I would like briefly to note an important historical issue. As Dreyfus 1994 has outlined, an important element of twelfth- to fourteenth-century rhetoric is the articulation of a shared community and identity among inhabitants of Tibetan cultural zones, particularly as found within the "treasure" traditions. While these traditions themselves stemmed from groups outside of the sociopolitical mainstream, their mythic paradigms were in many cases appropriated by political powers (most famously in the ideology of the Dalai Lama as Avalokiteśvara ruling over a unified Tibet). Thus the creation of cultural identity as well as solutions to political disunity were essentially tantric in nature, involving the rhetorical manipulation of an ideology of an overarching transcendent maṇḍala embracing many smaller localized maṇḍalas. See, for example, Samuel's (1993: 61–63) discussion of the "galactic polity" (of course, this model derives from nontantric Buddhist societies, and I am only arguing that its specific form in Tibet was irreducibly tantric in flavor). These interlocked maṇḍalas were embodied in the web of sacred sites within which Tibetans of all types engaged in common actions (circumambulation, pilgrimage, making offerings, etc.) while an important yet often neglected subculture of monastic and lay practitioners thrived as semipermanent residents of isolated elements of this network (caves, headlands of valleys, etc.). This appropriation of the treasure cult's mythic rhetoric in relation to its current prominent role in again articulating Tibetan cultural identity in the face of oppressive authorities bears further thought.

97. See Dreyfus 1994.

98. I find the opposition between Tibetan "traditional" culture and an extrinsic "modernity" deeply problematic, unless this "modernity" is understood as highly rhetorical and embodying a very biased agenda, whether Chinese communist or Euro-American. This is not to deny that some version of this dialectic was present in pre-1950 Tibet, indeed even in the eleventh century, but rather to resist the tendency to lump all of Tibetan culture under the homogeneous rubric of our concept of "traditional." Dialectics between movements presenting themselves as "modern" and other cultural strata as "traditional" have been present in Tibet from at least the eleventh century onward (see Mumford 1989). I have tried to stress this at different points in my text but at times have found myself forced into language that suggests my acceptance of such a split. This note serves as a caveat.

99. Samuel 1993: 149–54.

100. See Gyatso 1996: 150. Also see Gyatso 1986 for an interesting study of lineage and interpretation in the treasure tradition.

101. In other words, simply announcing oneself to be a Terton and producing the supposed Ter is a relatively simple matter; getting others to accept the claim is more complex. A dominant factor in the process of "accreditation" is the acceptance of the individual's claim by high-ranking Nyingma lamas, who make their opinions on the relative validity of the "revelations" known in ways formal and informal; of course, the support of those who are already recognized Terton in their own right is particularly important. This support is far more than simply rhetorical, since these teachers may also begin to utilize the rediscovered rituals, contemplative handbooks, and so forth, in teaching their own students, thereby helping to create an institutionalized set of lineages that will perpetuate these traditions in future generations. See Gyatso 1996: 151 and Thondup 1986: 157–60 for remarks on the

accreditation of a Terton. Aris 1988 has a fascinating study of the biography of Pemalingpa (*Pad ma gling pa;* 1450–1521), one of the most famous Terton, which focuses on his own struggle for legitimacy and acceptance. However, Aris's assumption of self-conscious deception on the part of the Terton reduces a multifaceted phenomena to a single simplistic model and largely ignores the equally interesting issues of hermeneutics, visionary experiences, and canonicity that are pertinent.

102. E.g., Thondup 1986: 157: "One cannot judge Tertons as inauthentic because of their imperfect and mercurial character, even to the slightest extent. . . . [A]mong the authentic Tertons there are many who are loose in speech and behavior and who, without the least hesitation, get involved in many activities that people will condemn."

103. As Schwartz 1994a: 737 notes, "The Chinese have come to realize that virtually every expression of religion [in Tibet] carries a message of political protest. Indeed, one of the salient aspects of current protest has been the ability of Tibetans to engage the secular Chinese state in a political confrontation on Tibetan terms, where religion is pitted against anti-religion. Tibetans have found that even the most innocent display of religiosity can be used to convey a powerful message of opposition to the regime. The Chinese state has been forced to contradict its own expressed policy of toleration, and Tibetans have been quick to seize on this as evidence that there is in fact no religious freedom in Tibet. Tibetans have thus been able to overcome their objective powerlessness by drawing the Chinese into a symbolic competition on terms where Tibetans control the meaning of the symbol."

At a mundane level, individuals in eastern Tibet with sufficient financial resources have found making major contributions to the rebuilding of temples and monasteries to be one of the few permissible and highly visible ways to express nationalistic sentiment. This understanding of the action has been made explicit in numerous discussions both with donors and with others. The reanimating of Tibetan mythohistorical beliefs and practices after its long suppression during the Cultural Revolution has been closely linked to this reviving landscape of stūpas, temples, and monasteries, such that Khenpo's actions in this light have clearly understood political implications. By "Tibetan Camelot," I refer to the close association of Ter with the mythoromantic elaboration of the activities of the dynasty's two principal kings, Songtsen Gampo (seventh century) and Tri Songdetsen (ninth century). In important Ter cycles, the first of these kings was claimed as an incarnation of the bodhisattva Avalokiteśvara, the same patron saint who later took birth in Tibet as the Dalai Lama, the "future" king of Tibet, while the second was identified with Mañjuśrī. As mentioned above, see Kapstein 1992: 86, 88 for his suggestion that Arthurian legends are an apt analogue for understanding these elaborate mythic romances.

104. See Schwartz 1994b: 226–31 for an interesting overview of the potential for Tibetan resistance to Chinese rule within popular religion. Also note the 1992 arrest of a woman in Lhasa simply claiming to be possessed by an important goddess (Dreyfus 1994: 218; Schwartz 1994b: 227).

105. Schwartz 1994a: 735 for a similar analysis pointing out a crucial difference between the nature of political activity of monasteries in Central Tibet in pre-1959 and under Chinese rule. The earlier "others" were simultaneously fellow Tibetans in positions of political authority, Tibetans participating in the "modernist" (*gsar ma*) instead of "ancient" lineages of Buddhism, and the new Indic models of Buddhism they were assimilating into their own inherited traditions of Buddhism formerly drawn from Central Asia and China as well as India. The striking contrast between these familiar others and the modern variants of the

"other" should be clear; the latter has a much stronger valence of being coercive, antireligious, and foreign.

106. A new generation of nonmonastic scholars, poets, and novelists has rapidly emerged in the past two decades in Tibet who are often employed in academic bureaus or as teachers in various government institutions. See Stoddard 1994 for brief, but interesting, comments on the subject. This very important development of a contemporary vernacular literature that includes modern critical scholarship as well as traditional and innovative narrative genres has in most ways remained distinct from the revival of traditional Buddhist literary genres such as scholastic commentaries, ritual manuals, tantric poetry, and the like. While this scholarship and composition, unlike contemporary Ter, has directly incorporated the new "modernity" into both its content and form, my own impression is that the lack of institutional support and other sociopolitical constraints had led to a high degree of frustration among its practitioners, at times verging on a sense of despair. It remains to be seen what creative synthesis may occur in the future between these lay scholars and their monastic counterparts, as well as what distinctively Tibetan variant of the new global modernism may emerge. See Ström 1994: 846–47 for speculation as to the nature of such a synthesis in Tibetan refugee communities in India. I agree with Ström that the Central Institute of Higher Tibetan Studies is a theoretically interesting development in this light, though I think much of its potential remains unrealized.

107. Tantric Buddhism involves rhetorically advocating antinomian behavior, such as ritual murder, transgressing against social norms, and sexual intercourse in religious settings. The degree to which this rhetoric should be interpreted literally or symbolically was a source of tension in the Tibetan renaissance, with Nyingma groups often being attacked as adhering to literal-minded interpretations. Contemporary "transgression" is focused instead on past transgressions of Buddhist norms caused by the Chinese-forced destruction of traditional Buddhist culture in the Cultural Revolution (colonially induced) and the transgressions of Tibetan nationalists breaking Chinese laws in their defense of Tibetan autonomy and rights (colonially defined). Thus the nature of "transgression" to which current and ancient Ter is linked is quite different.

108. Traditional Tibetan books consist of rectangular loose-leaf pages. The same holds true for seemingly modern variants such as Kusum Lingpa's discovery of treasure teachings for the protector deities of Mount Shasta (source Dr. Lawrence Epstein, in conversation). Khenpo Jikphun visited the United States and Europe in 1993 for several months, during which time I saw him for about a total of ten days in Washington, D.C., Maryland, and Boston; I also heard a number of reports from participants in events centered around him at other locations in the United States. I was struck by his ability to relate to American audiences, which in part derives from his speaking skills and charisma, impressive even in translation. Particularly notable were his repeated attempts to integrate America, and Americans, into the Ter cult through references to a vibrant mix of prophecies, karmic connections, and human rights; he made a number of statements about strong karmic connections with American Buddhist communities, particularly the well-known Vajradhatu centers of the late Chogyam Trungpa Rinpoche. Finally he established a close relationship with Sogyel Rinpoche, the author of the popular *Tibetan Book of Living and Dying*, who is said to also be an incarnation of Lerab Lingpa. Despite the considerable enthusiasm he generated, in the absence of consequent trips or an institutional basis, it remains unclear whether that enthusiasm will generate any systematic community. Based on these experiences, as well as his demonstrated ability to galvanize Chinese Buddhist interest in the PRC, I would

say that he exhibited considerable ability to integrate Chinese or American versions of "modernity" in personal interactions and oral teachings, even if he has not shown the inclination to do so in the content, genres, or forms of his writings and revelations.

CHAPTER 4

For facilitating the present research I wish to thank the Committee for Scholarly Communication with China (Washington, D.C.) and the Tibet Academy of Social Science (Lhasa). Invaluable logistical support at the Drigung Powa Chenmo was offered by S.M. and N.T., to whom I am deeply grateful. The revision of this chapter for the present publication has benefited from the perceptive comments of Professor Vincanne Adams (Princeton University), Orville Schell (University of California, Berkeley), and fellow contributors to the present volume.

1. The Tibetan calendrical system, like the Chinese, uses a twelve-year animal cycle. The monkey year is of particular importance for Tibet owing to its associations with the ape who was the mythical progenitor of the Tibetan people and because it is also the year consecrated to Guru Padmasambhava, the Indian master of esoteric Buddhism who played an important role in Tibet's conversion to Buddhism during the eighth century. Certain other important pilgrimages also are organized during the monkey year, especially the famous pilgrimage to Tsa-ri, to the north of Bhutan, on which see Stein 1988; Riccard et al. 1994: chap. 10; Huber 1994c.

2. In fact, the current "liberal" religious policy was officially sanctioned only in 1982, with the promulgation of the party directive known as "Document 19," for a translation of which see McInnis 1989: 8-26.

3. For testimony concerning traditional pilgrimage in and around Lhasa, see, e.g. David-Neel 1983; Richardson 1993.

4. Large-Blondeau 1960, though of course reflecting only the rather limited sources available during the period in which that article was written, remains nevertheless valuable precisely because it surveys the most important and prominent pilgrimages, which had gained the attention of foreign visitors to Tibet early on. For general background, see also Dak-pa 1987. Stein 1988 discusses many sites in Tibet, China, and other parts of Asia that may be usefully compared with those considered here. The articles presented in Huber 1994a represent some of the most up-to-date work on Tibetan pilgrimage, with extensive references to earlier contributions. It is expected that forthcoming work of Huber, and of Katia Bouffetrille (Paris), will greatly augment our knowledge of the traditions and practices of Tibetan pilgrimage.

5. The name Terdrom (*Gter-sgrom*) is of relatively recent origin and literally means "treasure chest," referring to the place as a site of discoveries of Ter (on which see chapter 3). The older name, and the one most frequently met with in the historical literature, is the near-homonym Tidro (*Ti-sgro*), abandoned no doubt in part because it is an obscure term. It means perhaps "pigeon quill," alluding to the shape of the rock spires rising above the valley (see Fig. 4.1). The names of the valley are discussed in Dkon-mchog-'phel-rgyas 1991: 12.

6. This is of course not the place to enter on a general discussion of current scholarly reflection on pilgrimage. Naquin and Yü 1992: 35-38 provide an excellent bibliographic survey of contemporary studies of pilgrimage in different religious cultures.

7. Chan 1994: 544-69 provides useful travel information and maps of the area.

8. Aris 1979: 3-41 includes an excellent analysis of these traditions. Refer also to Gyatso 1987.

9. On the Uru Shei Lhakhang and its early history, see Richardson 1952-53, 1983.

10. Refer to Tucci 1971: 195-201 for a brief account of Drigung among the principal fiefs of Central Tibet. During my visits to Lhasa in 1990 and 1992 I was repeatedly told that large numbers of the indigents then begging in the city were from Drigung or from Uyuk (*'u-yug*), to the west of Lhasa. Both are characterized by poor conditions for agriculture, when compared with the richer river valleys, and meager pastures, relative to the more prosperous nomadic regions of the plateau.

11. A traditional introduction to the Kagyü tradition, representing the Drigung lineage in particular and including hagiographical accounts of Phakmotrupa and Kyopa Jikten Gönpo, may be found in Könchog Gyaltsen 1990.

12. On the spread of the Drigung Kagyü in the Kailash region, see Dkon-mchog-bstan-'dzin 1992: 43-72. The doctrinal contributions of Kyopa Jikten Gönpo have not yet been as well studied as they deserve to be; some aspects pertaining to Buddhist epistemology are discussed in Kuijp 1987.

13. The main centers of the sect in Ladakh are Lamayuru and Phiyang (*phyi-dbang*) monasteries, briefly discussed in Snellgrove and Skorupski 1977: 20-22, 122-25. The treatment of the latter, despite some interesting photographs, is particularly inadequate.

14. This is the Drigung Chetsang Rinpoche, whose main center is established in the city of Dehra Dun, Uttar Pradesh State. The second-ranking Drigung hierarch, the Drigung Chungtsang Rinpoche, resides in Tibet but was in India during the revival described in this chapter. Ayang Rinpoche, representing an important eastern Tibetan branch of the tradition (from the Nangchen district), has established a monastic settlement at Byllakuppe, near Mysore, in Karnataka State.

15. Pad-rgyal 1989: 128-31 supplies the traditional biographical account of Dorje Gyelpo. Dkon-mchog-'phel-rgyas 1991: 50 states that his activities at Terdrom commenced during an earth-monkey (*sa-sprel*) year, which in Dorje Gyelpo's lifetime could only have been 1308, a date that is possible if these activities preceded his ascension to the Drigung throne in 1314. Pad-rgyal's account (p. 129) does in fact mention his residence at Terdrom a few lines before recounting his enthronement.

16. The notion of opening or reopening a religious site is a mystical and geomantic one, referring to the disclosure of the location's special powers and potentialities. Compare David Germano's remarks above, chapter 3.

17. On the cult of this deity, see Dudjom Rinpoche 1991: 1:710-16 and Boord 1993, the bibliography of which details other relevant sources and investigations. The rites of Vajrakīla are considered particularly efficacious means to remove obstacles to both material and spiritual success.

18. Dkon-mchog-'phel-rgyas 1991: 50.

19. For a brief hagiography of Rinchen Püntsok, see Dudjom Rinpoche 1991: 1:676-77. On the phenomenon and significance of treasure discovery, refer to chapter 3 above.

20. Dkon-mchog-'phel-rgyas 1991: 24-26 explains the configuration of the cave and its symbolic associations.

21. Dkon-mchog-'phel-rgyas 1991: 50. The biographies of the brothers are given in Pad-rgyal 1989: 240-88. Könchok Rinchen was the first of the Chetsang line of incarnations and Rikdzin Chödrak the first of the Chungtsang line who have alternately served as the lineage holders of Drigung down to the present time.

22. Shaw 1994: 117–22 summarizes traditional accounts of the origins of this teaching. In the final paragraph of this section, Shaw's assertion that "all but the intelligensia . . . are not aware that [the longevity teachings of Siddharajñī] are based on the revelations and teachings of a woman" does not square with my own observations. I found that both monks and laypersons generally referred to Siddharajñī using her honorific title Ma-gcig (Grub [-pa'i]-rgyal[-mo]), the "sole mother" Siddharajñī, which leaves little room for misunderstanding.

23. Dkon-mchog-'phel-rgyas 1991 spells this as *'ja'-tshug-ma*, meaning perhaps "Rainbow Ascent," an interpretation that I also received from some pilgrims orally. However, interviews with lamas of the Drigung lineage, the works cited in note 28 below, and the actual practice of using a stalk to test the opening in the fontanel that is induced by the powa, all support the spelling and translation offered here.

24. Guenther 1963: 201.

25. David-Neel 1931; Evans-Wentz 1958.

26. Brauen-Dolma 1985: 247. In note 6 on the same page, Brauen-Dolma cites Michael Aris's description of a public teaching of powa in Bhutan as "an outbreak of religious hysteria."

27. Dkon-mchog-'phel-rgyas 1991: 50.

28. Könchok Gyaltsen 1988: 119–27 summarizes the powa instructions and their history. Accounts of Nyinda Sangye are given in Gu-ru Bkra-shis 1990: 480–81; 'Jam-mgon 1976: 524–25.

29. David-Neel 1931. When visiting Dhagpo Kagyu Ling, the center of the Karma Kagyü tradition in Dordogne, France, in August 1979, I was asked to translate the powa teachings of the resident lama on behalf of a French disciple, who, following a couple of days of practice in retreat, experienced the characteristic opening of the fontanel, accompanied by a clearly visible swelling from which there was some bleeding.

30. It should be noted, however, that the Drigungpas were among the few Kagyü traditions favored by the Fifth Dalai Lama, who effected the unification of Tibet during this period. On the Great Fifth's sectarian relationships, refer, e.g., to Smith 1970: 16–18; Dudjom Rinpoche 1991: 1:682–84. The experiences of Rikdzin Chödrak during this period, as reported in Pad-rgyal 1989: 279–81, reflect the deeply troubling events that affected Tibet: in 1641–43 the hardships wrought by the Mongolian and Tibetan forces engaged in civil war and several successive years of hail brought severe famine to the populace and caused many deaths, "the unprecedented evil being such that some women ate the flesh of slain dogs." Rikdzin Chödrak succored the people as best he could and in 1645 entered into formal ties with the Fifth Dalai Lama.

31. Dkon-mchog-'phel-rgyas 1991: 50–51. In the present translation some expansion and explanation have been added, without annotation, wherever the Tibetan is so terse as to preclude clear understanding if interpreted more literally.

32. Tashi Tsering (Dharamsala), oral communication.

33. Schwartz 1994b: chaps. 6–7; Goldstein 1995: 46–52.

34. I arrived at the festival on 10 August 1992, that is, after it was already under way. In what follows, references to events in the preceding days are based on interviews with participants and the schedules publicly posted at Drongur Monastery.

35. During the late 1950s several prominent lamas from eastern Tibet disappeared immediately after meeting with Chinese authorities, and it was widely rumored that, had the Dalai Lama not escaped from Tibet in 1959, he would have met with the same fate. (See,

e.g., Donnet 1994: 33–36.) Turning to the post–Cultural Revolution period, some Tibetan lamas living abroad have experienced difficulty with Chinese visas and travel papers in recent years, and dissident lamas within Tibet, as is well known, have sometimes been arrested, imprisoned, and tortured. The disappearance of Gendun Choekyi Nyima, the Dalai Lama's candidate for the office of Panchen Lama, in the summer of 1995 is currently offered by some as evidence that the kidnap of religious figures regarded by the authorities as somehow troublesome is still a very real possibility, though in 1992 events had not yet taken this turn. In any event, the untroubled return of the Chungtsang Rinpoche to Tibet a year or so after the revived Drigung Powa Chenmo suggests that his position is a relatively secure one and that the worries expressed by some on his behalf were indeed not warranted.

36. A refugee Kagyü lama living in Nepal with whom I spoke afterward (September 1992), who was familiar with the reputation of the Drigung Powa Chenmo as it was performed in 1956 and before, was specifically concerned to learn from me, for instance, whether during the culminating teachings large numbers of persons were observed in trance, unconscious, or otherwise profoundly affected. The fact that, despite my observation of considerable and deeply felt religious fervor, no such occurrences took place in the immediate area in which I was seated (though they may well have elsewhere) he regarded as an indication of the diminished spiritual power (*byin-brlabs*) of the teaching.

37. On the fraternities of "fighting monks" in some of the larger Tibetan monasteries, see Goldstein 1964. "Monk policemen," however, need not be drawn from the ranks of the *rdab-rdob*, and the latter category is not recognized in all monasteries.

38. It appears to be very widely believed by local political authorities in Tibetan regions of China, including both ethnic Tibetan and Han cadres, that the protests in Lhasa during the late 1980s were at least in part aroused by the presence of foreign spectators, even if direct foreign agitation was not involved. In some parts of eastern Tibet, in particular, this is frequently mentioned ("unofficially" at least) as one justification for maintaining restrictions on foreign visitors. Cf. Schwartz 1994b: 38–42.

39. Engaging in trade in connection with pilgrimage is accepted practice in the Tibetan world and is not regarded as contradicting the religious aims of pilgrimage, unless worldly gain is one's primary motivation (*kun-slong*).

40. As Melvyn Goldstein notes in Chapter 2 above, the distributions of offerings in connection with these ceremonies are essential for the maintenance of the monks (and, in this case, nuns as well).

41. The schedule as I give it here reflects the actual program that was followed. This in fact does accord with the written program posted at the monastery, except in the matter of the teaching of the powa itself, on which occasion the Soktrül Rinpoche actually conferred the teaching instead of the lama who had been scheduled to do so but who fell ill the day before. Dkon-mchog-'phel-rgyas 1991: 51–52 provides the following summary of the traditional program.

> During the eighth day there is the initial preparatory empowerment. When the assembled public is very numerous there are about thirty thousand, but if not then roughly twenty thousand. On the ninth day there is the empowerment of the Sage, the Vajrāsana empowerment. On the day of the great festival of the tenth day, the two lords of refuge don the ceremonial garb of Oḍḍīyāna and Za-hor, and also the Central Asian woven cape called Nechuma that was offered to Kyopa Rinpoche by the emperor, and they set up the parasol of peacock feathers that the emperor

offered. [In this regalia] they confer the *torma*-empowerment of the peaceful guru, the empowerment of longevity, etc.

On the eleventh and twelfth, if there are none with special requests, they bestow such [initiations] as those of the Six Syllables, the longevity empowerment, Lo-gyon, the Wrathful Guru, and the three wrathful ones together. On the thirteenth, the great Drigungpa's profound and uncommon Great Generation of Spirit is conferred, this being a rite for generation of the enlightened attitude. On the fourteenth, if there are none with special requests, such empowerments as those of Tārā, Māricī, and Mañjuśrī are conferred.

On the fifteenth is the so-called Drigung Powa Chenmo, a profound doctrine renowned throughout all the numberless districts. The entire populace, high and low, harbors great hopes of obtaining the Powa Chenmo. Anywhere throughout the east, center, or west of Tibet, one who has obtained the Drigung Powa Chenmo is counted as being fortunate. In order to obtain it, many people, without regard to sectarian affiliation, travel from afar, undertaking many hardships. Up to that [date], every morning each day, when the great empowerment is performed, the two lords of refuge, as is desired, bestow each day's empowerment. In the afternoon, in the lower part of the great empowerment tent, they bestow guidance on the so-called background doctrines, i.e., the venerable Kyopa Rinpoche's Heart of the Teaching (*bstan-snying*) and Single Intention of the True Doctrine (*dam-chos dgongs-gcig*), as well as whatever teachings of the doctrine are desired by the faithful, without regard to sectarian affiliation. To those from the meditation colleges, according to the stages of their practice, they bestow the cycles of experiential cultivation, and the empowerment and instructions of the Further Profundity (*yang-zab*, the main *terma*-cycle of Rinchen Püntshok), etc. They also bestow the full monastic ordination, etc. It is the custom that during an interval [in the program of teaching], in the Terdrom assembly tent, Auspicious Whorl, the two lords of refuge join the assembly, at which time prayers for their longevity are offered by the entire assembly.

42. See Kapstein 1992 on the some of the distinctively nationalistic dimensions of the Tibetan Avalokiteśvara cult.

43. By "nonmonastic religious" I mean to refer to the not insubstantial numbers of Tibetans who have some ritual proficiency but are not ordained monks or nuns. Some of these persons, such as the adepts of Cutting seen in Fig. 4.3, may well have a formal religious designation applied to them, in this case *sngags-pa*, "mantra-adept." Others, like the two men seated in Fig. 4.5, may be for all intents and purposes ordinary laypersons who are distinguished by having mastered a ritual repertoire.

44. The "eight great charnel grounds" (*dur-khrod chen-po brgyad*) were thought to be major centers of tantric practice in medieval India. Many of the important pilgrimage routes in Tibet include locations metonymically identified with these sites. Occasionally one hears of them being used as the sites for "sky burials," the dismemberment of the deceased who is then fed to vultures, as well, but this is by no means essential to the function of the site in pilgrimage.

45. See note 22 above.

46. See Kapstein 1995, for example, where I have examined some of the rituals connected with artistic production. Though I would not deny that Turner's themes of liminality and communitas might be invoked in connection with the materials studied there as well, they are certainly much less prominent than the structures of order that I sought to emphasize in my analysis. Turner 1977b summarizes the main features of his theory of rit-

ual. Turner and Turner 1978 investigates pilgrimage in Christian culture, and Turner 1977a examines the relationship between pilgrimage and death.

47. The Tibetan people are often popularly depicted as having an admirable ecological sensibility, and indeed, I would concur that this was largely true of traditional Tibetan society. It remains a question, however, to what extent this was due to the relatively low-tech features of that society and to what extent to a deliberately cultivated view of nature. What I saw in the aftermath of the Drigung Powa some might regard as sad evidence that Tibetan Buddhists, given plastic, glass, and cardboard, are unfortunately no more ecologically aware than are most other contemporary peoples. Some of the monastic leaders of Drigung, whom I met afterward, did say that they had not foreseen a problem that, after all, had not existed in earlier times, and so were not adequately prepared to address it.

48. Goldstein 1989: 5–6 observes that "the government maintained no police or magistrate force in the rural areas," and "there were only 400 to 500 fully gazetteered lay and monk officials administering a country that contained at least one million inhabitants in an area that was almost as large as Western Europe." Goldstein's remarks apply, of course, just to the area of political Tibet ruled from Lhasa. See also Dawa Norbu 1985.

49. Having had the privilege to have participated on a number of occasions in discussions between H.H. the Dalai Lama and leading Jewish rabbis, I have more than once noted the surprise expressed by the latter on learning that, for instance, Tibetan Buddhism does not possess a common prayer book. While sectarian and lineage differences are not in particular what is at stake here (Judaism and Islam, for instance, are no less divided than Tibetan Buddhism in this regard), one may note nonetheless that tradition maintains that even when the political forces dominating Tibet gave the ecclesiastical leadership the opportunity to bring about sectarian unity by force this was refused. See, e.g., Thu'u-bkwan 1984: 451–52 on Khubilai Khan's failed attempt to arrange for the paramountcy of the Sa-skya-pa sect under Chos-rgyal 'Phags-pa. Even the Fifth Dalai Lama and his successors, who went further in the direction of bringing about religious unity than had any other Tibetan leaders, still left much latitude for sectarian difference.

50. Lcang-skya 1989: 11–12.

51. Ortner 1978: 157. I emphasize Ortner's earlier work here only because it clearly exemplifies some assumptions that appear to be very widespread in thinking about the Tibetan state and its relation with religion. However, the theoretical approach elaborated in Ortner 1989, from which I have learned much in connection with the present chapter, clearly suggests a very different perspective from that developed in the earlier work. Cf. also the critical discussion of views of the Tibetan state in Samuel 1993: 139–46.

52. Ortner 1978: 159.

53. Ortner 1989 suggests a similar perspective.

54. Lincoln 1989: 74.

CHAPTER 5

Research for this paper was funded by grants from the National Program for Advanced Study in China, the Graduate School Research Fund, University of Washington, and the State Nationalities Affairs Commission of the PRC. It was undertaken by the authors together with other members of the Research Group on Pilgrimage in eastern Tibet, Southwest Nationalities Institute, Chengdu, Sichuan, PRC. We thank Keith Dede, Kevin Stewart, and Charlene Makley for their comments on an earlier draft. We are especially grateful to Melvyn Goldstein and Matthew Kapstein for their deft editing of this chapter.

1. Repgong has various Tibetan spellings, e.g., Re-skong, Reb-skong, Reb-gong. It is part of Chinese Tongren in Qinghai Province, in the Tibetan subethnic area called Amdo by Tibetans.

2. Alternatively, *glu rol* is spelled *klu rol*, "nāga music." Explanations of the name differ even between villagers.

3. In fact, we were told, before the "democratic reforms," villages were likely to levy a substantial fine on households that did not attend.

4. Samuel 1993.

5. Ibid., 176ff.

6. See, e.g., Stein 1972; Tucci 1980.

7. Samuel's recent illuminating work (1993) attempts to trace the coevolution of these two modes of religious action in Tibetan thought, society, and culture.

8. We do not know whether this is an old or new prescription, but many claimed that it was old. There are certainly at least three reasons for this monastic absence. Ronggön has a reputation for close observation of the rules of discipline, and the timing of the luröl corresponds generally to that of summer retreat when monks are supposed to be attending closely to their studies instead of lollygagging about watching nonmonastic festivities. Indeed, on one occasion we observed a tutor drag two young acolytes out of Shachung's temple, down a long flight of steps, and back to Ronggön by their ears. Second, we were told that the monks regarded the organization and conduct of the ritual to be strictly in the hands of laymen and that the presence of shamans was sufficient to its conduct. Alternatively, others maintained that it was the very presence of shamans whom the monks hold in some contempt that kept them away. Third, the once-prevalent practice of animal sacrifice, in which villagers slaughtered male goats and/or burned alive live cocks in wicker cages, and represented today by the offering and burning of elaborately fashioned dough figures, clearly contravenes monastic vows. We were told that the custom of sacrificing live animals was halted by Rdzong dkar sprul sku of Rong Monastery, although we are uncertain as to when. Our guess is around the mid-1940s. Stewart, Banmadorji, and Huangchojia 1995: 233, notes that animal sacrifice during the luröl (Laru) festival in the Zhangjia area ended in the 1980s.

9. Bell 1992: 120.

10. Ibid., 121.

11. Ibid., 184.

12. Rnam sras 1991: 157–59.

13. See, e.g., Shakabpa 1967: 49ff.

14. Aris, in Rock 1992: 13.

15. Ibid.

16. The one story, quoted in Rnam sras 1991, that differs significantly from the others is from the village of Gling rgya, to the north of the area we studied, where a village wise man or shaman led the young men and women of the village to dance at a distant spring, so that the guardian klu might be pleased and release the water to the settlement's fields. This myth catches another of glu rol's primary themes, generational order and leadership.

17. 'Jigs med theg mchog 1988.

18. Ibid., 37ff. Many claim that they are ultimately descended from Khri srong lde btsan's soldiers. For example, we were told that Sog ru was a back area for troops during the battle with a Chinese army at Rgan rgya during Khri srong's time. A military chief is reputed to have married a girl from Sog ru, and at least one clan or tribe, Ri tsha tsho ba, with about twenty families in this village, claims descent from this alliance.

19. Ibid., 46. On the eight *gnas,* see Riccard et al. 1994: 22 n. 4 and 'Jigs med theg mchog 1988: 47ff.

20. 'Jigs med theg mchog 1988: 66–68.

21. The Rong po tsho ba are the twelve Reb-skong "tribes" (*shog kha*) located in seven villages: Mtsho bzhi, Sog ru, 'Ja mo, The bo, Rong po lha sde, Sa dkyil, and Bis pa. What is considered to be glu rol proper is performed only in four of the Rong bo villages:

The bo, for the deity A myes Gnyan chen
Bis pa, for A myes Gnyan chen
Sa dkyil, for A myes Bya khyung
Sog ru, for A myes Stag lung.

The remaining villages traditionally participate in one or more of these four. Of the remaining three Reb-skong villages:

'Ja mo worships Dpal ldan lha mo and a *yi dam,* Gza' Dgra can.
Mtsho bzhi, mostly Rnying ma pas, worships Dpal ldan lha mo.
Rong po lha sde has a *la-rtse* in the middle of the monastery.

Sa dkyil, the site of our principal inquiries, is a big village with 163 households and 710 people, apart from cadres who work outside. There are about 400 men and 200 people over the age of fifty, sixty-eight of whom are males. The village is presently encroached on by Tongren, the county town. Much of the village agricultural land has been leased to the town, which is pushing southward into the village, for public buildings.

Despite claims in Sa dkyil attesting to the antiquity of their glu rol, we subsequently learned from Padma 'bum of Indiana University that the village began its own independent festivities only about sixty years ago, after a fight with Sog ru, with which it had previously held a joint ritual.

Glu rol rituals are also performed by members of the Tu nationality in Gnyan thog, to the north of the Tongren area. See Rnam sras 1991 for a discussion of yet other places in the Dgu River vicinity.

22. This general description may act as a template for what also occurs in Sog ru village, across the river from Sa dkyil. Their *gzhi bdag* is A myes Stag lung. Additionally, villages pay courtesy visits to each other during the individual rituals, e.g., on 6/23, The bo village visits Sog ru, and the visit is returned the next day.

23. In general, a bodhisattva is a being who has committed himself to the thought of enlightenment and to helping other beings achieve it. Of the ten stations or planes (*sa*) on the bodhisattva path, attainment of the eighth (the Immovable; *mi gyo ba*) designates the one from which the aspirant cannot slide back.

24. A myes Gnyan chen also is the subject of competing Tibetan and Chinese myths. The latter hold that he was an exiled Chinese imperial prince.

25. We are much indebted to Kevin Stewart and Charlene Makley for information on the role of shamans. See Stewart, Banmadorji, and Huangchojia 1995 for a description of the shaman at Zhangjia village. Makley (personal communication) says that when she ob-

served the luröl at Sog ru in 1995, two shamans, a senior and a junior one, both young men, were in full possession state. This was not the case when we were there four years previously.

Generally, people distinguish between a *lha pa* and a *lha pa tshab* on the basis of whether he is actually in a possession state: *lha babs* (the deity has descended) or *khog pa nang bzhugs* (the deity resides internally).

26. See, e.g., Anagnost 1994.

27. Indeed, at Sa dkyil, local party leaders from the village were omnipresent at the rituals, but their participation in them tended to be superficial. As primary organizers they were highly visible, everywhere checking up on things, making sure that the organizational plan was carried out smoothly and that everything came off in proper fashion. Yet they did not actually participate fully in the dances but seemed content to act principally as spear carriers, if they acted at all. We suspect that in one sense their engagement in the administration of, but lack of full participation in, the ritual shows that given the new policies of more local autonomy in decision making in the contemporary setting, their authority has been somewhat undermined, and they fall back to the village to seek a new base of authority. At the same time, in ethnic minority areas higher authority wants local leaders to participate and not to be separate from the masses. Thus two functions fall to them: to demonstrate solidarity, participation, and identification with the masses and at the same time to play supervisory roles.

28. A myes nang was originally established by Skal ldan rgya mtsho who, it is said, regarded the deity so highly that he made the temple the same height as his chambers in Rong Monastery. The temple was destroyed in 1958 and restored in 1980 at the cost of 75,000 yuan.

29. Labdze (*la-rtse*) are among the most common ritual structures in Tibet. They are generally constructed of stone piles and contain the ritual implements described below. For a description of these rituals and their role in national identity formation, see Karmay 1994: 112-20.

30. See, e.g., Epstein 1975; Stewart, Banmadorji, and Hunagchojia 1995.

31. The names of the dances described here are from Sa dkyil. They differ from village to village, but generally their structure seems to be similar.

32. See Rnam sras 1991: 167, which refers to *pe hwa'i ru gling* in the villages of Dga' gsar and Sgo dmar. We are uncertain as to what *pe hwa'i ru* (alt., *phe hwa*) refers.

33. Two young men perform a dance on stilts, one set leopard spotted, the other tiger striped. The dance is said to tell the story of two klu, one spotted, the other striped, who emerged from the holy lake Dar rgyas g.yu mtsho in Xunhua to celebrate the peace accords referred to above. Alternatively, this dance is said to commemorate the occasion, reported in a vision of Skal ldan rgya mtsho, when the bodhisattvas Spyan ras gzigs and 'Jig rten mgon po manifested themselves in the forms of these creatures and sported in sheer delight at the auspicious beauties of the Rgan rgya area.

34. On this dance, see Rnam sras 1991: 159. Makley points out (personal communication) that at Sog ru, the Thugs rje chen po is performed as a line dance by all generations together. They exit in generational order, "compelling testimony to the emphasis on generational unity," she writes.

35. These are not dances but skits that spoof both hilarious and serious incidents (arguments, gluttony, adultery, laziness, greed, etc.) that have occurred in the villages during the

year. Their public display purges the village of ill feelings and resentments and gives things a fresh start. In the course of one of these skits, in Sog ru village, we saw the only explicit reference to Tibetan ethnicity, in which an outrageously dressed "hunter," armed to the teeth with an outlandish assortment of weaponry, is done in by his quarry, a deer portrayed by a man dressed in an old gas mask fitted out with horns of juniper branches. The utterly incompetent "hunter" bore a sign saying "Tibetan nationality" (*bod kyi mi rigs*).

36. Sog ru is divided into village quarters. The young men of each quarter take turns annually.

37. Though common in parts of South and Southeast Asia, the ritual use of skewers to pierce the cheeks, back, and even occasionally the abdomen is extremely uncommon in Tibet. Chime Radha Rinpoche told us that he has observed the custom in Zangskar, a border area of western Tibet, during the course of a ritual associated with local mountain deities as well. There may be some actual association between these far western reaches and Amdo, since some of the local populace claims this was their original homeland and that they stem from old garrisons that hailed from the far west during the imperial period. Whatever the case, it appears to be an archaic practice preserved only in Tibetan border or frontier areas.

38. Viewed from the perspective of current economic realities, Sa dkyil has virtually abandoned all agricultural or pastoral activities. Although about eighty-five people actively farm, the village has essentially blended into the town of Tongren. Some 1,000 mu of former agricultural land has been sold to the government. The sales have brought the village some 850,000 yuan, which it has collectively invested in such things as tractors, mills, markets, some 200 rooms of hotel space, and a restaurant. Some villagers have also invested in private ventures. From these collective investments the village distributes about 72,000 yuan to the village, yielding a household income of over 600 yuan.

39. Ironically, this ritual act, formerly regarded as prophylactic against diseases entering the mouth, is now seen by the young men in the more modern perspective as a potential source of illness.

40. See McKhann 1995.

41. For an analysis of Tibetan intellectuals in the contemporary context, who are subject to much the same bind, see Upton 1995. This dilemma of choice between ethnic tradition and modernity is further exacerbated by the fact that the youth especially seem quite aware that their ritual customs are peculiar and awe-inspiring even for most Tibetans. Thus, the Tibetanness in which they are enveloped through the ritual is also a Tibetanness that other Tibetans generally consider primitively bloody and not exemplary of Tibetan Buddhism or culture.

42. Anagnost 1994: 235.

43. Ibid., 229; Gladney 1994a.

44. See, e.g., Gladney 1994b; Litzinger 1992, 1994; Oakes 1991, 1992; Swain 1990.

45. See, e.g., Xiao Zhenwei and Liu Jinghong 1994: 27: "One particularly thrilling ritual carried out during the June Festival is for Buddhist Masters [*sic!*] to pierce steel pins through the cheeks of young Tibetans. The Masters do so upon request by young people who believe that [it] will help prevent diseases from entering the body through the mouth. . . . While removing the pins [they] withdraw the pins without the slightest drop of blood, and no observable scarring." See also Cai Xingmin 1987.

46. Feuchtwang and Wang Ming-ming 1991.

CHAPTER 6

1. These events are discussed at length in Barnett and Akiner 1994: pt. 4; Donnet 1994: chap. 4; Goldstein 1995: 25–52; and Schwartz 1994b.

2. Stein 1972: 191–229.

3. Hobsbawm 1992: chap. 2 speaks of "popular proto-nationalism," where I am using the expression "national identity." Hobsbawm's usage has been retained in studying Tibet by Dreyfus 1994. Terminology in this area, however, is by no means standard; see Connor 1994: esp. chap. 4.

4. Smith 1982: chap. 1 introduces the biological concept of polythetic definition to the study of religion, and early Judaism in particular, noting that attempts at monothetic definition (definition specifying a single differential quality) "have been deliberately tampered with for apologetic reasons" (p. 5). Attempts to define nationalities and ethnic groups have often been similarly motivated, frequently with grave consequences.

5. Thus, for instance, Tibetan is one of five languages (the others are Chinese, Mongolian, Uygur, and Kazak) found on Chinese currency notes, used for the publications of National People's Congresses, etc. See Ma Yin et al. 1985: 62–68.

6. Ma Yin et al. 1985: 1, for instance, describes China as "a unified multi-national state in which the Han people make up the vast majority."

7. See especially Hobsbawm 1992: 122ff. In practice, of course, Soviet and Chinese communism both came to make abundant use of nationalist rhetoric, particularly in giving support to anticolonial "wars of national liberation." The theoretical conflict between nationalism and communism, to which I refer here, therefore often has remained a concern of theory alone.

8. The degree and sources of division among the Chinese are of course subject to wide-ranging interpretation. In the wake of the Tiananmen Square tragedy of 1989, for instance, the prominent journalist Liu Binyan wrote that "China is no longer what it was in the thirties and forties, when warlords could bully people as they liked. Local armies are no longer backed up by foreign imperialists. Any head of the army, in order to have a solid base and keep up the living standards of the army, can only continue reform and opening to the outside world. Of course, the possibility of feudal separatist rule and fascist dictatorship by a few conspirators with the military forces cannot be ruled out" (1989: 171). Liu thus regards extreme divisiveness among the Han as a distortion, fostered in earlier times by foreign imperial interests and more recently by some military and political factions, if at all.

9. Hobsbawm 1992: chap. 4, for instance, centers the rise of modern nationalism in the period from 1870 through 1918, and examples from Eastern Europe and the tsarist Russian empire are prominent throughout.

10. See especially Goldstein 1989: 449–63 on the Tibet Improvement Party founded in 1939.

11. Ma Yin et al. 1985: 175 puts it this way: "while protecting the people's normal religious activities, the government will crack down on any counter-revolutionary sabotage perpetrated in the name of religion."

12. See, e.g., Robert Barnett, "Symbols and Protest: The Iconography of Demonstrations in Tibet, 1987–1990," in Barnett and Akiner 1994: 238–58; Schwartz 1994b: chap. 2.

13. We must avoid, however, overemphasizing or privileging the role of religion in Tibetan identity formation. There are many Tibetans who are outspoken regarding Tibetan identity, including many who are dedicated nationalists, who are not particularly religious,

or are skeptical or frankly unbelieving. The uniqueness of Tibetan language, culture, and lifestyle and pride in a history of relative autonomy provide more than a sufficient ground for their sentiments quite apart from religious belief. Moreover, some Tibetans argue that despite the nationalist convictions demonstrated by activist members of the clergy, other lamas have placed their religious, sectarian, or personal interests far in advance of the Tibetan national interest, though few would question their Tibetan identity on these grounds, except for polemical effect. This is not the place to adjudicate such views, but it is important to note that the relationship between religion and nationalism is sometimes a contested area for Tibetans themselves.

14. The general phenomena with which we are concerned here have significant parallels in other contexts that have been much discussed by social scientists. Clifford Geertz, for instance, has, in a pair of justly famed articles, described religion and ideology (where "ideology" referred primarily to nonreligious systems of modern political "belief") as "cultural systems," suggesting that the two may sometimes compete for preeminence within precisely the same sphere (Geertz 1973: chaps. 4, 8; see also chap. 6). This suggestion has been made fully explicit by Mark Juergensmeyer (1993: chap. 2), who has spoken in this context of "competing ideologies of order," where religions, liberal capitalism, and communism may all be understood as what he terms "ideologies of order." Huntington's (1993) notion of a "clash of civilizations" flows from similar reflections. The analyses proposed by these and other scholars, despite differences of emphasis, all show that where a traditional religious culture finds itself in conflict with a modern, secular ideology, difference and hence identity are accentuated in a manner that they are not when tradition is left unchallenged.

15. E.g., Dreyfus 1994; Kapstein 1992.

16. The role of recent Tibetan-language publication enterprises in China is a fascinating and difficult topic that has not yet been studied in depth. Beginnings may be found in Heather Stoddard, "Tibetan Publications and National Identity," in Barnett and Shirin 1994: 121-56; and Kapstein forthcoming.

17. The great abyss separating the Tibetan awareness of the sacrality and uniqueness of their land and Han Chinese conceptions of the place of Tibet was most strikingly brought home to me during my second visit to Tibet, in 1985. I had learned enough Chinese to make small talk with the driver of the bus I was in, who had first come to Tibet with the army in the early 1960s and who, though rather taciturn, tried to be straightforward and polite to this foreign "guest." Whenever I pointed to a mountain or a stream or a village off the road, however, and inquired after its name, he shrugged and always gave the same answer: *mei you mingzi,* "It has no name."

18. Cf. Juergensmeyer 1993: 61 on "the impact of Muslim teachers in relating the traditional truths of Islam to modern ideas."

19. See Hobsbawm 1992: 59-63, following Benedict Anderson. Consider, too, the contributions to Bhabha 1990.

20. Juergensmeyer 1993: 47 discusses the antipathy between modern nationalism and some currents of contemporary Muslim thought. Hobsbawm, speaking of Catholicism during the period of Italian unification in the nineteenth century, comments that "the Holy Church could hardly be expected to turn itself into a localized national, let alone nationalist, establishment, least of all under Pius IX." Elsewhere, I have written of the eighteenth-century Buddhist clergy of Amdo, northeastern Tibet, whose hierarchs were ideologically committed to a multiethnic Manchu empire, with Tibetan Buddhism playing a unifying role among ethnic Manchus, Mongolians, and Tibetans, that for them this "represented the

synthesis of a peerless salvific vehicle with a universal temporal order" (Kapstein 1989: 236). No more than the Church under Pius IX could the Buddhism of these lamas be considered a localized national religion.

21. Germano's remarks on the situation in 1996, added to the final revision of his chapter before the manuscript was sent to the press, suggest a recently more politicized atmosphere in the community he studies as well.

22. The phrase comes from the Polish sociologist Edmund Wnuk-Lipiński, cited in Kubik 1994: 4, 234.

23. Nowak 1984: esp. 65–66. See also Goldstein 1975.

24. I do not wish to suggest that this is a peculiarly Tibetan phenomenon. Indeed, it is probably more often the case that nations, tribes, and even families are most aware of their internal differences when dealing with one another but tend to hang together when others are involved. Answers to questions of identity may depend in large measure on who is asking.

25. The scholar and poet Don-grub-rgyal, whose suicide was referred to above by Germano, is frequently mentioned as an example of the rise of nationalist sentiment among educated younger Tibetans in China.

26. The Panchen Lama dispute is surveyed in Tibet Information Network 1996: chap. 6. Reports of the 1996 campaign, and other recent news, are posted on the World Wide Web at www.tibet.org, which includes reports from the Tibet Information Network. Researchers using current reports on Tibet, from whatever source, must of course exercise some caution: in the absence of relatively open journalism, it is often not possible to check their veracity.

27. Nowak 1984: esp. 24–31. Goldstein 1975: 178 remarks that "the Dalai Lama has been portrayed [in the refugee community] as the symbol or quintessence of Tibetan national identity."

28. Kubik 1994. The innovation involved here, and its implications for the revival of Tibetan Buddhism more generally, may be highlighted by comparing it with the distribution in Poland of the icon of the Black Madonna, beginning in 1957, a case studied by Kubik (pp. 108–19). The Black Madonna pilgrimage was uniformly organized by the Polish Church and was promoted with the explicit support of a powerful international body, the Roman Catholic church. This to some extent inhibited the ability of the Soviets to control or repress the pilgrimage as it moved throughout Poland. Indeed, one of the intriguing aspects of the role of Catholicism in the nurturing of modern Polish nationalism has been its ability to draw on the Church's supranational character, and so effectively to act as a transcendental source legitimating nationalist aspirations, thus contrasting with its role in nineteenth-century Italy, mentioned in note 20 above.

29. However, interesting questions are also raised by the consideration of religious revivals in non-Tibetan lands that have traditionally adhered to Tibetan Buddhism, e.g., Mongolia, Buryatia, and Kalmykia, and the relationships between these and events in Tibet. See also note 20 above. Nevertheless, the supranational role of Tibetan Buddhism institutionally is sufficiently restricted so that there can be no question of comparing it in this regard with Roman Catholicism.

30. The present Dalai Lama, like several of his predecessors (notably the Fifth, 1617–82, and Thirteenth, 1876–33), has sought to rise above sectarianism and so has frequently emphasized his non-Gelukpa connections, going so far as to permit himself to be photographed in the ceremonial regalia of Tibet's ancient Bön religion, an image that was, at

least until recently, widely displayed in Bonpo monasteries and shrines throughout Tibet and the neighboring provinces.

31. A thorough examination of the late Panchen Lama's controversial life, career, and legacy is a real desideratum for contemporary Tibetan studies. The examples of his interventions on behalf of Tibetan Buddhism cited here are chosen from among the many instances indicated to me during visits to Tibet. The real devotion many Tibetans felt toward the Panchen Lama was evident during the two occasions (both in 1985) when I was able to meet him at audiences that he granted in Lhasa and Shigatse.

32. See Shakabpa 1967: 172–76, 183, 186, 192, 230, on the use of lotteries in the selection of Dalai Lamas during the Manchu period. The controversy over the recognition of the Panchen Lama is summarized there on p. 306, and in Goldstein 1989: 683–84, 760–63.

BIBLIOGRAPHY

Alton, John. 1997. *Living Qigong.* Boston: Shambhala.

Anagnost, Ann S. 1994. "The Politics of Ritual Displacement." In Charles F. Keyes, Laurel Kendall, and Helen Hardcare, eds., *Religion and the Modern States of East and Southeast Asia.* Honolulu: University of Hawaii Press.

Anon. 1986. "The Education of a Monk." *Chö-Yang: The Voice of Tibetan Religion and Culture* 1 (1): 41–45.

Aris, Michael. 1979. *Bhutan.* Warminster: Aris and Phillips.

————. 1988. *Hidden Treasures and Secret Lives.* Delhi: Motilal Banarsidass.

Aziz, Barbara Nimri. 1978. *Tibetan Frontier Families: Reflections of Three Generations from D'ing-ri.* Durham: Carolina Academic Press.

Barnett, Robert, and Shirin Akiner, eds. 1994. *Resistance and Reform in Tibet.* Bloomington: Indiana University Press.

Batchelor, Stephen, trans. 1979. *A Guide to the Bodhisattva's Way of Life by Shantideva.* Dharamsala: Library of Tibetan Works and Archives.

Bell, Catherine. 1992. *Ritual Theory, Ritual Practice.* New York: Oxford University Press.

Bell, Sir Charles. 1931. *The Religion of Tibet.* Oxford: Oxford University Press.

Bhabha, Homi K., ed. 1990. *Nation and Narration.* London: Routledge.

Boord, Martin J. 1993. *The Cult of the Deity Vajrakīla.* Buddhica Britannica Series Continua, no. 4. Tring, U.K.: Institute of Buddhist Studies.

Brauen-Dolma, Martin. 1985. "Millenarianism in Tibetan Religion." In Barbara N. Aziz and Matthew Kapstein, eds., *Soundings in Tibetan Civilization,* 245–56. New Delhi: Manohar.

Bush, Richard C. 1970. *Religion in Communist China.* Nashville: Abingdon Press.

Cai Xingmin. 1987. "Jeri zhilu (Journey to a Festival)." *Zhongguo lüyu (China Tourism)* 79 (January): 18–31.

Chan, Victor. 1994. *Tibet Handbook: A Pilgrimage Guide.* Chico, Calif.: Moon Publications.

Cleary, Thomas, trans. 1993. *The Flower Ornament Scripture.* Boston: Shambhala.

Connor, Walker. 1994. *Ethnonationalism: The Quest for Understanding.* Princeton: Princeton University Press.

Dak-pa, Ngawang. 1987. "Les pèlerinages bouddhiques au Tibet." In Jean Chélini and Henry Branthomme, eds., *Histoire de pèlerinages non-chrétiens—Entre magique et sacré: Le chemin des dieux,* 264–77. Paris: Hachette.

David-Neel, Alexandra. 1931. *Initiations and Initiates in Tibet.* London: Rider.

———. 1983. *My Journey to Lhasa.* London: Virago Press. Reprint of 1927 edition.

Davidson, Ronald M. 1981. "The Litany of Names of Mañjuśrī." *Mélanges Chinois et Bouddhiques* 20: 1–69. Brussels: Institute Belge des Hautes Études Chinoises.

———. 1990. "An Introduction to the Standards of Scriptural Authenticity in Indian Buddhism." In Robert Buswell, ed., *Chinese Buddhist Apocrypha,* 291–325. Honolulu: University of Hawaii Press.

———. 1994. "The Eleventh-Century Renaissance in Central Tibet." Paper presented at the University of Virginia.

Dawa Norbu. 1985. "An Analysis of Sino-Tibetan Relationships, 1245–1911: Imperial Power, Non-coercive Regime and Military Dependency." In Barbara N. Aziz and Matthew Kapstein, eds., *Soundings in Tibetan Civilization,* 176–95. New Delhi: Manohar.

———. 1991. "China's Dialogue with the Dalai Lama, 1978–90: Prenegotiation Stage or Dead End?" *Pacific Affairs* 64 (3):351–72.

Dkon-mchog-bstan-'dzin. 1992. *Gangs ri'i gnas bshad shel dkar me long.* Lhasa: Bod ljongs mi dmangs dpe skrun khang. Originally written in 1896.

Dkon-mchog-'phel-rgyas. 1991. " 'Bri gung gzhu stod gter sgrom gyi gnas yig." *Bod ljongs nang bstan* 10 (2): 3–57.

Don grub rgyal. 1994. *Lang tsho'i rbab chu dang ljags rtsom bdams sgrigs.* Ed. Padma 'Bum. Dharamsala: A myes rma chen Bod kyi rig gzhung zhib 'jug khang.

Donnet, Pierre-Antoine. 1994. *Tibet: Survival in Question.* Trans. Tica Broch. London: Zed Books.

Dorje, Gyurme, and Matthew Kapstein. 1991. *The Nyingma School of Tibetan Buddhism,* vol. 2. Boston: Wisdom Publications.

Dreyfus, George. 1994. "Proto-nationalism in Tibet," In Per Kvaerne, ed., *Tibetan Studies,* 1: 205–18. Oslo: Institute for Comparative Research in Human Culture.

Dudjom Rinpoche, Jikdrel Yeshe Dorje. 1991. *The Nyingma School of Tibetan Buddhism: Its Fundamentals and History.* 2 vols. Annotated translation by Gyurme Dorje and Matthew Kapstein. Boston: Wisdom Publications.

Dung dkar, B. 1983. *Bod kyi chos srid zung 'brel skor bshad pa* (Social History of the Dual Religious Secular Form of Government in Tibet). Beijing: Mi rigs dpe skrum khang.

Epstein, Israel. 1983. *Tibet Transformed.* Beijing: New World Press.

Epstein, Lawrence. 1975. "Blood and Thunder: Theories of Causation in Tibet." *Tibet Society Bulletin* 9: 40–45.

Evans-Wentz, W. Y. 1958. *Tibetan Yoga and Secret Doctrines.* Oxford: Oxford University Press.

Feuchtwang, Stephan, and Wang Ming-ming. 1991. "The Politics of Culture or a Contest of Histories: Representations of a Chinese Popular Religion." *Dialectical Anthropology* 16: 251–72.

Freemantle, Francesca, and Chogyam Trungpa. 1987. *The Tibetan Book of the Dead.* Boston: Shambhala.

Geertz, Clifford. 1973. *The Interpretation of Cultures.* New York: Basic Books.

Germano, David. 1994. "Architecture and Absence in the Secret Tantric History of rDzogs Chen." *Journal of the International Association of Buddhist Studies* 17 (2): 203–335.

————. Forthcoming. *Mysticism and Rhetoric in the Great Perfection: The Transformation of Buddhist Tantra in Ancient Tibet.* Monograph in progress.

Gladney, Dru. 1994a. "Representing Nationality in China: Refiguring Majority/Minority Identities." *Journal of Asian Studies* 53(1): 92–123.

————. 1994b. "Salman Rushdie in China." In Charles F. Keyes, Laurel Kendall, and Helen Hardcare, eds., *Asian Visions of Authority: Religion and the Modern States of East and Southeast Asia,* 255–278. Honolulu: University of Hawaii Press.

Goldstein, Melvyn C. 1964. "A Study of the *ldab ldob.*" *Central Asiatic Journal* 9: 123–41.

————. 1971a. "Serfdom and Mobility: An Examination of the Institution of 'Human Lease' in Traditional Tibetan Society." *Journal of Asian Studies* 30(3): 521–34.

————. 1971b. "Taxation and the Structure of a Tibetan Village." *Central Asiatic Journal* 15(1): 1–27.

————. 1975. "Ethnogenesis and Resource Competition among Tibetan Refugees in South Asia." In Leo A. Despres, ed., *Ethnicity and Resource Competition in Plural Societies,* 159–186. The Hague: Mouton.

————. 1986. "Reexamining Choice, Dependency and Command in the Tibetan Social System: Tax Appendages and Other Landless Serfs." *Tibet Journal* 9(4): 79–112.

————. 1989. *A History of Modern Tibet: The Demise of the Lamaist State.* Berkeley: University of California Press.

————. 1990a. "The Dragon and the Snowlion." In Anthony J. Kane, ed., *China Briefing,* 129–168. Boulder: Westview Press.

————. 1990b. "Religious Conflict in the Traditional Tibetan State." In L. Epstein and R. Sherburne, eds., *Reflections on Tibetan Culture: Essays in Memory of T. V. Wylie,* 231–247. Lewiston, N.Y.: Edwin Mellen.

————. 1994. "Change, Conflict and Continuity among a Community of Nomadic Pastoralists in Western Tibet, 1950–90." In R. Bartlett and S. Akinar, eds., *Resistance and Reform in Tibet,* 76–111. London: C. Hurst.

————. 1995. *Tibet, China and the United States: Reflections on the Tibet Question.* Occasional Paper of the Atlantic Council of the United States. [Available on the World Wide Web at http://www.cwru.edu/orgs/tibet/.]

Goldstein, Melvyn C., William Siebenschuh, and Tashi Tsering. 1997. *The Struggle for a Modern Tibet: The Autobiography of Tashi Tsering.* Armonk, New York: M. E. Sharpe.

Guenther, Herbert V. 1963. *The Life and Teaching of Nāropa.* Oxford: Clarendon Press.

Gu-ru Bkra-shis. 1990. *Gu bkra'i chos 'byung.* Beijing: Krung go bod kyi shes rig dpe skrun khang.

Gyatso, Janet. 1986. "Signs, Memory and History: A Tantric Buddhist Theory of Scriptural Transmission." *Journal of the International Association of Buddhist Studies* 9(2): 35–73.

————. 1987. "Down with the Demoness: Reflections on the Feminine Ground in Tibet." *Tibet Journal* 12(4): 38–53.

————. 1993. "The Logic of Legitimation in the Tibetan Treasure Tradition." *History of Religions* 33(2): 97–134.

————. 1996. "Drawn from the Tibetan Treasury: The *gTer Ma* Literature." In José Cabezón and Roger Jackson, eds., *Tibetan Literature,* 147–69. Ithaca, N.Y.: Snow Lion.

Hanna, Span. 1994. "Vast as the Sky: The Terma Tradition in Modern Tibet." In Geoffrey Samuel, ed., *Tantra and Popular Religion in Tibet,* 1–13. New Delhi: International Academy of Indian Culture and Aditya Prakashan.

Harrell, Stevan. 1995. "Civilizing Projects and the Reaction to Them." In Stevan Harrell, ed., *Cultural Encounters on China's Ethnic Frontiers*, 3–36. Seattle: University of Washington Press.

Hobsbawm, E. J. 1992. *Nations and Nationalism Since 1780: Programme, Myth, Reality.* 2d ed. Cambridge: Cambridge University Press.

Huber, Toni, ed. 1994a. *Powerful Places and Spaces in Tibetan Religious Culture. Tibet Journal* 19(2–3).

———. 1994b. "Putting the *gnas* Back into *gnas-skor:* Rethinking Tibetan Buddhist Pilgrimage Practice." In Toni Huber, ed., *Powerful Places and Spaces in Tibetan Religious Culture. Tibet Journal* 19(2–3): 23–60.

———. 1994c. "Why Can't Women Climb Pure Crystal Mountain? Remarks on Gender, Ritual, and Space at Tsa-ri." In Per Kvaerne, ed., *Tibetan Studies*, 1: 350–57. Oslo: Institute for Comparative Research in Human Culture.

Huntington, Samuel P. 1993. "The Clash of Civilizations?" *Foreign Affairs* 72(3): 22–49.

International Campaign for Tibet. 1990. *Forbidden Freedoms: Beijing's Control of Religion in Tibet.* Washington, D.C.

International Campaign for Tibet. 1996. *A Season to Purge: Religious Repression in Tibet.* Washington, D.C.

Jackson, David. 1994. *Enlightenment by a Single Means: Tibetan Controversies on the "Self-Sufficient White Remedy" (dkar po chig thub).* Vienna: Der Östrerreichischen Akademie der Wissenschaften.

'Jam-mgon Kong-sprul Blo-gros mtha'-yas. 1976. *Gter ston brgya rtsa.* In *Rin chen gter mdzod*, 1: 291–759. Paro: Ngodrup and Sherab Drimay.

'Jigs med theg mchog. 1988. *Rong po dgon chen gyi gdan rabs rdzogs ldan gtam gyi rang sgrags.* Xining: Qinghai Nationalities Press.

Jing Wei. 1989. *100 Questions about Tibet.* Beijing: Beijing Review Press.

Juergensmeyer, Mark. 1993. *The New Cold War? Religious Nationalism Confronts the Secular State.* Berkeley: University of California Press.

Kapstein, Matthew. 1989. "The Purificatory Gem and Its Cleansing: A Late Tibetan Polemical Discussion of Apocryphal Texts." *History of Religions* 28, no. 3 (February): 217–44.

———. 1992. "Remarks on the *Maṇi-bka'-'bum* and the Cult of Avalokiteśvara in Tibet." In R. Davidson and S. Goodman, eds., *Tibetan Buddhism: Reason and Revelation*, 79–93. Albany: SUNY Press.

———. 1995. "Weaving the World: The Ritual Art of the *Paṭa* in Pāla Buddhism and Its Legacy in Tibet." *History of Religions* 34(3): 241–62.

———. Forthcoming. "The Indian Literary Identity in Tibet." In Sheldon Pollock, ed., *Literary Cultures in History.*

Karmay, Samten. 1979. "The Ordinance of Lha Bla-Ma Ye-Shes-'Od." In Michael Aris and Aung San Suu Kyi, eds., *Tibetan Studies in Honor of Hugh Richardson*, 150–62. Warminster: Aris and Phillips.

———. 1980. "An Open Letter by Pho-Brang Zhi-Ba-'Od to the Buddhists in Tibet." *Tibet Journal* 5(3): 3–27.

———. 1994. "Mountain Cults and National Identity." In Robert Barnett, ed., *Resistance and Reform in Tibet*, 112–120. Bloomington: Indiana University Press.

Könchog Gyaltsen. 1988. *In Search of the Stainless Ambrosia.* Ed. Victoria Huckenpahler. Ithaca, N.Y.: Snow Lion.

———. 1990. *The Great Kagyu Masters: The Golden Lineage Treasury.* Ed. Victoria Huckenpahler. Ithaca, N.Y.: Snow Lion.

Kubik, Jan. 1994. *The Power of Symbols against the Symbols of Power: The Rise of Solidarity and the Fall of State Socialism in Poland.* University Park: Pennsylvania State University Press.

Kuijp, Leonard van der. 1987. "An Early Tibetan View of the Soteriology of Buddhist Episte-mology: The Case of 'Bri-gung 'Jig-rten mgon-po." *Journal of Indian Philosophy* 15: 57–70.

Kunsang, Eric Pema, trans. 1993. *The Lotus-Born: The Life of Padmasambhava.* Boston: Sham-bhala.

Large-Blondeau, Anne-Marie. 1960. "Les pèlerinages tibétains." In *Les Pèlerinages,* Sources Orientales 3: 199–245. Paris: Editions du Seuil.

LAWASIA Human Rights Committee and Tibet Information Network. 1991. *Defying the Dragon: China and Human Rights in Tibet.* London.

Lcang-skya Rol-pa'i rdo-rje. 1989. *Grub mtha' thub bstan lhun po'i mdzes rgyan.* Beijing: Krung go bod kyi shes rig dpe skrun khang.

Lincoln, Bruce. 1989. *Discourse and the Construction of Society: Comparative Studies of Myth, Ritual, and Classification.* New York: Oxford University Press.

Litzinger, Ralph. 1992. "Returning the 'Traditional' to a Socialist-Modern Landscape." Paper presented at the American Anthropological Meetings, San Francisco, December 2–6.

———. 1994. "Some Thoughts on Remembering and Forgetting in Representations of the Yao." Paper presented at the Annual China Studies Meeting, China Studies Program, University of California, Berkeley, February 24–25.

Liu Binyan, in collaboration with Ruan Ming and Xu Gang. 1989. *"Tell the World": What Happened in China and Why.* Trans. Henry L. Epstein. New York: Pantheon Books.

Ma Yin et al. 1985. *Questions and Answers about China's National Minorities.* Beijing: New World Press.

McInnis, Donald E. 1972. *Religious Policy and Practice in Communist China: A Documentary History.* New York: Macmillan.

———. 1989. *Religion in China Today: Policy and Practice.* Maryknoll, N.Y.: Orbis Books.

McKhann, Charles Fremont. 1995. "The Naxi and the Nationalities Question." In Stevan Harrell, ed., *Cultural Encounters on China's Ethnic Frontiers* 39–62. Seattle: University of Washington Press.

Makley, Charlene E. 1994. "Gendered Practices and the Inner Sanctum: The Reconstruc-tion of Tibetan Sacred Space in 'China's Tibet.'" *Tibet Journal* 19(2): 61–94.

Martin, Daniel. 1996. "The 'Star King' and the Four Children of Pehar: Popular Religious Movements of 11th to 12th Century Tibet." *Acta Orientalia Academiae Scientiarum Hung* XLIX (1–2): 171–195.

Mumford, Stan. 1989. *Himalayan Dialogue.* Madison: University of Wisconsin Press.

Naquin, Susan, and Chün-fang Yü, eds. 1992. *Pilgrims and Sacred Sites in China.* Berkeley: University of California Press.

Nebesky-Wojkowitz, René de. 1956. *Oracles and Demons of Tibet.* London: Mouton.

Nowak, Margaret. 1984. *Tibetan Refugees: Youth and the New Generation of Meaning.* New Brunswick, N.J.: Rutgers University Press.

Nyang Nyi-ma-'od-zer. 1988. *Chos 'byung me tog snying po sbrang rtsi'i bcud.* Gangs can rig mdzod 5. Lhasa: Bod ljongs bod yig dpe rnying dpe skrun khang.

Oakes, Timothy S. 1991. "The Cultural Space of Modernity: Ethnic Tourism and Place Identity in China." *Environment and Planning D. Society and Space* 11: 47–66.

———. 1992. "Cultural Geography and Chinese Ethnic Tourism." *Journal of Cultural Geog-raphy* 12(2): 3–17.

Ortner, Sherry B. 1978. *Sherpas Through Their Rituals.* Cambridge: Cambridge University Press.

———. 1989. *High Religion: A Cultural and Political History of Sherpa Buddhism.* Princeton: Princeton University Press.

Ots, Thomas. 1994. "The Silenced Body—the Expressive *Leib:* On the Dialectic of Mind and Life in Chinese Cathartic Healing." In Thomas J. Csordas, ed., *Embodiment and Ex-perience,* 116–38. Cambridge: Cambridge University Press.

Pad-rgyal = 'Bri-gung Bstan-'dzin Pad-ma'i Rgyal-mtshan. 1989. *Nges don bstan pa'i snying po mgon po 'bri gung pa chen po'i gdan rabs chos kyi byung tshul gser gyi phreng ba,* Gangs can rig mdzod 8. Lhasa: Bod ljongs bod yig dpe rnying dpe skrun khang. Originally written in 1800–03.

Petech, Luciano. 1990. *Central Tibet and the Mongols: The Yüan-Sa skya Period of Tibetan History.* Rome: Istituto Italiano per il Medio ed Estremo Oriente.

Riccard, Matthieu, et al., trans. 1994. *The Life of Shabkar: The Autobiography of a Tibetan Yogin.* Albany: SUNY Press.

Richardson, Hugh. 1952–53. "Tibetan Inscriptions at Ź'va-ḥi Lha Khaṅ." *Journal of the Royal Asiatic Society.* 133–54; 1–12.

———. 1983. *A Corpus of Early Tibetan Inscriptions.* London: Royal Asiatic Society.

———. 1984. *Tibet and Its History.* Boulder: Shambala.

———. 1993. *Ceremonies of the Lhasa Year.* London: Serindia Publications.

Rnam sras. 1991. "Mtsho sngon lho shar du dar ba'i drug pa'i klu rol skor gleng ba." *Krung go'i bod kyi shes rig* 4: 154–71.

Rock, Joseph F. C. 1992. *Lamas, Princes and Brigands: Rock's Photographs of the Tibetan Borderlands of China.* Ed. Michael Aris et al. New York: China House Gallery China Institute of America.

Roerich, G. N., trans. 1976. *The Blue Annals.* Delhi: Motilal Banarsidass.

Ruegg, D. Seyfort. 1984. "Problems in the Transmission of Vajrayāna Buddhism in the Western Himalaya about the Year 1000." *Acta Indologica* 6:369–81.

Samuel, Geoffrey. 1993. *Civilized Shamans: Buddhism in Tibetan Societies.* Washington, D.C.: Smithsonian Institution Press.

Schwartz, Ronald D. 1994a. "Buddhism, Nationalist Protest, and the State in Tibet." In Per Kvaerne, ed., *Tibetan Studies: Proceedings of the 6th Seminar of the International Association for Tibetan Studies,* 728–38. Oslo: Institute for Comparative Research in Human Culture.

———. 1994b. *Circle of Protest: Political Ritual in the Tibetan Uprising.* New York: Columbia University Press.

Shakabpa, Tsepon W. D. 1967. *Tibet: A Political History.* New Haven: Yale University Press.

Shaw, Miranda. 1994. *Passionate Enlightenment: Women in Tantric Buddhism.* Princeton: Princeton University Press.

Smith, E. Gene. 1970. Introduction to *Kongtrul's Encyclopedia of Indo-Tibetan Culture,* Śatapiṭaka Series 80. New Delhi: International Academy of Indian Culture.

Smith, Jonathan Z. 1982. *Imagining Religion from Babylon to Jonestown.* Chicago: University of Chicago Press.

Smith, Warren W., Jr. 1996. *Tibetan Nation: A History of Tibetan Nationalism and Sino-Tibetan Relations.* Boulder: Westview Press.

Snellgrove, David L., and Tadeusz Skorupski. 1977. *The Cultural Heritage of Ladakh.* Vol. 1: *Central Ladakh.* Warminster: Aris and Phillips.

Stein, R. A. 1972. *Tibetan Civilization.* Trans. J. E. Stapleton Driver. Stanford: Stanford University Press.

———. 1988. *Grottes-matrices et lieux saints de la déesse en Asie orientale.* Paris: École Française d'Extrême-Orient.

Stewart, Kevin, Banmadorji, and Huangchojia. 1995. "Mountain Gods and Trance Mediums: A Qinghai Tibetan Summer Festival." *Asian Folklore Studies* (Nagoya) 54(2): 219–37.

Stoddard, Heather. 1994. "Don grub rgyal (1953–1985): Suicide of a Modern Tibetan Writer and Scholar." In Per Kvaerne, ed., *Tibetan Studies: Proceedings of the 6th Seminar of the International Association for Tibetan Studies*, 825 – 34. Oslo: Institute for Comparative Research in Human Culture.

Ström, Axel Kristian. 1994. "Tibetan Refugees in India: Aspects of Socio-cultural Change." In Per Kvaerne, ed., *Tibetan Studies: Proceedings of the 6th Seminar of the International Association for Tibetan Studies*, 837 – 47. Oslo: Institute for Comparative Research in Human Culture.

Swain, Margaret. 1990. "Commoditizing Ethnicity in Southwest China." *Cultural Survival Quarterly* 14(1): 26 – 29.

Tambiah, Stanley J. 1976. *World Conqueror and World Renouncer.* Cambridge: Cambridge University Press.

Thondup, Tulku Rinpoche. 1986. *Hidden Teachings of Tibet: An Explanation of the Terma Tradition of the Nyingma School of Buddhism.* Ed. Harold Talbott. London: Wisdom Publications.

Thu'u-bkwan Blo-bzang-chos-kyi-nyi-ma. 1984. *Thu'u bkwan grub mtha'.* Lanzhou, Gansu: Kan su'u mi rigs dpe skrun khang.

Tibet Information Network and Human Rights Watch/Asia. 1996. *Cutting off the Serpent's Head: Tightening Control in Tibet, 1994–1995.* New York: Human Rights Watch.

Tibet Statistical Bureau. 1993. *Statistical Yearbook of the Tibet Autonomous Region.* Lhasa (in Chinese).

Tsultrim, Chhonphel Tersey. 1979. "One Month in Tibet." *Tibetan Review* (June): 12 – 27.

Tucci, Giuseppe. 1971. *Deb t'er dmar po gsar ma: Tibetan Chronicles by bSod nams grags pa.* Serie Orientale Roma 24. Rome: Istituto Italiano per il Medio ed Estremo Oriente.

———. 1980. *The Religions of Tibet.* Trans. Geoffrey Samuel. Berkeley: University of California Press.

Turner, Victor W. 1977a. "Death and the Dead in the Pilgrimage Process." In Frank E. Reynolds and Earl Waugh, eds., *Religious Encounters with Death*, 24 – 39. University Park: Pennsylvania State University Press.

———. 1977b. *The Ritual Process: Structure and Anti-structure.* Ithaca: Cornell University Press.

Turner, Victor W., and Edith Turner. 1978. *Image and Pilgrimage in Christian Culture: Anthropological Perspectives.* New York: Columbia University Press.

Union Research Institute. 1968. *Tibet 1950–1967.* Hong Kong: Union Research Institute.

Upton, Janet. 1995. "Home on the Grasslands? Tradition, Modernity and the Negotiation of Identity by Tibetan Intellectuals in the PRC." In Melissa Brown, ed., *Negotiating Ethnic Identities in China and Taiwan*, 98 – 124. Berkeley: University of California Center for East Asian Studies.

Wang Yao. 1994. "Hu Yaobang's Visit to Tibet, May 22 – 31, 1980." In Robert Barnett and S. Akiner, eds., *Resistance and Reform in Tibet*, 285 – 89. London: C. Hurst.

Welch, Holmes. 1972. *Buddhism under Mao.* Cambridge, Mass.: Harvard University Press.

Xiao Zhenwei and Liu Jinghong. 1994. "June Festival in Qinghai." *China's Tibet* 5(3): 25 – 29.

CONTRIBUTORS

Lawrence Epstein is an affiliate Assistant Professor of Anthropology at the University of Washington. He has conducted research and written on various aspects of Tibetan popular religion in refugee communities in India and in the Kham and Amdo regions of the PRC.

David Germano is Assistant Professor of Tibetan and Himalayan Studies in the Department of Religious Studies at the University of Virginia. Recent publications include a study of the Great Perfection (*rdzogs-chen*) tradition in the *Journal of the International Association of Buddhist Studies* and three studies of tantric contemplative and ritual practices in *Religions of Tibet in Practice* (Princeton). He is editor of the electronic *Nyingma Tantras Archives* at the University of Virginia and is completing two books on the Great Perfection traditions.

Melvyn C. Goldstein is John Reynolds Harkness Professor and Chairman of the Department of Anthropology and Director of the Center for Research on Tibet at Case Western University. He has conducted extensive research in Tibet on history, society, and language and is the author of more than eighty books and articles, including *A History of Modern Tibet, 1913–51: The Demise of the Lamaist State* (California, 1989), *Nomads of Western Tibet* (California, 1990), *Essentials of Modern Literary Tibetan: A Reading Course and Reference Grammar* (California, 1991), and coauthor of *The Search for Modern Tibet: The Autobiography of Tashi Tsering* (M. E. Sharpe, 1997).

Matthew T. Kapstein is Visiting Associate Professor in the Department of South Asian Languages and Civilizations and Numata Visiting Professor of Buddhist Studies in the Divinity School of the University of Chicago. His publications include primary texts, translations, and interpretive essays on many aspects of Indian and Tibetan religious culture. At present he is preparing a multivolume history of Tibetan religion and philosophy, *Buddhist Thought in Tibet: A Historical Sourcebook*.

Orville Schell is Dean of the Graduate School of Journalism at the University of California, Berkeley. His most recent book is *Mandate of Heaven*.

Peng Wenbin is a doctoral candidate in the Department of Anthropology at the University of Washington. He is currently doing fieldwork on ethnic tourism and the politics of representation in the PRC.

INDEX

Achi, 101
Amban, 19, 41
Amitāyus, 109
Anagnost, Ann S., 136
Ani Muntsho, 67, 87
Anye Magpön, 125, 130
Anye Nang, 128
Anye Nyechen, 125
Anye Shachung, 125, 126, 128, 130
Aris, Michael, 123, 176n.101
Atiśa, 85
Avalokiteśvara, 78, 108, 109, 176n.103

Batang Monastery, 8
Bell, Catherine, 122
Black Maṇḍala Lake, 100
Bon, 121
Brauen-Dolma, Martin, 99
Buddha Śākyamuni, 108, 109
Buddhism, Tibetan: contrasted with folk religion, 121; destruction and revival of, 6–11; minimal definition of, 116; role in society of, 5–6; sectarian differences in, 183n.49; state-sponsored, 73; tantric movements in, 73, 177n.107; tradition of burying artifacts in, 54. See also Monasticism, Tibetan
Bumpadöndrub, 125

Celibacy, 15, 68, 69, 72, 79
Chadrel Rinpoche, 147

Charnel grounds, 110, 111, 182n.44
Chetsang Rinpoche, 103. See also Drigung Chetsang
Chimphu, 82, 83
China, People's Republic of: changing Tibet policy of, 6–10, 11, 12–13, 14, 23, 26–27, 48–51; fascination with Tibetan Buddhism in, 86–87, 91, 173n.82; freedom of religious belief in, 2–3, 26; minority nationalities in, 141. See also Cultural Revolution
Chinese Buddhist Association, 7, 8, 158n.22
Chinese Communist Party: campaign against display of photos of Dalai Lama by, 146; conciliatory policy of, 27; gradualist policy of, 23; religious policy of, 1–2; Third Plenum of Eleventh Congress of, 1, 10. See also China, People's Republic of
Chungtsang Rinpoche, 103
Clear and Cool Mountains. See Wutai Mountains
Clear and Cool Rock Monastery, 172n.78
Crisis cults, 99–100
Cultural Revolution: associated by Tibetans with earlier dark period, 89; banning of religion during, 3, 102, 136; burial of religious objects during, 53; end of Drepung Monastery during, 23–25; in Tibet, 9–10
Cutting rite, 107, 110, 111

Ḍākiṇī, 167n.19; caves of 77, 78, 79; script, 74, 80

Index:	Andrew L. Christenson
Designer:	Ina Clausen
Compositor:	Impressions Book and Journal Services, Inc.
Text:	Baskerville
Display:	Baskerville
Printer:	Edwards Brothers, Inc.
Binder:	Edwards Brothers, Inc.